# Liberia

# WORLD BIBLIOGRAPHICAL SERIES

General Editors:

Robert G. Neville (Executive Editor)

John J. Horton

Robert A. Myers                                    Ian Wallace

Hans H. Wellisch                          Ralph Lee Woodward, Jr.

**John J. Horton** is Deputy Librarian of the University of Bradford and currently Chairman of its Academic Board of Studies in Social Sciences. He has maintained a longstanding interest in the discipline of area studies and its associated bibliographical problems, with special reference to European Studies. In particular he has published in the field of Icelandic and of Yugoslav studies, including the two relevant volumes in the World Bibliographical Series.

**Robert A. Myers** is Associate Professor of Anthropology in the Division of Social Sciences and Director of Study Abroad Programs at Alfred University, Alfred, New York. He has studied post-colonial island nations of the Caribbean and has spent two years in Nigeria on a Fulbright Lectureship. His interests include international public health, historical anthropology and developing societies. In addition to *Amerindians of the Lesser Antilles: a bibliography* (1981), *A Resource Guide to Dominica, 1493-1986* (1987) and numerous articles, he has compiled the World Bibliographical Series volumes on *Dominica* (1987), *Nigeria* (1989) and *Ghana* (1991).

**Ian Wallace** is Professor of German at the University of Bath. A graduate of Oxford in French and German, he also studied in Tübingen, Heidelberg and Lausanne before taking teaching posts at universities in the USA, Scotland and England. He specializes in contemporary German affairs, especially literature and culture, on which he has published numerous articles and books. In 1979 he founded the journal *GDR Monitor*, which he continues to edit under its new title *German Monitor*.

**Hans H. Wellisch** is Professor emeritus at the College of Library and Information Services, University of Maryland. He was President of the American Society of Indexers and was a member of the International Federation for Documentation. He is the author of numerous articles and several books on indexing and abstracting, and has published *The Conversion of Scripts and Indexing and Abstracting: an International Bibliography*, and *Indexing from A to Z*. He also contributes frequently to *Journal of the American Society for Information Science*, *The Indexer* and other professional journals.

**Ralph Lee Woodward, Jr.** is Professor of History at Tulane University, New Orleans. He is the author of *Central America, a Nation Divided*, 2nd ed. (1985), as well as several monographs and more than seventy scholarly articles on modern Latin America. He has also compiled volumes in the World Bibliographical Series on *Belize* (1980), *El Salvador* (1988), *Guatemala* (Rev. Ed.) (1992) and *Nicaragua* (Rev. Ed.) (1994). Dr. Woodward edited the Central American section of the *Research Guide to Central America and the Caribbean* (1985) and is currently associate editor of Scribner's *Encyclopedia of Latin American History*.

VOLUME 157

# Liberia

## D. Elwood Dunn

*Compiler*

**CLIO PRESS**

OXFORD, ENGLAND · SANTA BARBARA, CALIFORNIA
DENVER, COLORADO

British Library Cataloguing in Publication Data

Liberia. – (World Bibliographical series; vol. 157)
I. Dunn, D. Elwood    II. Series
016.96625


ISBN 1–85109–178–5


ABC-CLIO Ltd.,
Old Clarendon Ironworks,
35A Great Clarendon Street,
Oxford OX2 6AT, England.

ABC-CLIO Inc.,
130 Cremona Drive,
Santa Barbara,
CA 93116, USA.


Designed by Bernard Crossland.
Typeset by Columns Design and Production Services Ltd, Reading, England.
Printed and bound in Great Britain by
Bookcraft (Bath) Ltd., Midsomer Norton

# THE WORLD BIBLIOGRAPHICAL SERIES

This series, which is principally designed for the English speaker, will eventually cover every country (and many of the world's principal regions), each in a separate volume comprising annotated entries on works dealing with its history, geography, economy and politics; and with its people, their culture, customs, religion and social organization. Attention will also be paid to current living conditions – housing, education, newspapers, clothing, etc.– that are all too often ignored in standard bibliographies; and to those particular aspects relevant to individual countries. Each volume seeks to achieve, by use of careful selectivity and critical assessment of the literature, an expression of the country and an appreciation of its nature and national aspirations, to guide the reader towards an understanding of its importance. The keynote of the series is to provide, in a uniform format, an interpretation of each country that will express its culture, its place in the world, and the qualities and background that make it unique. The views expressed in individual volumes, however, are not necessarily those of the publisher.

## VOLUMES IN THE SERIES

# Contents

# Contents

# Preface

This bibliography attempts to reflect both the uniqueness of Liberia and its West African setting. It blends, as equally as possible, the nation's pre-Liberia experiences, and its American and other black New World impulses, as well as the historic encounter between Westernized black cultures and cultures indigenous to the area.

Country and people, history, politics, economics, foreign relations, literature, culture, and the arts all receive special attention in the volume, but a good number of other subjects are also covered. Within the annotations are details of numerous other works of value, and an index of authors, titles and subjects is provided. The aim of this work is to present the general reader and the specialist with a useful compilation of significant resources to enhance study of Africa's oldest republic, now ravaged by civil war.

The selection process for the volume involved drawing from an enormous body of material that might be categorized into the following: literature on pre-Liberia, or the nature and evolution of society prior to colonial settlement; literature on colonization, emigration, and the abolition of slavery; the Liberian settlement and the evolution of settler-indigene relations; and the more recent efforts at reconstituting civil society in the midst of pervasive conflict. The availability of published works has been the major factor in my choice, and though every effort was made to include most of the material in the public domain, I am conscious of the fact that worthy publications may, inadvertently, not have been included. The emphasis has been on English-language works, but some important French and German publications are included.

I have tried to be as exhaustive as possible, particularly in the Bibliographies section, and I have included many theses and dissertations, as well as periodicals (especially professional ones). The inclusion of all of the foregoing should in some way compensate for some of the omissions. The theses and dissertations, which also include important research papers, are listed alphabetically by author. Copies of these can be secured from the following addresses: in the United States – University Microfilm International, P.O. Box 1764, Ann Arbor, Michigan 48106; and in Europe – University Microfilm Ltd., 18 Bedford Row, London WC1R 4EJ.

The annotated entries are arranged alphabetically by the name of the author within each section or subsection. If there is neither author nor corporate author, entries are listed by the first non-article word in the title. Multiple entries by the same author are arranged alphabetically.

Users should note the absence of standardized nomenclature for many areas of Liberian studies. 'Indigenous-Liberian' and 'settler-Liberian', with no designation for Liberians of mixed parentage, seem to be the usages most widely employed to designate general ethnicity in Liberia. For the indigenous communities there are as yet no standardized nomenclatures, the attempt by the American anthropologist Svend E. Holsoe, notwithstanding (see Holsoe's *A standardization of Liberian ethnic nomenclature*. Philadelphia, Pennsylvania Institute for Liberian Studies, 1979. 28p., Liberian Studies Research Working Paper, no. 6). The annotations reflect this unsettled state of Liberian social consensus and of scholarship. Pre-Liberia refers to the period from antiquity to the colonial settlement in 1822; the Colonial period lasts from 1822 to 1839; the Commonwealth period covers 1839 to 1847; the First Republic refers to 1847-1980; and the Second Republic includes the years 1986 to 1990. From 1980 to 1986 there was a period of military rule, and from 1990 to 1994 there has been the period of Civil War, although the war actually began in December of 1989.

Users should also note the following current address for items published under the Liberian Studies Monograph Series/Institute for Liberian Studies: ARDEN Associates Corporation, P.O. Box 232, Landsdowne, PA 19050, USA. For government-provided information on the various functional sectors of society, consult the Annual Reports of the various Liberian government ministries. The Library of Congress carries most reports.

Debts of gratitude are due to many people who assisted in various ways and thus enabled this bibliography to be compiled. The inter-library loan system of the DuPont Library of The University of the South has been crucial in facilitating the project. I thank Sue Armentrout for remaining unwavering in responding to my inter-minable requests for loaned material. Two University of the South student assistants, Laurel W. Murchison and Scott Andrew Williams, cheerfully put in many hours carrying out chores in connection with this work. Professors Arthur Knoll and Reinhard Zachau, and German exchange student, Benedikt Sieberts, helped me with the German translations. The Print Services of The University of the South, particularly Tammy M. Scissom, is alone responsible for the computer formatting and other valuable technical services. I register here my thanks and sincere appreciation.

During the course of the collection and compilation I made use of the libraries of the University of Texas at Austin, Tulane University, Vanderbilt University, and the Library of Congress. I thank the following individuals for their contributions to my efforts: Svend E. Holsoe (for access to his personal collections on Liberia, and also for sharing with me particular items), Jo Mary Sullivan, Warren d'Azevedo, Beverly Ann Gray, and John Singler. To Similih M. Corder I owe a special debt of gratitude for providing the first drafts of most of the entries on Literature and for otherwise willingly consenting to consult with me on particular items. None of the individuals who rendered assistance is responsible for any errors of fact or judgement. Any such errors, or omissions, are entirely my responsibility.

I wish to thank WBS Executive Editor Robert G. Neville and his able staff for all editorial assistance, and William Kory, Geography Department, University of Pittsburgh, Johnstown, who kindly produced a map of Liberia on which the map in the present volume is largely based.

I thank my wife, Matilda Eeleen, for her continuing moral encouragement.

This reference study is dedicated to the memory of the thousands of Liberians who lost their lives in the Civil War.

*D. Elwood Dunn*
*Sewanee, Tennessee*
*June 1994*

# Introduction

Located along the western bulge of Africa, facing the Atlantic Ocean, the Republic of Liberia is a country of tropical rain forests and broken plateaux. Founded as a modern state in 1822, and becoming an independent entity in 1847, Liberia is the product of complex historical processes. The establishment of the country involved much more than the abolition of the Atlantic slave trade and the resettlement of 'freed American black slaves'. The Liberian enterprise was, indeed, made possible by the efforts of white and black Americans but a crucial role was also played by the leaders of the indigenous communities in the West African area that was eventually to become Liberia. Though the new nation was able to establish a place for itself in the 19th-century world, its settler leadership was soon faced with serious problems of internal social cleavages and the clash of cultures that ensued helped sow the seeds of later conflict. Liberia also suffered at the hands of other countries and was exploited by Western economic interests. Today, the country is ravaged by civil war, though measures are currently under way to resolve the conflict and reconstitute Liberian society.

## The country

Liberia extends from 4° 20'N to 8° 30'S, with a maximum breadth of 280 kilometres between Buchanan and Nimba. It occupies an area of 111,370 square km, and is bordered by Sierra Leone to the west, Guinea to the north, and Côte d'Ivoire (Ivory Coast) to the east. The coastline is 535 km long but it does not provide easy access from the Atlantic; the modern ports of Monrovia, Buchanan, Harper and Greenville provide the primary entrance points to the country. Liberia's physical features are varied. Flat coastal plains rise steadily to a plateau area before developing into densely forested mountainous regions whose highest points are Mt. Wutivi (1,380 metres), the Nimba Mountains (1,752 m) and the Wologizi Range (1,381 m). Of the seven rivers flowing towards the coast, only the Cavalla or Cavally is navigable along its total length, the rest being obstructed by rapids. All the rivers have sandbars at their mouths.

Liberia has two rainy seasons, one in the southeast, and the other (from May to October) in the rest of the country. There is an average of 465 cm per year of rainfall in Monrovia and along the northeast coast, and 224 cm per year towards the southeast and the interior. Flooding is common during the wet season. Average temperatures tend more to the extreme in the hinterland than at the coast. The average mean temperature is 28°C (82°F).

Most of the land is given over to agriculture, with rice, cassava, rubber and bananas as the principal crops. Rubber is the principal cash crop though coffee and cocoa are harvested. Two forms of land tenure are in existence but the central government's leasing system dominates the traditional method of holding land under collective ownership. Forestry is also a concern with great potential, with 685,000 cubic metres of roundwood harvested in 1976 for industrial purposes – there are sixty suitable types of hardwood. Cattle and sheep farming are rare; traditionally they have not been pursued and this, combined with other factors such as the prevalence of the tsetse fly and a dearth of grazing land, has ensured that animal husbandry has remained a neglected activity. Fishing is also a practice which provides a guaranteed income. Foreign investment in areas such as timber and rubber, as well as in mining play a major role in Liberia's political and economic life and, accordingly, are discussed in detail below.

## The people
Population growth in recent decades has been fairly rapid. In 1962 the total population figure stood at 1,016,443, rising to 1,503,368 in 1974, and 2,101,628 in 1984. Official estimates place the mid-1989 level at 2,508,000. In 1971 the annual birth and death rates per 1,000 were estimated to be 49.8 and 20.9, respectively. Distribution is uneven, with large areas in the southeast and west sparsely populated. In 1978 density per square mile was 39.9. The majority of people are employed in agriculture, forestry, hunting and fishing (541,555 in 1977) and migration is rare, extreme economic pressure usually proving the only factor forcing people to move. Unskilled workers form the main bulk of the economically active population.

## Ethnic compostion and religion
Liberia is one of the most ethnically diverse countries in the world. The main division has traditionally been between the settler-Liberians and the indigenous groups of which sixteen have been identified.

Throughout West Africa ethnic groups often range beyond national boundaries and many of these sixteen groups are not restricted solely to Liberia. Only the Bassa, Dei and Belle are not found outside the country. Other ethnic groups include the Bandi, Gio or Dan, Gola, Grebo, Kissi, Kpelle (the largest of the groups), Krahn, Kru (a sea-faring people), Loma, Mandingo, Mano, Mende and Vai, a group who invented the Vai script, a language with over a hundred characters.

Although English is the official language of the country, within Liberia some twenty-eight native languages and dialects are spoken which are divided into: West Atlantic or Mel (Gola and Kissi); Kruan (Kru, Grebo, Krahn, Bassa, Dei and Belle); and Mande (Ma, Dan, Kpelle, Loma, Bandi, Mende, Vai and Mandingo). In addition to standard English mainly spoken by the small percentage of literate and semi-literate Liberians, there are many forms of a developing lingua franca, 'Liberian English'. It is used widely in the country especially in intergroup relations.

The figures on Liberian religious affiliations vary enormously and many surveys have been carried out with widely differing results. It is therefore difficult to reach many firm conclusions but indisputably the three major religions are: the African traditional religions (ATR), reputed to be over half the population; Islam; and Christianity (the smallest of the three groups). However, by virtue of the fact that settler-Liberian values have dominated other areas of life, Christianity has certainly been a major influence since the last century. Notwithstanding this, the politics of social realignment may alter this position under post-civil war conditions.

## The economy

As indicated above, the majority of Liberians are engaged in agriculture and consequently the industrial sector of the economy is not adequately developed in spite of the attempt in 1964 to implement 'Operation Production' which was designed to increase agricultural production and intensify industrialization. Nonetheless, development plans were not formulated until the mid-1970s, and the industrial sector is still very underdeveloped. In 1980 only 1 per cent of the population was employed in manufacturing which contributed 5 per cent to the GDP in 1986.

According to figures published in the *Europa World Yearbook, 1989* (p. 1639), Liberia's GNP (Gross National Product) in 1987 was US $1,030m ($440 per head). Since 1980, GNP per head had decreased in real terms by 5.2 per cent per annum. Similarly GDP (Gross

Domestic Product) had fallen by 1.3 per cent p.a. during the period 1980-1986.

It would not be an overstatement to say that Liberia's economy has always been intertwined with those of its more powerful overseas neighbours, both in Europe and especially America, and not always to Liberia's advantage. Timber, mining and rubber are all areas where foreign companies became heavily involved. This involvement often resulted in the formation of 'enclave economies' characterized by the exploitation of Liberian land by overseas companies with little profit accruing to Liberia itself.

The first major company to exploit Liberia's resources was the Firestone Rubber Company. In 1925 Harvey S. Firestone made clear his intention to purchase what was then the British-owned Mount Barclay Plantations. His decision to acquire this land was dependent on Liberia's agreement to take out a loan from Firestone of US $5 million. Liberia's Secretary of State at the time, Edwin Barclay was compelled to sign three agreements with Firestone and its specially created Finance Corporation of America, which would oversee the loan, under the following conditions: one million acres of land would be leased by Liberia for a period of ninety-nine years at a cost of eight cents per acre; the loan was to be repaid over a forty-year period at a rate of seven per cent interest, to allow Liberia to cancel all its other foreign debts; further extensions to the loan were to be made available should Liberia fail to meet all its obligations, but only on the condition that a foreign receiver be appointed to monitor financial management. A receiver was appointed until 1952, when the loan was finally liquidated.

During the late 1960s, Liberia was finally in a position to bargain with Firestone regarding further changes to the agreement which had been modified on several occasions. The outcome of this was a unified agreement, incorporating all previous arrangements. It was signed in August 1976 and will remain in force until 1 October 2025, although provision does exist for its termination.

Although three-quarters of the labour force is concentrated in agriculture, this sector is so dominated by inefficient subsistence activities that more than half of the country's grain has to be imported. Liberia's status as a 'flag of convenience' for some 2,450 ships, or one-fifth of the world's maritime tonnage, ensures that the merchant marine sector makes a major contribution to the country's economy. Notwithstanding this, and in spite of external assistance, including a donation by the United States government in the 1980s of nearly $500m, corruption, fiscal indiscipline, inadequate administrative capacity and external factors (a global decrease in commodity prices, for example) combined with the effects of the civil war have devastated the Liberian economy. External debt rose very rapidly (by 1988 it was higher than GDP, and nearly 900 per cent of total export earnings); debt service ended and capital flight accelerated. In addition, exports and imports fell and the banking and credit system ceased to function.

War-ravaged Liberia is currently (1994) in a state of administrative paralysis. The government in Monrovia is relying largely on the royalties from a dwindling maritime programme while the administration in Gbarnga is continuing as best it can on the revenue from timber, iron ore, rubber and other resources. The bulk of the population, however, is dependent on international charity for its very survival. Though a government of national unity (the Liberian National Transitional Government) representing the major factions was installed on 7 May 1994, it was still consolidating its position the following summer.

## History

Through data gleaned from archaeological work and the gathering of oral traditions it may be estimated that the part of the tropical rainforest and coastal areas of West Africa which today form Liberia had been inhabited for several millennia prior to the creation of the state in the early nineteenth century.

The earliest inhabitants appear to have been part of the Niger-Congo-speaking group, later to develop into *Mel* speakers (Kissi and Gola). *Kruan* speakers (Dei, Kuwaa [Belle], Bassa, Wee [Krahn], Kru [Klao], and Grebo [Glebo]) and *Mande* speakers (Mano, Dan, Kpelle, Loma, Bandi, Mende, Vai, and Mandingo) are said to have entered the area in successive waves in response to socio-political and economic disturbances in the great Sudanic communities.

Collectively, these indigenous communities were socio-politically structured either as incipient states or chieftancies (Gola, Vai, Bassa, Kpelle, for example); sometimes they were structured without a chief or headman, in a 'stateless' arrangement of 'age groups' or 'sets' (such as Grebo or Kru) . Trade links existed between the peoples inhabiting the interior and the coastal area and until 1364 there were occasional visits by European traders. After this date, and up until 1413, merchants from Dieppe (Normandy, France) established trade posts on the seaboard of what became Bassa and Sinoe counties.

The Portuguese entered the trading activity in 1461 and quickly established a monopoly which lasted for a century. However, following challenges from Europe's other maritime powers – France, Britain and the Netherlands – the Portuguese were eventually driven out.

The Portuguese period had been marked by the naming of geographical features such as rivers (Mesurado, Cestos, Sanguin), promontories (Cape Mount, Cape Palmas, Cape Mesurrado), and regions

('Malaguetta Coast' named for the spice or pepper that was a major trade item). The English and Dutch preferred to call the spice 'grains of paradise' and eventually adopted the name 'Grain Coast' by which the area became universally known until 1824.

With the break in the Portuguese monopoly in 1598, trade between West Africa and maritime Europe and the New World expanded with far-reaching consequences for Africa. The legitimate trade in Europe's crafted and processed merchandise bartered for African hides, spices and gold was in time eclipsed by the transatlantic slave trade. This enforced removal from Africa to the New World of millions of Africans also included people indigenous to the Grain Coast. Some six decades before this trade effectively ended in the nineteenth century, there occurred a controversial return from America of some of the descendants of Africans earlier sold into slavery.

The circumstances of this 'back to Africa' enterprise are extensively documented, though the scholarship on the links between the repatriation movement in America and the settlement in Africa is rather scant. It was in response to a number of social forces in American society between 1690 and the early 1800s that various deportation/colonization/emigration schemes developed. They all eventually culminated in the creation in 1816 of the American Society for the Colonization of the Free People of Color of North America (ACS), and it was the ACS and its auxiliaries in collaboration with the United States government and a number of prominent Americans, that enabled the black repatriation to take place. It was those who were repatriated who came to constitute the core of Liberia's settler population. However, repatriation still occurred in the face of black-American opposition, and this dissension appears to have been influential: only a relatively small number (less then 20,000) were actually repatriated to Africa up until the outbreak of the American Civil War, at which time any significant emigration ended.

In 1790 there were 31,000 free blacks in the northern American States, and 80,000 in the southern states, a number which had doubled to 160,000 by 1820. The free blacks constituted only a part of the group that was repatriated: slaves were freed on condition of repatriation, and recaptured Africans who had illegally been sold following the abolition of the slave trade in 1807 were also returned.

The beginnings of settler Liberia were precarious. The ACS and the US government, supported by three presidents – Thomas Jefferson, James Monroe and James Madison – had collaborated over a twenty-four-year period to set in motion this 'back to Africa' venture. In 1824, two years after the first settlers arrived in the Liberia colony, the population stood at only 390, settled in small communities along the Grain Coast. The efforts of the US government to nurture the settlement that they had helped create were insufficient; black settlers were now considered expatriates, with apparently no American obligation of protection owed to them. In reality they never were American citizens under the constitution and never would be.

As important as the New World experience was to the making of modern Liberia, it must be seen as only a part of the whole picture. Consideration must also be given to the existing indigenous societies. Indeed, the suspicion and conflict created by the early encounters between the colonizers and the original inhabitants of the area set the scene for the ensuing attempts to achieve peaceful cohabitation. Negotiations for land were complicated and were often marked by conflict. Nevertheless, in spite of the tension engendered by these efforts at co-existence, the immigrant leadership gradually began to lay the foundations for a new state.

As the initiators of this new venture, it was largely the immigrants who determined the model, or the social order, upon which the Liberian state would be built. The initial and dominant model projected the country as an outpost of the Western world devoted to Africa's regeneration through Western civilization and Christianity. As the new Liberia developed, however, there was a shift in the balance of power and influence. Originally the ACS was the dominant element, creating a colonial relationship between themselves and the settler entity. Nonetheless, in the years that followed authority was assumed first by the settler merchant class and then by a personalized presidency as the state expanded into the hinterland regions and consolidated its position.

While the power-base for the new Liberia was developing, however, an alternative model (dating back at least to the 1850s) was evolving. Challenging the notion of building Liberia as a replica of the West in Africa, the articulators of this plan saw the majority indigenous population as essential to the creation of a prosperous and stable society. Accordingly, it called for the development of indigenous human resources, the expansion and protection of internal trade, and the subordination of civilizing/Christianizing considerations to all elements of cultural and racial nationalism.

The Liberian leadership's decision not to incorporate this model into society led to many later problems as the new Republic of Liberia made the transition from dream to reality. The first of the settlements was founded at Cape Mesurado, having been obtained in 1821 by Eli Ayres and Robert Stockton (the principal agents of the ACS) from the rulers of the Mahnbahn and the Dei. This settlement was renamed Monrovia, and remains today the seat of government. The collective settlements first became united as the Commonwealth of Liberia in 1838. Other territories soon joined. Maryland-in-Liberia, which had declared itself as an independent republic, joined Liberia as a county in 1857. By the turn of the century, Liberia had consolidated its position both as a new country on the African continent and in the field of international relations. Multi-party elections had taken place, exploration to the interior had been undertaken, and Liberia established relations with a number of sovereign states. However, the country was not a signatory of the Berlin Conference of 1885 and was obliged to remain on the sidelines whilst the continent was carved up among European powers. By the time of its centenary celebrations in 1947, Liberia was a member of the United Nations and a fully integrated member of the international community. The country further consolidated its position over the following decades, in apparent unity. However, the military coup d'état of 1980 and the outbreak of civil war in 1989 laid bare the roots of social conflict, much of which dated back to the very beginnings of Liberia.

The Tubman years (1944-71), whilst not entirely peaceful, had allowed Liberia to develop increased domestic security. President Tubman unveiled a three-point plan: an alignment to the West with respect to the Cold War; the assertion of an Open Door policy, enabling extensive foreign investment in Liberia; and a move toward greater National Unification, drawing aboriginal Liberians into what was an essentially settler-created society. In this connection, for example, universal suffrage was granted to all Liberians although overall power still lay with the settler contingent.

Nevertheless, the relative tranquillity of the Tubman presidency gradually dissipated during President Tolbert's rule (1971-80). Whilst attempting to sustain elements of Tubman's policies and initiating some new progressive policies of his own, Tolbert's government met with growing criticism from the developing opposition movements. The cracks first began to show when a proposal by the administration to increase the price of rice sparked a bloody riot on 14 April 1979. This led Tolbert to claim emergency powers, and to postpone a forthcoming mayoral election.

### The Civil War

The descent into anarchy came with the storming of the presidential palace in 1980, by a group of non-commissioned officers of the Armed Forces of Liberia (AFL) which came to be led by Samuel Kanyon Doe. An indigenous Liberian of Wee (Krahn) ethnicity, Doe was appointed by his colleagues chairman of the People's Redemption Council (PRC). Tolbert was assassinated and Doe assumed the succession. He declared himself to be '. . . committed to the establishment of equal opportunities for all without discrimination, wherein the resources of the country are used for the benefit of the people'. Unfortunately, these stirring words belied the cruelty of Doe's régime which followed the pattern set by his seizure of power. In all, thirteen former government officials were publicly executed and all political activities were outlawed. In 1981, all ministers were commissioned into the army, thus creating a military administration and casting doubt over the earlier announcement that there would be a return to civilian rule by 1986. Three years later in August 1984 Doe founded the National Democratic Party of Liberia (NDPL) and formally announced his candidature for the presidency. Meanwhile, the administration remained unstable, since what was claimed to be Doe's avowed intention of eradicating government corruption resulted in dismissals and executions. Moreover, many viewed such actions as a mere smokescreen behind which Doe hid whilst consolidating the position of his administration. The fact that the ban on political parties was later lifted as a preliminary to the 1985 elections adds weight to this charge. In the period before the election in October 1985 eleven parties had been formed, albeit in the face of institutionalized opposition. Two were eventually outlawed – the Liberian People's Party (LPP) and the United People's Party (UPP) – and polling was marred by the harassment of voters and accusations of ballot rigging. Many were not happy with the outcome of the election, but nevertheless, on the 6 January 1986 Doe was inaugurated as the legitimate President of Liberia.

The mid- to late 1980s were a time of political uncertainty. Rumours of insurrection were rife and summary imprisonment, dismissals for corruption and interference in the political process (the banning of parties and other activities, election fraud) all seemed to be commonplace. Bill Berkeley's *Liberia: a promise betrayed* (New York: Lawyers Committee for Human Rights, 1986) comments that 'Almost from the moment they seized power, soldiers of the Liberian armed forces have been a law unto themselves. Looting, arson, flogging, arbitrary arrests, persistent reports of rape – all of these abuses have been attributed on a wide scale to soldiers loyal to President [Samuel K.] Doe. Reports of summary executions, meanwhile, have been colored by credible eyewitness descriptions of horrific brutality, including castration and dismemberment' (p. 1). Coups and rumours of coups also punctuated the proceedings – there were reported attempts to overthrow the government in 1983, 1985 and 1988. Foreign relations also broke down from time to time in the light of these atrocities.

By 1989, the situation was no better; opposition parties were thwarted at every turn, and their leaders were either imprisoned or forced into exile. Moreover, human rights abuses were being carried out on an enormous scale and could no longer be ignored by the outside world. These violations had come to the attention of the USA who had earlier offered economic aid in return for the release of political prisoners. Once again aid was refused pending fundamental changes in the system.

Spurred on by outside support, the LAP (Liberian Action Party), the UPP and the UP (United Party) formulated what was to be a last-ditch attempt to assert their democratic prerogative with a proposition demanding changes in the Doe government and asserting the rights of freedom of speech and of political expression. They also insisted that the law be upheld and rejected Doe's attempts to create an authoritarian, one-party régime. The optimism was short-lived as Doe's administration struck back, the president maintaining that 'power comes from God' and that it was he [Doe] who had the Divine Right to rule.

Typically, the descent into civil war was marked by confusion and uncertainty. When pushed to the limit, the United States seemed reluctant to carry out its threats to cut financial support, maintaining that the Liberian situation was not as bad as that of some other African countries. Faced with such apathy, the Liberian people began to voice their opposition to the Doe régime. The President's birthday celebrations were accompanied by rioting, whilst Liberian exiles in the USA demonstrated in the American capital urging action to end the 'brutal repression' and 'manipulation of the constitution'.

The insurrection officially started on 24 December 1989, when a rebel band calling itself the National Patriotic Front of Liberia (NPFL) attacked the border town of Butuo in Nimba County, killing a number of soldiers and immigration officers. This attack was symptomatic of the desperately tense situation. It was reported in *Jeune Afrique* that the rebels had not planned to attack but government arrests of the group's members in Monrovia forced them to rethink their position. Also characteristic of rebel insurgency was the fact that the group, despite having a name, was rather an *ad hoc* faction, drawing together various elements of Liberian dissatisfaction. Charles Taylor, a former government official, appeared to be the leader of the NFPL, supported by some who had taken part in earlier coup attempts.

Though widely reported by the Western media as an exclusively ethnic conflict, in truth the insurrection initially represented a confrontation between a loose coalition of opposition forces and Doe loyalists. The core of Doe's supporters were the Armed Forces of Liberia which had been purged of most of its non-Krahn soldiers. The NPFL led the opposition and under its wing came a host of Liberians bent on ending Doe's brutal régime.

During 1990 the war intensified. People lived in fear of indiscriminate attacks as government paranoia, caused by the overwhelming awareness that defeat was probable, increased. Even the USA, whose relative complacency had done little to avert the outbreak of war, was forced to withdraw support, positioning a naval and military force off the Liberian coast to aid American citizens should the need arise. Continuing the trend of foreign concern, the Economic Community of West African States (ECOWAS) formulated a peace plan for Liberia which envisaged the Community's intervention, in the face of what was becoming an increasingly convoluted struggle.

By this time the rebels, under the leadership of Taylor, had won what was estimated to be eighty per cent of the country. This objective achieved, the common aim was removed, thus exposing other factions within the previously united rebel camp. A breakaway group, the INPFL, led by Prince Yormie Johnson, opened its own attack on the capital Monrovia, and was substantial enough to pose a real threat to the objectives of the other two forces. ECOWAS, however, was still determined to bring a peaceful resolution to the conflict. The presence of monitoring forces, namely the Economic Community Monitoring Group (ECOMOG), was a major component of this plan and whilst it was welcomed by both Doe and Johnson, Taylor was frustrated by the proposal and in his desperation, threatened the member-countries (Nigeria, Ghana, Guinea, Sierra Leone and The Gambia amongst others). ECOMOG troops were admitted into the country on 24 August 1990 and an interim government was subsequently installed in Monrovia. However, this was done explicitly against the wishes of Taylor and nominally against those of Doe. Whilst Doe's National Democratic Party of Liberia (NDPL) attended the deliberations which established the interim government, Doe himself remained in the Executive Mansion, still asserting his presidency.

The ECOWAS Peace Plan for Liberia, armed with this interim government, ECOMOG, and political support from the United States, embarked initially on a diplomatic offensive to secure support from hesitant Francophone states, notably Côte d'Ivoire and Burkina Faso, persuading Taylor to 'come aboard', and urging Doe to accept standing offers to have him airlifted out of the country. Neither Doe nor Taylor seemed interested in these overtures, and the strain was beginning to show within ECOWAS, notably along linguistic lines.

On the ground, in Monrovia, there came a new twist to the crisis. On 9 September 1990 Doe decided to venture out of the Executive Mansion to visit the ECOMOG Commander at the Monrovia port where the West African forces were headquartered. Whether he wished to negotiate or effect a compromise remains a mystery. At the port he was captured by Johnson's troops in a pitched battle which left almost the entire presidential entourage dead. Doe himself was later tortured to death at the hands of Prince Johnson's men.

Unfortunately, the loss of Doe did not lead to a material change in the situation. Ceasefire negotiations continued, culminating in the first agreement to stop hostilities on 28 November 1990. The Liberian people were finally given a respite, and the diplomats a challenge.

Notwithstanding this, a long-term solution was not found. Almost two years later the ceasefire was broken and hostilities were resumed. To the three warring factions was added a fourth, the United Liberation Movement of Liberia (ULIMO). By November 1992, the INPFL of Prince Johnson was no longer a factor in the war, and Taylor's NPFL seemed to be confronted by ULIMO, AFL, and an increasingly active ECOMOG. As 1992 drew to a close, the civil war was at a crucial turning point – the African solution embodied in the ECOWAS Peace Plan was being severely tested, whilst the wider international community was distancing itself from the necessity of modifying or replacing the Plan. Thus Liberia's future hung very much in the balance, dependent on external factors as much as internal ones.

The peace process, however, continued and at Cotonou, in Benin, a significant agreement on ending the civil war was reached in mid-1993. Signed by all the principal internal parties to the conflict and endorsed by the international factilitators (ECOWAS, OAU and UN), it envisaged the establishment of a power-sharing transitional government (the Liberian National Transitional Government, or LNTG), the disarming of all warring factions and the holding of national elections within six months of the government's installation.

In accordance with the Cotonou agreement, the LNTG was installed on 7 March 1994 and disarmament has begun, though as yet on a very small scale. Complications continue to mar the process as internal power struggles manifest themselves. Deadly splits have appeared in some groups (such as ULIMO) and, at the same time, new assertive groups such as the Liberia Peace Council and the Lofa Defense Force have emerged. Meanwhile, outside the country those international organizations who are striving for peace are preoccupied with trying to reconcile the major differences between the various factions.

When the civil war is finally concluded, whatever the outcome, Liberian society will require major reconstruction. One hopes that those involved in this process will have learned the painful lessons of Liberia's more distant and recent history, the consequences of which have cost the lives of so many.

# List of Theses and Dissertations

Mohammed Allieu Abdulah, 'The Mano River Union: A study of sub-regional strategy for economic cooperation and development in West Africa', PhD, University of Maryland, 1984. 257p.

James Frederick Abel, 'National Ministries of Education', PhD, George Washington University, 1930. 158p.

Arthur Abraham, 'Mende government and politics under colonial rule, 1890-1937', PhD, Centre for West African Studies, University of Birmingham, 1974. [Also published as a book under the same title, Freetown: Sierra Leone University Press, 1978].

Sarah Adams, 'An observation of English and Kru phonology', MA, San Francisco State College, 1965.

Carlos A. Ajavon, 'Technical construction and its part in the economic development of Liberia', BA, Cuttington College, 1954.

Ida Ajavon, 'Recommendations for the improvement in the science curriculum and instruction in the junior high schools of Liberia', MA, San Francisco State College, 1965.

Harrison Oladunfoye Akingbade, 'The role of the military in the history of Liberia 1822-1947', PhD, Howard University, 1977. 349p.

Monday Benson Akpan, 'The African policy of the Liberian settlers, 1842-1932: A study of the native policy of a non colonial power in Africa', PhD, Ibadan University, 1968. 475p.

Austin Dwadu Amegashie, 'Liberian agricultural programs: The theory and practice of marketing and food distribution systems', PhD, University of Florida, 1978. 186p.

Simon Obe Anekwe, 'Investment, trade and national security in the relations of Liberia and the United States', MA, New York University, 1953.

Richard R. Ashburn, 'A study of the diplomatic relations between the United States and Liberia between 1925 and 1936', MA, Bowling Green State University, 1960. 97p.

Harden P. Ballantine, 'Americans and education in early Liberia', MA, Columbia University, 1966/67. 156p.

Seth Dojo Bansa and Elike Botsoe Takyi, 'Attracting, recruiting, and retaining teachers in Liberian schools', EdD, Columbia University, 1967. 315p.

Victor Kevin Barbiero, 'The transmission dynamics of onchocerciasis on the Firestone Rubber Plantation, Harbel, Liberia', PhD, The Johns Hopkins University, 1982. 196p.

Anthony Barclay, 'Fiscal performance and economic growth: the buoyancy of the tax structure in Liberia', PhD, University of Wisconsin-Madison, 1986. 159p.

Daniel Erasmus Barclay, 'Foundations of education in higher educational institutions in Liberia', PhD, Southern Illinois University at Carbondale, 1982. 139p.

Toye Cornelius Barnard, 'The position of Liberia on major issues before the United Nations', MA, Western Reserve University, 1962. 152p.

James Wallace Beckman, 'Some models of individual decision-making among the Kpelle and other peoples of Liberia West Africa', PhD, University of California, Irvine, 1973. 89p.

Mildred Chaffee Beckman, 'Slavery in Liberia', MA, Ohio State University, 1936. 108p.

Lloyd Nelson Beecher, Jr. 'The State Department and Liberia, 1908-1941: A heterogeneous record', PhD, University of Georgia, 1971. 262p.

Beryl Larry Bellman, 'Village of curers and assassins: On the production of Fala Kpelle cosmological categories', PhD, University of California, Irvine, 1971. 336p.

Peter Ben, 'Can Liberia import the effective school's research?', MA, Cornell University, 1990.

Charles R. Bennett, 'The American Colonization Society in Kentucky, 1829-1860', PhD, University of Kentucky, 1980. 224p.

Edward Benson, 'The applicability of tropical silvicultural systems to the Liberian high forests', MF, New York State College of Forestry at Syracuse University, 1962. 107p.

Rosetta Benson, 'The development of teacher education in Liberia', MA, Fresno State College, 1966. 87p.

Jochen Berdehoft, 'Zur Epidemiologie der klinischen Symptomatik in verschieden Endemiegebieten, Lymphatische Filariasis in Liberia' ('About the epidemiology of clinical symptomatics in various endemic areas: Lymphatic filiariasis in Liberia'), Universität Hamburg, 1983. 62p.

J. W. Berge, 'Contributions to the petrology of the Goe Range area, Grand Bassa County, Liberia', Uppsala University, 1962.

Joseph L. Bettie, 'Suggested methods and instructional materials for use in teaching mathematics in the secondary schools in Liberia', MA, San Francisco State College, 1965.

Amos Jones Beyan, 'The American Colonization Society and the formation of political, economic and religious institutions in Liberia, 1822-1900', PhD, West Virginia University, 1985, 186p.

Timothy Y. Zeze Beyan, 'The psychological principles involved in the process of human learning', BA, Cuttington College, 1958.

Khalipha Mohammed Bility, 'Planning education and training for health services delivery: A model for primary health care in Liberia', PhD, University of Pittsburgh, 1988. 293p.

Kathleen Diane Billman, 'The dance of loyalty: Loyalty issues in cross-cultural and pastoral care with Liberian immigrant families', PhD, Princeton Theological Seminary, 1992. 300p.

Robert Barnett Binswanger, 'The development of a Peace Corps training program to meet the request of Liberia for fifty elementary school teachers, 1963', PhD, Harvard University, 1964.

John Bernard Blamo, 'Nation-building in Liberia, as revealed by symbol analysis', PhD, Boston University, 1969. 364p.

John Bernard Blamo, 'The impact of industrialization on Liberian society', MA, International Graduate School, University of Lund, Sweden, 1964. 97p.

David Grant Blanchard, 'The impact of external domination on the Liberian Mano economy: An analysis of Weber's hypothesis of rationalism', PhD, Indiana University, 1973. 299p.

Carole Hazel Bledsoe, 'Women and marriage in Kpelle society', PhD, Stanford University, 1976. 148p.

Donald M. Bluestone, 'Colonization is our middle name: The American Colonization Society and American expansion into Africa 1780-1880', MA, University of Wisconsin-Madison, 1965. 236p.

Isaac Opoku Boadi, 'Origin of mega-gold placer deposits in the light of data on the Bukon Jedeh deposit, Liberia, and on the Tarkwa deposit, Ghana', PhD, New Mexico Institute of Mining and Technology, 1991. 236p.

Patrick Thomas Bogba, 'Technical vocational education and manpower development as instruments in Liberia's national development', EdD, State University of New York at Buffalo, 1979. 307p.

Jerome Zack Boika, 'National development in Liberia and the role of the broadcast media, 1950-1980: A descriptive study', PhD, Wayne State University, 1983. 251p.

LeRoy Zobon Bokai, 'A survey of teacher's perceptions of, and beliefs about, promoting critical thinking in Liberian high schools', EdD, Columbia University, 1989. 154p.

Fatorma Karmo Bolay, 'Biological control and fauna assessment of *Anopheles bambiae*, vector of malaria breeding in rice fields in Liberia, West Africa', PhD, The Johns Hopkins University, 1989. 199p.

George Saigbe Boley, 'An analysis of scholastic achievement, educational, job and income expectation of selected secondary school students in three Liberian counties', EdD, The University of Akron, 1977. 183p.

E. Rame Bowen, 'An intensive study to improve articulation of work in elementary shorthand with first placement positions in Liberia', MA, San Francisco State College, 1965.

Hannah Abeodu Bowen 'An investigation of Liberian literature: Its history and development', BA, Cuttington College, 1956. 68p.

Willis Boyd, 'Negro colonization in the national crisis, 1860-1870', PhD, University of California-Los Angeles, 1953. 513p.

Theophilus Rotimi Brainerd, 'An economic analysis of sea-food trade in West Africa', PhD, University of Rhode Island, 1990. 327p.

Deborah Anne Brautigam, 'Chinese agricultural aid in West Africa: A technical, economic and institutional analysis of three Chinese rice projects in Liberia, Sierra Leone and Gambia', PhD, Fletcher School of Law and Diplomacy (Tufts University), 1987. 650p.

Lawrence Bart Breitborde, 'The social structural basis of linguistic variation in an urban African neighborhood', PhD, University of Rochester, 1978. 516p.

Mary Elizabeth Brenner, 'Arithmetic and classroom interaction as cultural practices among the Vai of Liberia', PhD, University of California, Irvine, 1985. 371p.

Rubell Essien Brewer, 'The laboratory investigation of parasites in *Periplaneta americana* and an observation of the most effective available insecticide at Cuttington College for its Control', BA, Cuttington College, 1958.

Larry Ray Brim, 'The eagle, the sparrow and the vultures: America's policy and perceptions in Liberia, 1909-1933', MA, Northern Illinois University, 1974. 67p.

Agnes Brinkmann, 'Zur Epidemiologie der Dermatomykosen in Liberia' ('About the epidemiology of dermatomycosis in Liberia'), PhD, Universität Hamburg, 1973. 10p.

Madison Spencer Briscoe, 'Some ecological aspects of Liberia as interpreted from the vegetation and ground and aerial photography with special reference to the distribution of Parasites', PhD, Catholic University of America, 1950. 165p.

Samuel Irving Britt, 'The children of salvation: Struggle and cosmology in Liberian prophet churches', PhD, University of Virginia, 1992. 769p.

Amanda Lee Brooks, 'Captain Paul Cuffe, 1759-1817 and the Crown Colony of Sierra Leone: the linimality of the Free Black', PhD, University of Chicago, 1988.

Patrick Doe Bropleh, 'Rural resources and Liberian economic development', PhD, Duke University, 1974. 203p.

Patrick Doe Bropleh, 'Applicability of point sampling to the forests of Liberia', MF, Oregon State University, 1967. 54p.

Christopher Michel Brown, 'Liberia's rubber outgrowers: an economic appraisal', PhD, Fletcher School of Law and Diplomacy (Tufts University), 1989. 279p.

David W. Brown, 'Domination and personal legitimacy in a district of Eastern Liberia', PhD, University of Manchester, 1979. 502p.

E. A. Brown, 'EST implications for the English-language syllabus of Liberian junior high schools', MEd, University of Manchester, 1978.

George Washington Brown, 'The economic history of Liberia', PhD, University of London, 1938. 680p.

Mary Antoinette Grimes Brown, 'Education and national development in Liberia, 1800-1900', PhD, Cornell University, 1967. 249p.

Robert Harry Brown, 'Some problems in the teaching of African literature at the tertiary level in Liberia and their pedagogical implications', MA, University of London, 1982. 180p.

Robert Harry Brown, 'A sociolinguistic study of language attitudes among selected tertiary Liberian bilinguals and their attained proficiency in ESL', PhD, University of Essex (UK), 1989. 388p.

George Daniel Browne, 'A helpful handbook of testing and evaluation for Liberian secondary school teachers', BA, Cuttington College, 1958.

George Daniel Browne, 'A missionary approach to the African animist: The spirit world', STM, Episcopal Theological Seminary, Alexandria, Virginia, 1964. 63p.

Beverlee Pickett Bruce, 'Transcending boundaries: An anthropological study of the AME Church in Monrovia, Liberia', PhD, Harvard University, 1978. 160p.

David Alan Bruckner, 'Comparative studies of the Liberian and Puerto Rican strains of *Schistosoma mansoni*', ScD, The Johns Hopkins University, 1973. 122p.

Winifred P. L. Brunskine, 'Food habits and customs of some Liberian tribes', BA, Cuttington College, 1955.

Elizabeth Joyce Buchanan, 'The development of operational thinking in elementary school children: An examination of some aspects of Piaget's theory among urban Liberian children', PhD, Columbia University, 1979. 238p.

George David Buelow, 'The ethnographic novel in Africa', PhD, University of Oregon, 1973. 263p.

Shirley Ann Burchfield, 'Improving energy data collection and analysis in developing countries – a comparative study in Uganda, Liberia, and Sudan', PhD, University of Texas at Arlington, 1986. 365p.

Ruth Lonstaff Burgess, 'A proposed social studies book of children of Liberia, West Africa', MA, Kennedy School of Missions, 1954. 135p.

Ida Famattah Burphy, 'The snakes of Liberia', BA, Cuttington College, 1954.

Carl Patrick Burrowes, 'Press freedom in Liberia, 1830-1970: The impact of modernity, ethnicity and power imbalances on government-press relations', PhD, Temple University, 1994. 732p.

J. Sebastian B. Bush, 'The impact of Firestone Plantations Company on the economy of Liberia', BA, Cuttington College 1954.

Augustus Feweh Caine, 'A study and comparison of the West Africa Bush School and the Southern Sotho Circumcision School', MA, Northwestern University, 1959. 152p.

Penelope Campbell, 'Maryland in Africa: The Maryland State Colonization Society, 1831-1857', PhD, Ohio State University, 1967. 426p.

S. Jabaru Carlon, 'Educational plans for Liberia: An assessment of public elementary education during the decade of the sixties, with particular emphasis on planned goals and their achievement', PhD, University of Wisconsin-Madison, 1973. 314p.

Burgess Carr, 'The comparative growth and performance of two groups of Rhode Island Reds; one group fed with a diet made from locally available feedstuffs, and the other group fed with imported commercial feed', BSc, Cuttington College, 1958.

Jeanette Ellen Carter, 'Household organization and the money economy in a Loma community, Liberia', PhD, University of Oregon, 1970, 212p.

John Walter Cason, 'The growth of Christianity in the Liberian environment', PhD, Columbia University, 1962. 561p.

Carolyn M. Cassio, 'Development of elementary education in Liberia, Africa', MA, Newark State College, 1960/61. 156p.

Frank Robert Chalk, 'America, Liberia and the Stevenson Act: A study of the American response to rubber restriction in the 1920's', MA, University of Wisconsin-Madison 1962. 178p.

Frank Robert Chalk, 'The United States and the international struggle for rubber, 1914-1941', PhD, University of Wisconsin-Madison, 1970. 363p.

Eric S. Charry, 'Musical thought, history, and practice among the Mande of West Africa', PhD, Princeton University, 1992. 375p.

Florence Alletta Chenoweth, 'Small farmers' response to economic incentives: A case study of small farmers in Liberia', PhD, University of Wisconsin-Madison, 1986. 265p.

Jean Chevrier, 'Aperçu sur Liberia' ('Glimpse of Liberia'), Doct. D'État-Droit, Université de Paris, 1951. 199p.

Jim A. Chezem, 'The unification policy in Liberia', MA, American University, 1964. 151p.

George Tucker Childs, 'The phonology and morphology of Kisi', PhD, University of California, Berkeley, 1988. 404p.

Ronald James Church, 'The railways of West Africa: A geographical and historical analysis', PhD, University of London, 1943. 277p.

Thomas Joseph Ciborowske, 'A cultural and developmental study of concept formation learning', PhD, University of California-Irvine, 1971. 106p.

Emilia Joyaux Clapham, 'The establishment and development of Liberia', MA, University of California-Berkeley, 1926. 159p.

Charles Amstard Clarke, 'Administrative centralization and its imparct on planning political participation and service delivery to hinterland areas in Liberia', DPA, Public Administration, American University, 1974. 266p.

Joshua D. Cleon, 'The effects of an experimental curriculum development project in statistics on the achievement and attitude of tenth grade students in Liberia', PhD, University of Illinois at Urbana-Champaign, 1983. 312p.

Melton S. Clinton, 'A brief survey of the Lutheran Mission in Liberia with an appraisal of its religious, educational, literacy and medical programs', BA, Cuttington College, 1956.

William Davis Coale, Jr., 'West German transnationals in tropical Africa: The case of Liberia and the Bong Mining Company', PhD, Boston University, 1977. 303p.

Johnetta Betsch Cole, 'Traditional and wage earning labor among tribal Liberians', PhD, Northwestern University, 1967. 328p.

Robert Eugene Cole, 'The Liberian élite as a barrier to economic development', PhD, Northwestern University, 1967. 336p.

Albert Byrleton Coleman, 'A descriptive analysis of the factors of rural-urban balance in developing countries: The role of education – a case study of Liberia', PhD, Southern Illinois University at Carbondale, 1982. 189p.

Arthur James Kuscuiski Coleman, 'A survey of the status of teachers in elementary and secondary schools of Liberia and a suggested plan for improving teacher education', PhD, University of Pennsylvania, 1960. 186p.

Ciyata Dinah Coleman, 'Exports and partial economic growth in Liberia: Effects of rubber and iron ore', PhD, Southern Illinois University at Carbondale, 1986. 110p.

Stephen Keith Commins, 'Peasant producers and rural development projects: a Liberian study', PhD, University of California, Los Angeles, 1988. 312p.

Al-Hassan Mohammed Conteh, 'The dynamics of migration to Monrovia: Patterns and determinants', M Phil., United Nations, Cairo Demographic Centre, 1980. 255p.

Al-Hassan Mohammed Conteh, 'Migration and household structure in Liberia', PhD, University of Pennsylvania, 1993. 204p.

Frederick Cooper, 'Ethnicity and stratification in Liberia: An essay in modern African social history', Senior Honors Essay, Harvard University, 1969. 158p.

Susan F. Cooper, 'The selection and organization of curricular knowledge at the University of Liberia during 1951-1985', PhD, University of Pittsburgh, 1991. 254p.

Jeannie Eliza Copping, 'Liberia: An American experiment in colonization', MA, Auburn University, 1970. 91p.

Harold Steven Bresford Corbin, 'An apologetic for music education in the elementary schools of Liberia', BA, Cuttington College, 1958.

Michael W. Corkran, 'A preliminary archaeological and ethnographic analysis of Sabo ceramics', MA, University of North Carolina-Chapel Hill, 1973. 65p.

Suzanne Marie Cowin, 'A descriptive phonological study of the Spanish of Liberia, in the Province of Guanacaste, Costa Rica', MA, Florida Atlantic University, 1978, 90p.

Martin Boyd Coyner, 'John Hartwell Cocke of Bremo . . .', PhD, University of Virginia, 1961. 617p.

Jamesetta M. Cummings, 'A handbook of art and craft for the elementary schools in Liberia', BA, Cuttington College, n.d.

Gerald Elwin Currens, 'The Loma farmer: A socio-economic study of rice cultivation and the use of resources among a people of northwestern Liberia', PhD, University of Oregon, 1974. 279p.

Kathleen Addison d'Azevedo, 'Kwi cooking influences of the West African cooking tradition', MA, California State University-San Francisco, 1973. 381p.

Warren Leonard d'Azevedo, 'Continuity and integration in Gola society', PhD, Northwestern University, 1962. 302p.

John Michael D'Amico, 'Spiritual and secular activities of the Methodist Episcopal Church in Liberia, 1833-1933', PhD, St. John's University, 1977. 491p.

Gilbert Ralsron Dale, 'The history of education in Liberia', PhD, University of Missouri Columbia, 1947. 452p.

Paul Mason Daniel, 'A study of the African lizard *Agama africana* Hallowell', MA, University of Miami, Ohio, 1954. 79p.

Jonathan Robert Davis, 'Quantitative studies on the transmission of onchocerciasis by *Simulium sanctipauli* and *Simulium yahense* in Harbel, Liberia (black flies)', PhD, The Johns Hopkins University, 1987. 287p.

Ronald Wayne Davis, 'Historical outline of the Kru Coast, Liberia, 1500 to the present', EdD, Indiania University, 1968. 289p.

Emily Rose De Groat, 'Culture and education in Liberia, West Africa', MA, New Jersey State Teachers College, Newark, 1955. 117p.

Cecily Delafield, 'Arts and crafts education for Liberian schools', EdD, Columbia University, 1967. 267p.

James Cohen Dennis, 'The growth of rice in upland soil both as known amounts of humus mixed in the soil and humus burned with 200 lbs. of fertilizer per acre of 10-10-10 and without fertilizer', BA, Cuttington College, 1958.

McKinley A. Deshield, Jr., 'Shifting cultivation in the tropics with particular emphasis on Liberia', MA, Cornell University, 1962. 92p.

Sadie Deshield, 'Elementary school guidance implications of child-rearing practices in Liberia', MA, Catholic University of America, 1961. 29p.

Sylvester Warren Dickson, 'Liberia: A study of geographic regions', MA, University of Illinois, 1936.

Holger Dietz, 'Vorkommen darmpathogener Bakterien bei authoch-thonen und zugereisten Personen mit und ohne Dairrhoe in Liberia/ Westafrika' ('Occurence of intestinal pathogeneous bacteria in independent and migrant people with and without diarrhoea in Liberia'), PhD, Universität Hamburg, 1978. 43p.

Joseph T. Diggs, 'Malaria and the helminth diseases of Liberia', BA, Cuttington College, 1958.

Osborne K. Diggs, 'Treaties, conventions and agreements concluded between Liberia and the United States from 1847-1955', MA, Atlanta University, 1955.

Eva Carol Dixon, 'A Liberian history workbook for use with the text *The Liberian Hinterland* by Doris Henries for Grades Eleven and Twelve', BA, Cuttington College, 1958.

Eva Carol Dixon, 'A proposed social studies program for Liberian elementary school children', MA, Millersville State Teachers College, 1963. 262p.

Samuel Kanyon Doe, 'A survey of Liberian–U.S. relations', BA, University of Liberia, 1988. 55p.

William Doe, 'English manual for West African primary school teachers', MA, University of California-Los Angeles, 1965.

Jacob S. Dogbeh, 'The need for introducing industrial education in Liberian public schools', MA, San Francisco State University, 1965/66. 156p.

P. Oare Dozier, 'The politics of knowledge: Selected black critiques of Western education 1850-1933', PhD, University of Massachusetts, 1985. 306p.

Julian Iman Dreyden, 'The effects of urbanization, socioeconomic status, and school funding on the dropout rates of elementary school students of Liberia', EdD, Morgan State University, 1988. 178p.

Bo Roland Duberg, 'Forces influencing educational policy making in Liberia: Socio-economic changes and educational relevance', EdD, Columbia University, 1978. 255p.

Bo Roland Duberg, 'Schooling, work experience and earnings: A study of determinants of earnings in a Third World corporate setting', PhD, Stockholm University, 1983. 165p.

Clara V. Dunbar, 'The major social problems of treating and controlling leprosy in the Ganta and Bolahun areas of Liberia', BA, Cuttington College, n.d.

David Cushing Duniway, 'The relations of the United States government to the origin and foundation of Liberia', MA, University of California-Berkeley, 1934. 161p.

Daniel Elwood Dunn, 'The foreign policy of the Republic of Liberia as reflected in selected political questions in the United Nations', PhD, American University, 1972. 345p.

David James Dwyer, 'The comparative phonology of Southwestern Mande nominals', PhD, Michigan State University, 1973. 288p.

David J. Edelman, 'Liberia's development prospects for the 70's: The relationship of economic development to economic nationalism', MA, Cornell University, 1974. 155p.

Dolores Costello Edwards, 'The effect of ecological conditions on the incidence of termites in the Cuttington area', BA, Cuttington College, 1958.

Vivian Joseph Edwards, 'Folk tales from Liberia: A supplementary reader in English for students at Cuttington College, Liberia, West Africa', PhD, Columbia University, 1959. 212p.

Satch oba Ejike, 'Direct investment disputes and United States corporate multinationalism in post-colonial Africa, 1959-1979', PhD, Ohio State University, 1989. 346p.

Luckson Ewhiekpamare Ejofodomi, 'The missionary career of Alexander Crummell in Liberia: 1853 to 1873', PhD, Boston University, 1974. 279p.

Gifty N. Elliott, 'The study of the external features of certain reptiles in the Totota area', BA, Cuttington College, 1958.

Gerald Michael Erchak, 'The Kpelle early learning environment', PhD, Harvard University, 1976. 244p.

Roland I. Erickson, 'Geology of Bomi Hills, Liberia, Africa', MA, University of North Dakota, 1954. 158p.

Pantea Etessami, 'Mutagenesis studies on the genome of cassava latent virus', PhD, University of East Anglia (UK), 1989. 237p.

Edwin Owen Fahnbulleh, 'A critical appraisal of recent educational programs with special emphasis on the discovery of bases for an implementation in-service program in Liberia', MA, North Carolina College at Durham, 1955. 38p.

Maamusu M. Fahnbulleh, 'The history of the education of African girls and women', BA, Cuttington College, 1953.

Eberhard Fischer, 'Der Wandelökonomischer Rollen bei den Westlichen Dan in Liberia' ('The change of economic roles in the Western Dan in Liberia'), PhD, Universität Basel, 1967. 489p.

Henry P. Fisher, 'The Catholic Church in Liberia', MA, Catholic University of America, 1929. 87p.

Miles Mark Fisher, 'The Negro Baptists and foreign missions', BD, Northern Baptist Theological Seminary, 1923.

George R. Flora, 'Come over into Liberia to help us', MA, Northwestern Lutheran Theological Seminary, 1950. 150p.

David Michael Foley, 'Liberia's international status and United States policy 1906-1926', MA, Auburn University, 1961. 168p.

Martin Joseph Ford, 'Ethnic relations and the transformation of leadership among the Dan of Nimba, Liberia', PhD, State University of New York at Binghantom, 1991. 337p.

Nancy Kaye Kirkham Forderhase, 'The plans that failed: The United States and Liberia, 1920-1935', PhD, University of Missouri-Columbia, 1971. 170p.

Early Lee Fox, 'The American Colonization Society, 1817-1840', PhD, The Johns Hopkins University, 1917. 223p.

Barbara Frank, 'Mande leatherworking: A study of style technology and identity', PhD, Indiana University, 1988.

Christa Frank, 'Filariasis in einer Küstenzone Liberias: Eine Kontrolluntersuchung nach Ablauf eines Jahres; Diagnostische und therapeutische Feldstudien' ('Filiarisis in a coastal zone in Liberia: an investigation after one year; diagnostic and therapeutic field surveys'), PhD, Universität Hamburg, 1976. 79p.

Larry Eli Frankel, 'The choices of Kpelle families at certain critical points in the educational careers of their children', EdD, Columbia University, 1979. 274p.

Donald Bruce Franklin, 'The white Methodist image of the negro in Liberia, 1833-1848', EdD, Columbia University, 1975. 105p.

Austin M. Freeman, 'Survey of public administration technical assistance training programs in selected underdeveloped areas for the purpose of recommending a training program for Liberia', MA, George Washington University, 1957. 131p.

Cecilia M. Z. Freeman, 'A model program for teacher education in Liberia', EdD, University of Pittsburg, 1985. 251p.

Edward A. Freeman, 'Evangelical missions in Liberia', ThM, Central Baptist Seminary, 1950. 54p.

James B. Freeman, 'Returns from our agricultural development, 1949-1954', BA, Cuttington College, 1954.

Samuel Vaani Freeman, 'Thirty years of hospital development in Liberia', BA, Cuttington College, 1958.

Ruth Fricke, 'Zukunftserwartungen liberianischer Schuljugend – Versuch eines Beitrages zum Verständnis junger Westafrikaner' ('Future expectations of Liberia's school children – an attempt to understand young West Africans'), PhD, Universität Bonn, 1978. 314p.

Richard Melvin Fulton, 'The Kpelle of Liberia: A study of political change in the Liberian interior', PhD, University of Connecticut, 1969. 285p.

Polycarp Gadegbeku, 'Multiple freezing and thawing of rat serum infested with *Trypanosoma lewsi*', MA, Howard University, 1959.

Frederick Sayon Gbegbe, 'Teacher characteristics associated with the implementation of the Sepa approach to teaching science in Liberia', PhD, University of Illinois at Urbana-Champaign, 1980. 205p.

Dumalo-Banang Gding, 'A study of selected twentieth-century symphonies and original composition: Symphony No. 1 (Liberia)', DA, University of Northern Colorado, 1984. 278p.

Yilma Gebremariam, 'A multidimensional analysis of regional integration and cooperation: The case of Economic Community of West African states', PhD, University of Southern California, 1989.

S. Momolu Getaweh, 'The conceptualization of family size goals among the Mende in Sierra Leone and the Vai in Liberia', PhD, Boston University, 1978. 419p.

Animesh Ghoshal, 'Export commodities and economic development: The Liberian rubber industry', PhD, University of Michigan, 1974. 205p.

James Lowell Gibbs, Jr., 'Some judicial implications of marital instability among the Kpelle', PhD, Harvard University, 1960. 439p.

James Maurice Gifford, 'The African colonization movement in Georgia, 1817-1860', PhD, University of Georgia, 1977. 258p.

Charles Shuttlesworth Gordon, 'Economic problems in a developing society: Liberia', MA, University of California-Berkeley, 1960. 129p.

Lawrence Denog-Beh Grear 'An evaluation of adequacy of the census data in Liberia', PhD, University of Texas at Austin, 1987. 156p.

Nehemiah Carter Greene, 'The effect of soil preparation, soil improvement and shade on the production of tomato at Cuttington College', BA, Cuttington College, 1958.

Ralph Greenwood, 'The Presidency of William V. S. Tubman, President of Liberia, 1944-1971', PhD, Northern Arizona University, 1993. 272p.

Doris D. Duncan Grimes, 'Economic development in Liberia', MA, New York University, 1955.

Joseph Saye Guannu, 'Liberia and the League of Nations: The crisis of 1929-1934', PhD, Fordham University, 1972, 282p.

Esther Livne Guluma, 'Liberian women in administrative and managerial positions', PhD, University of Keele, 1984. 346p.

Gordon Mackay Haliburton, 'The Prophet Harris and his work in Ivory Coast and Western Ghana', PhD, University of London, 1966.

Rirouz Hamidian-Rad, 'A multisector dynamic optimization model for Liberian economic development', PhD, Catholic University of America, 1989. 162p.

John P. Hammond, 'Community development for Robertsport, Liberia', Master of Architecture, University of Idaho, Moscow, Idaho, 1975.

Winston Penn Handweker, 'The Liberian internal market structure', PhD, University of Oregon, 1971. 423p.

John H. Hanson, 'The press on Liberia', MA, Syracuse University, 1972. 115p.

Motuba Israel Harding, 'Improving elementary school principalships in Liberia', MA, Illinois State Normal University, 1957. 69p.

George Way Harley, 'Native African medicine', PhD, Hartford Theological Seminary Foundation, Connecticut, 1938.

Wilber Christian Harr, 'The negro as an American Protestant missionary in Africa', PhD, Divinity School, University of Chicago, 1945. 214p.

Patrick Joseph Harrington, 'Secret societies and the Church: An evaluation of the Poro and Sande secret societies and the missionary among the Mano of Liberia', PhD, Gregorian University, Rome, 1975. 312p.

Katherine Harris, 'The United States, Liberia and their foreign relations to 1847', PhD, Cornell University, 1982. 360p.

Lynn Patrick Hartzler, 'Higher education for imitative roles in educational development projects: An exploratory study', PhD, Stanford University, 1971. 412p.

Gesin Hasen, 'Therapieversuche mit Metrifonate bei mit *Schistosma haematobium* infezierten Minerarbeitern und ihren Angehörigen in Liberia' ('Therapeutic tests with metrifonate in mine workers and their relatives infected with *Schistosoma haematobium*'), PhD, Universität Hamburg, 1979.

Thomas E. Hayden, 'Changing marriage patterns among the Sekleo Kru of Liberia', PhD, Howard University, 1976. 370p.

Raymond Charles Hayes, 'The relation of ethnic politics to the creation of the modern geography of Liberia', M.Litt, Oxford University, 1980. 2 vols. 347p.

Leslie Clyde Hendrickson 'Kinship, achievement and social change in tribal societies: Report of 1300 interviews with rubber workers in Liberia, West Africa', PhD, University of Oregon, 1970. 348p.

Thomas Christian Hendrix, 'The love of liberty: A study of the religious factor in the 19th-century settlement of Afro-Americans in Liberia', PhD, University of Illinois at Chicago, 1985. 457p.

James Jerome Hennelly, 'The Free Port of Monrovia and its impact on the Republic of Liberia, 1943-1971', PhD, St. John's University, 1973. 513p.

Robert G. Henry, 'Adult education as an instrument of social change in Liberia', MA, Indiana University 1966. 73p.

Dieter Heuskel, 'Direktinvestitionen als entwicklungsrelevante Projekt-realisierungen in Entwicklungsländern: dargestellt am Beispiel der mineralischen Rohstoffindustrie' ('Direct investments as develop-mental projects in developing countries as exemplified by the raw minerals industry'), PhD, Universität Bonn, 1979. 291p.

Stephen Shisizwe Hlophe, 'Class, ethnicity and politics in Liberia: The impact of an emergent technocratic class on the Liberian oligarchy from 1944-1975', PhD, McGill University (Canada), 1979. 317p.

Joseph S. Hne, 'Garvey and the administration of Liberian President Charles King, 1919-1924', MA, Morgan State University, 1991. 142p.

Eva Naomi Hodgson, 'The Presbyterian mission to Liberia, 1833-1900', PhD, Columbia University, 1980. 386p.

Advertus Arthur Hoff, 'Higher education for a changing Liberia: An analysis of emerging needs, with proposals for an expanded, strengthened program', EdD, Columbia University, 1959. 375p.

Edward Julius Hoff, 'A proposed program for in-service teacher education in Liberia', MA, Illinois State Normal College, 1957. 68p.

Joanna Tenneh Diggs Hoff, 'The role of women in national development in Liberia, 1800-1900', PhD, University of Illinois at Urbana-Champaign, 1989. 160p.

William Stateman Hoff, Jr., 'The role of the University of Liberia in national development, 1960-1980', PhD, University of Illinois at Urbana-Champaign, 1987. 311p.

Edmund Hogan, 'Catholic missionaries and Liberia', PhD, National University of Ireland, Cork, 1977. 535p. (Also published as a book by Cork University Press in 1981. 268p.)

Edmund Hogan, 'The African Missions in Ireland, 1877-1916', MA, University College, Cork, 1973. 212p.

Willard N. Hogan, 'The United States, Liberia and the League of Nations since 1926', MA, University of Kentucky, 1934. 102p.

Joseph Edward Holloway, 'Liberian diplomacy in Africa: A study of inter-African relations between 1957 to 1966', PhD, University of California-Los Angeles, 1980. 255p.

Svend Einar Holsoe, 'The cassava-leaf people: An ethnohistorical study of the Vai people with particular emphasis on the Tewo chiefdom', PhD, Boston University, 1967. 298p.

Dean Arthur Holt, 'Change strategies initiated by the Protestant Episcopal Church in Liberia from 1836 to 1950 and their differential effects', EdD, Boston University, 1970. 393p.

George Holmes Honadle, 'Organization design for development administration: A Liberian case study of implementation analysis for project benefit distribution', PhD, Syracuse University, 1978. 315p.

James Franklin Hopewell, 'Islam and the forest: A study of Muslim penetration into French Guinea, Sierra Leone, and Liberia before 1850', PhD, Columbia University, 1958. 187p.

Tometro Hopkins, 'Issues in the study of Afro-Creoles: Afro-Cuban and Gullah', PhD, Indiana University, Bloomington, Indiana, 1992. 337p.

Jules Charles Horwitz, 'A case study of the Firestone Tire and Rubber Company in Liberia', MA, University of Chicago, 1959. 98p.

Harold Houghton, 'The role of technical education in the economic development of Liberia and Israel', MA, San Francisco State University, 1968/69.

Lawrence Cabot Howard, 'American involvement in Africa South of the Sahara, 1800-1860', PhD, Harvard University, 1956. 347p.

Mary Ellen Hughes, 'The rural mimeo newspaper experiment in Liberia', MS, University of Wisconsin, 1969. 187p.

K. Hussemann, 'Die Republik Liberia and ihre Beziehungen zum Eingeborenenleben' ('The Republic of Liberia and its relations with its indigenous citizens'), PhD, Berlin, 1949. 123p.

Clarence Hutchinson, Jr., 'The Liberian economy and major American concession agreements', MA, University of Pittsburgh, 1955. 78p.

Uche C. Isiugo-Abanihe, 'Child fostering in West Africa: Prevalence, determinants and demographic consequences', PhD, University of Pennsylvania, 1983. 260p.

George L. Jackson, 'Correctional conditions in Liberia, Angola, and Mozambique', MA, San Diego State University, 1969. 125p.

Linda Collier Jackson, 'The relationship of certain genetic traits to the incidence and intensity of malaria in Liberia, West Africa', PhD, Cornell University, 1981. 342p.

Robert Thaddeus Jackson, 'Anemia of pregnancy in Liberia, West Africa: A therapeutic trial', PhD, Cornell University, 1981. 247p.

Raymond B. Jallah, 'The native methods of food production of Liberia', BA, Cuttington College, 1954.

Abraham Lamina James, 'National integration and the Liberian political process, 1943-1985', PhD, University of Pennsylvania, 1990. 313p.

Lydia Angela Jarosz, 'The nutritional implications of changing sociocultural patterns of infant feeding in the Republic of Liberia', PhD, University of Minnesota, 1985. 315p.

Bankole Jarrett, 'Untersuchungen zur körperlichen Leistungsfähigkeit liberianische Studenten' ('Investigations about the physical capabilities of Liberian medical students'), PhD, Universität Hamburg, 1972. 33p.

Paul R. Jeffy, 'Foreign aid and economic growth in Liberia', BA, Cuttington College, 1968.

Frances M.S. Jennings, 'The early activities of the Maryland State Colonization Society in Liberia, 1831-1834', MA, Columbia University, 1951. 183p.

Knud Rosmussen Jensen, 'The education aspect of the Lutheran Mission in Liberia', MA, New York University, 1927. 93p.

Joe Bernard Jimmeh, 'The transfer of administrative training institutions of Africa: The Institutes of Public Administration of Ghana, Western Nigeria, and Liberia', PhD, Syracuse University, 1987. 505p.

Frances T. Jinlack, 'A project manual on public health administration and supervision in Liberia', Thesis for Certificate, Personnel Training Department of Health, Manila, Philippines, 1967.

A. E. Nyema Jones, 'Origin and distribution of elements in laterites and lateritic soils', PhD, University of Chicago, 1963. 125p.

A. E. Nyema Jones, The exploration and development of the mineral resources of Liberia', BA, Cuttington College, 1955. 60p.

Hannah Abeodu Bowen Jones, 'The struggle for political and cultural unification in Liberia, 1847-1930', PhD, Northwestern University, 1962. 327p.

Joseph Mills Jones, 'A macroeconomic study of the Liberian economy: a short-run analysis', PhD, The American University, 1976. 121p.

Wede Sareta Jones, 'Analysis of faculty development in higher education in the United States of America and implications for faculty development in Liberal Arts Colleges in Liberia', EdD, Columbia University, 1986. 344p.

Charles Baylus Justice, III, 'The social structure of Greenville: Prestige and mobility in a Liberian coastal town', PhD, Wayne State University, 1980. 155p.

I. Sorie Kondowa Kajue, 'Transformation of Liberian peasantry under peripheral capitalism', PhD, University of Manchester (UK), 1987. 304p.

John M. Kallon, 'Contextualism of Christianity in Africa: A participatory Bible study of Exodus for the Kpelle of Liberia', DMin., United Theological Seminary, 1987. 257p.

Edith Zoe Kamara, 'Progress of teacher education in Liberia, 1928-1958', MA, University of Michigan, 1960.

Ronald Kaminsky, 'Untersuchungen zur Biologie, Ökologie und Infektion von Tsetsefliegen (Diphtera, Glossinidae) in einem Regenwaldgebiet Liberias' ('Investigations about the biology, ecology and infection of tsetse flies in a Liberian rain forest area'), PhD, Universität Göttingen, 1983. 144p.

Robert Kappel, 'Ökonomie, Klassen und Staat in Liberia. Entwicklung gesellschaftlicher Widersprüche im peripheren Kapitalismus im 19. und 20. Jahrhundert' ('Economy, classes and government in Liberia. Development of social contradictions in peripheral capitalism in the 19th and 20th century'), PhD, Universität Bremen, 1982. 370p.

Joseph S. Kappia, 'Developmental and political news coverage in the Liberian press', MS, San Jose University, 1989. 66p.

Martin Karpeh, 'Gesundheitsprobleme Liberias' ('Health problems in Liberia'), PhD, Universität Bremen, 1963. 68p.

Nmano B. Kawah, 'Diseases and insect vectors in Liberia', BA, Cuttington College, 1956.

Melvin D. Kennedy, 'Relations between the United States and Liberia, 1816-1920', MA, Clark University, 1930. 165p.

Edward B. Kesselly, 'The Organization of African Unity as a functioning system', PhD, University of Manchester, 1971.

Nathaniel Ejiogu Kevin, 'Financial treaties and foreign investment in Liberia', MBA, New York University, 1957.

George Klay Kieh, 'Dependency and the foreign policy of a small power: An examination of Liberia's foreign policy during the Tolbert administration, 1971-1980', PhD, Northwestern University, 1986. 287p.

Phyllis Ann Kilbourn, 'Responses to the psychological trauma of Children in war: appropriateness of resources from the social and religious agencies [Liberia]', EdD, Trinity Evangelical Divinity School, 1993. 321p.

J. Dwalu Kimber, 'Liberia and the missionaries', BA, Cuttington College, 1954. 57p.

Edmund Nah Kloh, 'Analysis for specific influences on students' acquisition of written and spoken English in selected public schools in Liberia, a multi-dialect setting', EdD, Texas Southern University, 1988. 171p.

Erasmus Helm Kloman, Jr., 'The investment climate in three West African countries: Liberia, The Ivory Coast and Ghana', PhD, University of Pennsylvania, 1962.

Peter Hans Koch, 'Die Shiftingcultivation und ihre Luftbildauswertung. Eine vergleichende Übersicht zur "Shifting Cultivation" und Luftbildausbildauswertung aus dem Hinterland von Monrovia' ('A comparative survey about shifting cultivation and aerial photo interpretation in the humid tropics with an agrarian geographic aerial photo interpretation from the hinterlands of Monrovia'), PhD, Universität Zürich, 1970. 137p.

Jon Nognwulo Kolleh, 'Industry in Liberia: Implications for junior high schools through the colleges', MA, San Francisco State University, 1973. 157p.

Jon Nognwulo Kolleh, 'The need for technical education in Liberia: implications for manpower development', PhD, Ohio State University, 1975. 209p.

Konia Tweninmic Kollehlon, 'Residence background, internal migration and fertility in Liberia', PhD, University of Maryland, 1982. 311p.

Stephen Nge Konfor, 'Study abroad as a strategy of manpower development: The propensity of African students to remain in the United States after graduation (a closer look)', PhD, Wayne State University, 1989. 259p.

Augustine Konneh, 'Indigenous entrepreneurs and capitalists: The role of the Mandinka in the economic development of modern-day Liberia', PhD, Indiana University, 1992. 189p.

Peter V. Konneh, 'The role of Bolahun in the educational program of Liberia', BA, Cuttington College, 1953.

Thomas Gesae Koon, 'Development of a conceptual model for the creative teaching of social studies in the secondary schools of Liberia', EdD, Social Science Education, University of California, Los Angeles, 1980. 234p.

Emmanuel Seeku Koroma, 'A survey study of the Liberian mineral resources of iron ore, gold, and diamonds, and the possible means of their development', BA, Cuttington College, 1958.

Emmanuel Seeku Koroma, 'Appraisal of public education in Liberia with recommendations for improvements of instruction', MA, Illinois State Normal University, 1963. 90p.

Werner Korte, 'Organisation und gesellschaftliche Funktion unabhängiger Kirchen in Afrika' ('Organization and social function of independent churches in Africa. Examples from Liberia and the attempt at a general theory'), PhD, Universität Giessen, 1974. 588p.

Joseph D. Z. Korto, 'Analysis of a policy formulation process for external aid to education: The case of the World Bank and Liberia', PhD, The Catholic University of America, 1991. 199p.

Paul M. Korvah, 'Patterns of child care among the Loma and Kpelle tribes of Liberia', BA, Cuttington College, 1955.

Moussa Kourouma, 'International trade flows and economic interdependence in the West African Market', PhD, Rensselaer Polytechnic Institute, 1990. 138p.

Fodee Kromah, 'The geology and occurrences of iron deposits in Liberia and the impact of mining on the environment', PhD, Cornell University, 1974. 208p.

Alfred Akki Kulah, 'The organization and learning of proverbs among the Kpelle of Liberia', PhD, University of California, Irvine, 1973. 151p.

Arthur Flomo Kulah, 'Theological education in Liberia: Problems and opportunities', ThD, Wesley Theological Seminary, 1970. 174p.

Charles Ownsu Kwarteng, 'Challenges of regional economic cooperation among the ECOWAS states of West Africa', PhD, University of Pittsburg, 1989. 364p.

Henry Geeduoba Kwekwe, 'Liberia's national educational policy goals and factors affecting their achievement', EdD, University of Southern California, 1979. 190p.

George Nee Oko Lamptey, 'Public subsidization of non-public schools and the development of education in Liberia', EdD, Columbia University, 1990. 185p.

David F. Lancy, 'Work play and learning in a Kpelle town', PhD, University of Pittsburg, 1974. 453p.

George F. Landry, 'Realistic expectations of seminarians preparing for the Mission of Cape Palmas, Liberia, Africa', MA, Catholic University of America, 1966. 60p.

Robert Selig Leopold, 'Prescriptive alliance and ritual collaboration in Loma society', PhD, Indiana University, 1991. 388p.

Jefferson D. Lewis, 'A survey of the earthworms in the Suacoco area', BA, Cuttington College, 1958.

William Henry Lewis, 'The progress made by Liberia from 1847 to 1900...', MA, Ohio State University, 1930. 118p.

Wolfgang Liedke, 'Beziehungen zwischen Produktivkräften und Produktionsverhältnissen bei Völkern Nordghanas, Obervoltas und im Hinterland Liberias' ('Relations between productive forces and production relations amongst peoples of Northern Ghana, Upper Volta and the hinterlands of Liberia'), PhD, Universität Leipzig, 1975. 296p.

Thomas Wills Livingston, 'Edward Wilmot Blyden, West African cultural nationalist: His educational activities and ideas', PhD, Columbia University, 1972.

Frank Brown Livingstone, 'The explanation of the distribution on the sickle cell gene in West Africa with particular reference to Liberia', PhD, University of Michigan, 1957. 163p.

Melvin Long, 'Monrovia, Liberia's plan for the career development of its citizens', MA, California State University, Long Beach, 1977. 93p.

Ronald W. Long, 'A comparative study of the northern Mande languages', PhD, Indiana University, 1971. 190p.

John Louis, 'The helping role of American education advisors in a West African country: Implications for cross-cultural urban education', PhD, Wayne State University, 1972. 145p.

Martin Lowenkopf, 'Political modernization and integration in Liberia', PhD, University of London, 1969. 359p.

M. Townsend Lucas, 'The Liberian presidential election of 1955', MA, Howard University, 1960. 165p.

Stephen Rudy Luckau, 'A tonal analysis of Grebo and Jobo', PhD, Stanford University, 1975. 186p.

Peter Luthe, 'Epidemiologische Untersuchungen an Schulkindern in Liberia/Westafrika: ein Bericht über ernährungsweisen und dem Gesundheitszustand der Mundhöhle' ('Epidiomological investigations in students in Libera/Western Africa: A report about nutrition and the health of the oral cavity'), PhD, Universität Marburg, 1978. 70p.

Judson Merrick Lyon, 'Britain and the crisis of Liberian independence, 1903-1909', PhD, University of Connecticut, 1977. 244p.

Hans Jörg Maasch, 'Erhebungen und Experimente zur Übertragung von *Wucheria bancrofti* durch verschiedene Stechmückengenera in einem Küstengebiet in Liberia' ('Investigations and experiments about the transmission of *Wucheria bancrofti* through various kinds of mosquitoes in a coastal area in Liberia'), PhD, Universität Hamburg, 1973. 55p.

Karl-Joachim Mahncke, 'Methodische Untersuchungen zur Kartierung von Brandrodungsflächen im Regenwald von Liberia mit Hilfe von Luftbildern' ('Methodological investigations about the cartography of fire clearing in the Liberian rain forest with aerial photos'), PhD, Universität München, 1973. 57p.

Mae Haha Makor, 'The treatment and control of yaws in the Kpain and Sanodwele areas of Liberia', BA, Cuttington College, 1958.

Woah-tee J. Mamodee, 'An analysis of the problems in producing trained teachers for Liberia, (1980-1989)', University of Maryland, 1989. 94p.

Moses Mammadi Mamulu, 'A revised program of vocational education for Booker T. Washington Agriculture and Industrial Education with implications for Liberia', MA, Ohio State University, 1953. 111p.

Arthur Nanuh Manly, 'Liberia College, The University of Liberia: A descriptive history, 1851-1963', MA, Chapman College, 1965. 83p.

Fletcher Summerfield Manson, 'Liberia and her international relations', PhD, University of Pennsylvania, 1924.

Lynell Marchese, 'Tense aspect and the development of auxiliaries in the Kru language family', PhD, University of California-Los Angeles, 1979. 520p.

Lawrence Anthony Marinelli, 'Liberia: A current historical survey', PhD, St. John's University, 1965.

Jane Jackson Martin, 'The dual legacy: Government authority and mission influence among the Glebo of eastern Liberia, 1834-1910', PhD, Boston University, 1968. 477p.

Amelia T. Mason, 'An analytical survey of the Liberian educational systems', MA, Chapman College, 1965. 43p.

Melvin Justinian Mason, 'The role of Cuttington College in the development of Liberia', EdD, Michigan State University, 1965. 197p.

Fatima Massaquoi, 'Nationalist movements in West Africa', MA, Fisk University, 1940.

Andreas Walter Massing, 'Economic developments in the Kru culture area', PhD, Indiana University, 1977. 452p.

Gerhard Mayerhofer, 'Missbildungen und Anomalien des Gebisses Liberianischer Cercopithecidae' ('Deformations and anomalities in the teeth of Liberian Cercopithecidae'), PhD, Universität Göttingen, 1978. 118p.

Frederick Dean McEvoy, 'History, tradition and kinship as factors in modern Sabo labor migration', PhD, University of Oregon, 1971. 705p.

David Wayne McGrail, 'Mechanisms of sedimentation on the continental shelf of Liberia and Sierra Leone', PhD, Geology, University of Rhode Island, 1976. 129p.

Marie Tyler McGraw, 'The American Colonization Society in Virginia 1816-1832: A case study in Southern Liberalism', PhD, George Washington University, 1980. 250p.

Russell Uber McLaughlin, 'The economic development of Liberia between 1940 and 1955: A study of the role of United States public and private investment in economic development', PhD, University of Pennsylvania, 1958. 446p.

Diana Bralah McNeil, 'The Liberian Republic – the development of the nineteenth century experiment in government', MA, University of Southern California, 1910. 138p.

John Hanson Thomas McPherson, 'History of Liberia', PhD, Johns Hopkins University, 1890.

Charles Arthur Mehaffey, 'Teacher education in Liberia', PhD, Education, Bowling Green State University, 1980. 214p.

Gopal Krishna Mehrotra, 'A study of Liberia's population with special emphasis on ethnic and fertility variations', PhD, University of Pennsylvania, 1980. 283p.

Wolfgang Meins, 'Elephantiasis und Filariaasis in Endemiegebieten Liberias' ('Elephantiasis and filariasis in endemic areas in Liberia'), PhD, Universität Hamburg, 1983. 118p.

Scudder Mekell, 'Preliminary survey of social administration of the Kru, Grand Cess, Liberia, and comparison with the Grebo, Nimiah, Liberia', MA, University of Chicago, 1929. 68p.

P. Golafale Metzgor, 'Medical facilities and disease control in Liberia', BA, Cuttington College, 1955.

Robert James Minges, 'Land and labor problems of Liberia's economic development', MA, University of Chicago, 1949. 133p.

John Payne Mitchell, 'America's Liberian policy', PhD, University of Chicago, 1955. 367p.

John Payne Mitchell, 'Firestone in Liberia', MA, Boston University, 1953. 156p.

Lee O. Dia Mitchell, 'The impact of western civilization on the social, religious and political life of the Mah tribe', BA, Cuttington College, 1956.

Salome Susan Mitchell, 'International relations of Liberia since 1900', MA, University of Illinois, 1936. 159p.

James Kormoh Momah, 'An academic guidance handbook for Liberian schools', BA, Cuttington College, 1958.

Harry Fumba Moniba, 'Booker T. Washington, Tuskegee Institute, and Liberia: Institutional and moral assistance, 1908-1969', PhD, Michigan State University, 1975. 178p.

Lester Parker Monts, 'Music in Vai society: An ethnomusicological analysis of a Liberian ethnic group', PhD, University of Minnesota, 1980. 370p.

Hannah E. Moore, 'The role of the family in the Liberian hinterland', BA, Cuttington College, 1958.

Mary Moran, 'Civilized women: Gender and prestige among the Glebo of Cape Palmas, Liberia', PhD, Brown University, 1986. 215p.

Edwina Albertha Morgan, 'History of the educational development of Bassa', BA, Cuttington College, 1954.

Joseph Morris, 'A proposal for the improvement of Liberia's in-service education program', MA, 1958.

Joseph Getehmnah Morris, Sr., 'An investigation of some of the factors associated with persistence in teaching in Liberia', PhD, Cornell University, 1968. 161p.

Melvina M. Morris, 'A science course for the sixth grade in the elementary schools of Liberia', BA, Cuttington College, n.d.

H. G. Mudarovsky, 'Die Sprache der Kissien Liberia' ('The language of the Kissi in Liberia'), PhD, Universität Wien, 1948.

James Karvee Mulbah, 'Comparative growth of coffee liberica and coffee robusta with and without shade and fertilizer', BA, Cuttington College, 1958.

Paul F. Mulligan, Jr., 'Government functions in an underdeveloped free enterprise economy: The economic system of Liberia', PhD, Duke University, 1973. 407p.

William Alan Muraskin, 'Black Masons: The role of fraternal orders in the creation of a middle-class black community', PhD, University of California, Berkeley, 1970. 288p.

Peter John Murdza, Jr., 'The tricolor and the lone star: A history of Franco-Liberian relations 1847-1930', PhD, University of Wisconsin-Madison, 1979. 535p.

Peter John Murdza, Jr., 'The American Colonization Society and emigration to Liberia 1865 to 1904', MA, University of Wisconsin, 1972. 154p.

William Peter Murphy, 'A semantic and logical analysis of Kpelle proverb metaphors of secrecy', PhD, Stanford University, 1976. 259p.

Oumar Nabe, 'Military expenditures and socioeconomic development in Africa', PhD, Columbia University, 1983. 267p.

Stephen T. Nagbe, 'The evolution and development of clergy training in the Methodist Church and in Liberia', BA, Cuttington College, 1956.

Peter Lorkula Naigow, 'How the Voice of America's African Division perceives and programs for sub-Saharan Africa: A case study of criteria used in determining programming policies', PhD, University of Wisconsin, Madison, 1977. 237p.

James Christopher Gbayon Natt, 'The diffusion of the tripartite philosophy of government in the educational system of the Republic of Liberia', PhD, University of Michigan, 1978. 587p.

Valens Ndoreyaho, 'Untersuchungen zur Nährstoffversorgung von Pflanzen von Humidtropischen Böden des Lizenzgebietes der "Bong Mining Company"' ('Investigations about plant nutrition in humid-tropical soils in the licence area of the Bong Mining Company'), PhD, Universität Bonn, 1978. 173p.

Thelma Evangeline Nelson, 'Development of the executive branch of government in Liberia since 1942', MPA, School of Public Administration, 1969.

Debra Lynn Newman, 'The emergence of Liberian women in the nineteenth century', PhD, Howard University, 1984. 508p.

Fawoni Nguma, 'Missions and education in Liberia: A check list of annotated writings (1824-1977) on Western education in Liberia with emphasis on its mission origins', PhD, University of Missouri-Kansas City, 1979. 598p.

Anthony Jlanyene Nimley, 'The Liberian bureaucracy: a measurement of the relationship between executive appointment and bureaucratic performance', PhD, University of Maryland, 1976. 349p.

Jay Hamilton Nolan, 'Culture and psychosis among the Loma tribe of Liberia, West Africa', PhD, Stanford University, 1972. 276p.

Araba Kofi Noonoo, 'Relationship between children's self-esteem and their perception of parental behavior and God images among Liberians and African-Americans', PhD, Northwestern University, 1991. 158p.

Laura Cecilia Norman, 'Criteria for reorganization of secondary school curriculum in Liberia', MA, Illinois State Normal University, 1957. 72p.

Oscar Norman, 'Liberian tribal life', MA, Liberia College, 1941.

Elizabeth L. Normandy, 'Black Americans and U.S. policy toward Africa: Two case studies form the pre-world War II period', PhD, University of South Carolina, 1987. 473p.

Pathenia Emily Norris, 'United States and Liberia: The slavery crisis, 1929-1935', PhD, Indiana University, 1961. 279p.

Enoch G. David Nyakoon, 'Toward a theology of mission for Liberia: an appropriation of David Bosch's model', MTh, The Southern Baptist Theological Seminary, Louisville, Kentucky, 1993. 118p.

Patricia A. O'Connell, 'Bandi oral narratives', MA, Indiana University, 1976. 161p.

George Gordon Parker, 'A preliminary ethnological survey of the native tribes of Liberia', MST, Hartford Seminary Foundation, 1941. 113p.

John Patrick O'Grady, 'Hospital use among the Kpelle', MA, Stanford University, 1969. 150p.

Dorith M. Ofri-Scheps, 'On the object of ethnology: Apropos of Vai culture in Liberia', PhD, University of Berne, Switzerland, 1991.

Lazarus Chike Okeke, 'A history of the Protestant Episcopal Church in Liberia', BD, Cuttington College, 1955. 66p.

Lazarus Chike Okeke, 'Liberia and its health program', BA, Cuttington College, 1952.

James Okoro, 'The Mano River Union: A test of functionalism (Liberia, Guinea, Sierra Leone)', PhD, Southern Illinois University at Carbondale, 1984. 227p.

Corann Phelps Okorodudu, 'Achievement training and achievement motivation among the Kpelle of Liberia: A study of household structure antecedents', EdD, Harvard University, 1966. 313p.

Roy Olton, 'Problems of American foreign relations in the African area during the nineteenth century', PhD, Tufts University, 1954. 239p.

Peter Kent Opper, 'The mind of the white participant in the African Colonization Movement 1816-1840', PhD, University of North Carolina-Chapel Hill, 1972. 318p.

Ezekiel Oyeyipo, 'Foreign investment and development in small countries: A comparative study of six nations', MA, Vanderbilt University, 1972. 119p.

Diane Oyler, 'If you haven't eaten rice you haven't eaten: A brief history of agriculture education policy in Liberia', MA, University of Florida, 1989. 180p.

C. Siada Paasewe, 'The problem of school attendance in Grand Cape Mount County, Liberia', MA, Illinois State Normal College, 1959. 157p.

Panday Parekh, 'Operational concerns and primary health care: need for an interdisciplinary approach and constraints to its implementation in a developing country', University of California, Los Angeles, 1984. 113p.

George Gordon Parker, 'A preliminary ethnological survey of the native tribes of Liberia', MST, Hartford Seminary Foundation, 1941. 113p.

George Gordon Parker, 'Acculturation in Liberia', PhD, Hartford Seminary Foundation, 1944. 315p.

Barbara C. Patterson, 'Developments in government sponsored education in Liberia, 1944-1964', MA, Howard University, 1967.

Hollis Dwight Paul, 'Cognitive factors of rural-urban migration in Liberia: A case for the development of an experimental practice of anthropology', PhD, University of California, Irvine, 1972. 237p.

Charles O. Paulin, 'Diplomatic negotiations by American naval officers', PhD, Johns Hopkins University, 1903.

George Saa Pawa, 'The primitive rice culture in Liberia', BA, Cuttington College, 1954.

Lee E. Perkins, 'An evaluation of the vocational training program of the Foreign Assistance Project at Booker T. Washington Institute in Kakata, Liberia', PhD, University of Denver, 1959. 51p.

Clifton J. Phillips, 'Protestant America and the pagan world: The first half century of the American Board of Commissioners for Foreign Missions, 1810-1860', PhD, Harvard University, 1954. 360p.

Hilton Alonzo Phillips, 'Organization and administration techniques of the Liberian national government', MA, University of Southern California, 1948. 160p.

James E. Porter, 'Internal balancing and alignment with the U.S.: The cases of Kenya, Liberia, and Zaire', PhD, Johns Hopkins University, 1993.

Phillip W. Porter, 'Population distribution and land use in Liberia', PhD, London School of Economics and Political Science, 1956. 213p.

Robert William Price, 'The Black Republic of Liberia, 1822-1912: A ninety year struggle for international acceptance', PhD, University of Illinois-Urbana-Champaign, 1980. 262p.

Pearl Eileene Primus, 'An anthropological study of masks as teaching aids in the enculturation of Mano children', PhD, New York University, 1978. 234p.

Joellen Pryce, 'Background to United States neo-colonialism in Liberia', MA, Howard University, 1972.

Yvonne Ramboz, 'Relations intersectorielles dans le développement économique du Libéria' ('Intersectorial relations in the economic development of Liberia'), Doct. D'Etat-Droit, Université de Paris, 1960. 245p.

John G. Rancy, 'The impact of political suffrage upon the status of the Westernized women of Liberia', BA, Cuttington College, 1955.

Joanne Shirley Rankin, 'The development and testing of indigenous word problems for Grades Four-Six in Liberia, West Africa', PhD, University of Michigan, 1977. 332p.

James R. Reed, 'The interaction of government in private enterprises and voluntary agencies in the development of broadcasting in the Republic of Liberia from 1950 to 1970', MA, Temple University, 1970. 144p.

Anette Reimer, 'Thalassamie und Sichelzell-beta-Thalasammie in Liberia (Westafrika)' ('Beta thalassaemia and sickle cell beta thalassaemia in Liberia'), PhD, Universität Berlin, 1985. 86p.

Allan Gale Rice, 'Liberia, 1913', MA, Clark University, n.d.

Margaret Rich, 'Lightening foretells the sound of thunder: A study of Liberia's settlement years, 1820-1835', MA, State University of New York-Brockport, 1974. 137p.

James Coleman Riddell, 'Labor migration and rural agriculture among the Bbannah Mano of Liberia', PhD, University of Oregon, 1970. 158p.

Ben Augustus Roberts, 'Patterns of migration to, within, and from the United States: A case study of Liberian nationals', PhD, Arizona State University, 1986. 184p.

Bibi Zinnah Roberts, 'An experimental study of the effects and prevention of erosion on Cuttington's farm land', BA, Cuttington College, 1958.

Maria Rosalita Roberts, 'Roles of the public and private senior high school principals in Liberia, Africa', PhD, Education, Fordham University, 1979. 346p.

Rudolph L. Roberts, 'An analysis of selected factors affecting economic development in tropical Africa', MA, Ohio State University, 1964. 135p.

Edwin Lahai Rogers, 'The development of the fishing industry in Liberia', BA, Cuttington College, 1954.

Momo Kpaka Rogers, 'Liberian journalism, 1826-1980: A descriptive history', PhD, Southern Illinois University of Carbondale, 1988. 396p.

Isaac Barture Roland, 'Relationship between the Liberian social studies curriculum and both the National Unification and African Unity Movements, 1953-1980', EdD, Temple University, 1988. 232p.

Horst Rompf, 'Liberia als Arbeitskräftemarkt für Kamerun – ein Beitrag zu einem spezifischen Form kolonialer Expansionspolitik während der deutschen Kolonialzeit 1884-1914' ('Liberia as employment market for Cameroon – a contribution to a specific form of colonial expansion policy during the German colonial period 1884-1914'), PhD, Pädagogische Hochschule Magdeburg, 1985. 225p.

Rodney Anson Ross, 'Black Americans and Haiti, Liberia, the Virgin Islands and Ethiopia, 1929-1936', PhD, University of Chicago, 1975. 237p.

Eleanor Lasier Rowe, 'The knowledge of American nurses, serving in Ethiopia, Nigeria, and Liberia concerning the etiology and treatment of typhoid, typhus, and malaria', EdD, Boston University, 1975. 184p.

James Thomas Sabin, 'The making of the Americo-Liberian community: A study of politics and society in nineteenth-century Liberia', PhD, Columbia University, 1974. 300p.

Wesley L. Sadler, Jr. 'The Loma language', PhD, Hartford Theological Seminary Foundation, 1949. 178p.

Santosh Chandrs Saha, 'The romance of nationhood: an investigation of the attitudes of educated Africans toward Liberia, 1847-1980', PhD, Kent State University, 1993. 353p.

William Saa Salifu, 'An analysis of discipline problems in Liberian high schools: Types, incidence, and administrative response', EdD, State University of New York at Albany, 1984. 193p.

Amos C. Sawyer, 'Social stratification and orientations to national development in Liberia', PhD, Northwestern University, 1973. 209p.

Virginia Nyanaplu Sherman, 'A proposed program in social studies for the first grades of Liberia', MA Seminar Report, University of Wisconsin, 1958.

Cynthia Elizabeth Schmidt, 'Multiparty vocal music of the Kpelle of Liberia', PhD, University of California, Los Angeles, 1985. 336p.

John Schmitz, 'Open Door policy of Liberia', MA, Stockholm University, 1968. 82p.

Sterling C. Scott, 'Aspects of the Liberian Colonization Movement in Louisiana', MA, Tulane University, 1953.

Eli Seifman, 'A history of the New York Colonization Society', PhD, New York University, 1965. 209p.

Frederick V. Seitua, 'The development of the iron industry in Liberia', BA, Cuttington College, 1955.

Ruth Nyapa Seitua, 'A handbook for Vai mothers on the scientific care of the mother from conception to birth and the child from birth to two years', BA, Cuttington College, 1958.

Benedict Dotu Sekey, 'A history of Liberia College from the point of view of its Liberian setting', MA, Howard University, 1973. 145p.

L. Tanda Sendekpie, 'The labor force profile of Upper Lofa County: A case study', BA, Cuttington College, 1972. 11p.

Matthew Joko Sengova, 'A classification of tense, aspect, and time specification in the verb system of Mende', PhD, University of Wisconsin, Madison, 1981. 247p.

Amadu Sesay, 'International policies in Africa: A comparative study of the foreign policies of Liberia and Sierra Leone, 1957-73', PhD, London School of Economics, University of London 1978.

Patrick L. N. Seyon, 'Education, national integration and nation-building in Liberia', PhD, Stanford University, 1977. 470p.

El Mohamed Sheriff, 'A proposed plan for the improvement of vocational-technical education in Liberia', PhD, Iowa State University, 1978. 209p.

Charles Dunbar Sherman, 'The economic effects of foreign loans and concessions in Liberia', MA, American University, 1948. 223p.

Robert Gbanya Sherman, 'The monetization, growth and development of the Liberian economy through financial markets and institutions', DBA, Arizona State University, 1983. 214p.

Theresa Sherman, 'The use of instructional materials in the Liberian public schools', MA, San Francisco State College, 1965.

Virginia Nyanaplu Sherman, 'A proposed program in social studies for the first grades of Liberia', MA Seminar Report, University of Wisconsin-Madison, 1958.

Tom Wing Shick, 'The social and economic history of Afro-American settlers in Liberia, 1820-1900', PhD, University of Wisconsin Madison, 1976. 406p.

Joseph Dudu Siaplay, 'Fertility level and differentials among Golas of Liberia', MA, University of Ghana, 1976. 160p.

Phil Samuel Sigler, 'The attitudes of free blacks towards emigration to Liberia', PhD, Boston University, 1969. 222p.

John Victor Singler, 'Variation in tense-aspect modality in Liberian English', PhD, University of California, Los Angeles, 1984. 445p.

Farquema Amadu Sirleaf, 'Curriculum content for training individuals as skilled electricians in residential wiring at the multilateral high school system in Liberia', PhD, Texas A & M University, 1989. 103p.

Hassan Bailey Sisay, 'United States policy toward Liberia: 1923-1947', PhD, Southern Illinois University-Carbondale, 1976. 250p.

Hassan Bailey Sisay, 'United States-Liberian relations, 1923-1935', MA, Southern Illinois University-Carbondale, 1972.

Michael Robert Smith, 'An ethnographic account of literacy and written learning in a Vai town', PhD, Cambridge University, 1982. 346p.

Naomi M. Smith, 'A handbook and color slides', MA, Sacramento State College, 1967. 157p.

Sophie Evangeline Mends-Cole Smith, 'An assessment of the need for pupil personnel services as part of the secondary school system of Liberia', EdD, Columbia University, 1977. 175p.

Theophilus Nimley Sonpon, 'An analysis of teachers' perceived sources of job satisfaction at the Monrovia consolidated school system: A public school district in Liberia', PhD, University of California, Los Angeles, 1983. 205p.

Gilbert P. Spangler, 'Introduction, development, and experimental investigations of natural rubber in Liberia, West Africa', MA, Pennsylvania State College, 1946.

Nema Puo Tidi Anna Speare, 'Organizing a kindergarten curriculum for Liberia', MA, Illinois State Normal University, 1958. 58p.

Theodore R. Speigner, 'The economic activities of the United States in Liberia, 1900-1930', MA, University of Iowa, 1933. 52p.

Randolph Stakeman, 'The cultural politics of religious change: A study of the Kpelle of Liberia', PhD, Stanford University, 1982. 356p.

William Richard Stanley, 'Changing patterns of transportation development in Liberia', PhD, University of Pittsburgh, 1966. 218p.

Phillip John Staudenraus, 'The history of the American Colonization Society', PhD, University of Wisconsin, 1958. 417p.

Flumo Yanquoi Bonawu Stevens, 'Financial intermediaries and economic development: the Liberian case', PhD, University of Nebraska-Lincoln, 1974. 206p.

Ida Harris R. Stevens, 'A study of the status of elementary education in Liberia, West Africa', MA, Virginia State College, 1965. 47p.

James Robert Stevenson, 'Subsistence farming and the quality of life in a rural Liberian community', PhD, Southern Illinois University at Carbondale, 1981. 107p.

Reed F. Stewart, 'The Mande-speaking people of West Africa: a geographic approach to cultural classification', PhD, Clark University, n.d.

Ruth Marie Stone, 'Communication and interaction processes in music events among the Kpelle of Liberia', PhD, Indiana University, 1979. 323p.

Ruth Marie Stone, 'Music of the Kpelle people of Liberia', MA, Hunter College, 1972. 211p.

Verlon Lloyd Stone, 'The effects of color in filmed behavior sequences upon description and elaboration during feedback interviews by Kpelle school boys in Liberia', PhD, Indiana University, 1979. 279p.

David Leandor Stratmon, 'An administrative appraisal of the United States Public Health Mission in Liberia', PhD, University of Michigan, 1955. 286p.

Richard Norman Stuempges, 'The Sande secret society in northwestern Liberia (Wozi area): An agent of socio-cultural control', MA, Duquesne University, 1972. 131p.

Jo Mary Sullivan, 'Settlers in Sinoe County, Liberia and their relations with the Kru', PhD, Boston University, 1978. 456p.

Robert Joseph Swan, 'Thomas McCants Stewart and the failure of the Mission of the Talented Tenth in Black America, 1880-1923', PhD, New York University, 1990. 346p.

Barbara Myers Swartz, 'The Lord's Carpetbagger: A biography of

Joseph Crane Hartzell', PhD, State University of New York-Stony Brook, 1972. 648p.

Dwight Nash Syfert, 'A history of the Liberian coasting trade, 1821-1900', PhD, Indiana University, 1977. 321p.

Dominic Nmah Tarpeh, 'Local participation and institution building: The case of the Lofa County Agricultural Development Project in Liberia', PhD, State University of New York at Albany, 1984. 525p.

James Teah Tarpeh, 'The Liberian-Lamco joint venture partnerships: The future of less developed country and multinational corporation collaboration as a national strategy for host country development', PhD, University of Pittsburgh, 1978. 662p.

Stephen Byron Tarr, 'Efficiency in revenue generation: A measure of ability to promote economic development', PhD, University of Illinois, Urbana-Champaign, 1972. 255p.

Stephen Byron Tarr, 'The role of societal structure in Liberian economic development', MA, University of Illinois, 1970.

Emma Vivian Taylor', A comparative study of the economic, social, and family life of the Kpelle tribe in the towns of Gbarnga during the period between 1900 and 1945 and the period 1945 to the present', BA, Cuttington College, 1958.

John Peter Taylor, 'Liberia and the League of Nations, 1929-1939', PhD, Université de Genève, 1986. 526p.

Michele M. Teitelbaum, 'Officers and elders: A study of contemporary Kpelle political cognition', PhD, Rutgers University, New Brunswick, 1977. 163p.

Benjamin C. E. Temple, 'The economic feasibility of adopting low cost equipment in Liberian agriculture', MA, University of Illinois, 1972. 156p.

Gisela Thiem, 'Liberia, ein Beitrag zur Laenderkunde'('Liberia: A regional study'), PhD, Koeln, 1955.

James Thomas-Queh, 'La politique de contrôle sociale dans un pays en voie de développement: Analyse des lois, des institutions judiciaires et l'application de la justice pénale au Libéria' ('Policy of social control in a developing country: Analysis of laws, judicial institutions and the application of penal justice in Liberia'). Thèse pour le doctorat de 3ème cycle, Université de droit d'économie et de sciences sociales de Paris (Paris II), Paris, 1989. 510p.

James Thomas-Queh, 'Le peuple en révolte: Une étude de psychologie sociale sur le coup d'état au Libéria' ('The people in revolt: A social psychological study of the coup d'état in Liberia'). Mémoire pour le diplôme de l'Ecole des Hautes Etudes en Sciences Sociales, Paris, 1986. 183p.

Gordon C. Thomasson, 'Indigenous knowledge system, sciences and technologies, ethnographic and ethnohistorical perspective in the educational foundations for development in Kpelle culture', PhD, Cornell University, 1987. 399p.

Robert Gbatiae Tikpor, 'Traditional theism in African creation myths with the Bassa (Liberian) Djuankadju as central theme', STD, Pontificial University of St. Thomas Aquinas (Rome), 1981. 451p.

Henrique F. Tokpa, 'Education and other determinants of income among heads of households in rural Liberia', PhD, Florida State University, 1988. 232p.

Angeline Patricia Toles, 'An analysis and evaluation of the in-service education program in public schools of Montserrado County, Liberia, 1957-1958', MA, Atlanta University, 1959. 157p.

Walter Lewis Tompkins, Jr., 'The birth of Liberia: The Reverend Jehudi Ashmun's contribution to early United States influence in Africa', MA, American University, 1963. 85p.

Solomon Hartley Toweh, 'Prospects for Liberian iron ores considering shifting patterns of trade in the world iron ore industry', PhD, University of Arizona, 1989. 356p.

Edison Reginald Townsend, 'Problems of the Liberian press', MA, American University, 1952. 123p.

Oliver W. Tyler, 'Liberia – the League of Nation's plan of assistance', MA, Howard University, 1944. 99p.

Kalu Okoro Uche, 'Ebony kinship: Americo-Liberians, Sierra Leone Creoles and the indigenous African population, 1820-1900: A comparative analysis', PhD, Howard University, 1974. 298p.

Martin Ihoeghian Uhomoibhi, 'Imperial and League intervention in Sierra Leone and Liberia: Boundaries, finance and labour, 1890-1936', DPhil, Oxford, 1983. 328p.

Lester Utz, 'Pioneering in Africa: David Alexander Day, D. D., 1851-1897, his life and letters', BD, Lutheran Theological Seminary (Gettysburg, PA), 1941.

William Okefie Uzoaga, 'The impact of foreign loans on the Liberian fiscal system', MA, Cornell University, 1955. 52p.

Sarr Abdulai Vandi, 'Towards the utilization of mass media in community education programs in Liberia', PhD, State University of New York-Buffalo, 1977. 192p.

John S. Varfley, 'The role of the foreign retailers in Liberian business', BA, Cuttington College, 1958.

Evangeline D. Varnah, 'An appraisal of the missionary activities of the Foreign Mission Board of the National Baptist Convention Incorporated in Liberia', BA, Cuttington College, 1956.

James William Vogel, 'Late quaternary sedimentary faces of the southern Sierra Leone and Liberian Continental Shelf and Upper Slope, northwest Africa', PhD, University of Rhode Island, 1982. 375p.

Joseph G. Wachter, 'Early Negro colonization and America's west African settlers of 1820-1822', MA, Morgan State College, 1972. 278p.

Barbara-Yvonne Wagner, 'Arbeitsrecht in der Republic Liberia' ('Labour laws in the Republic of Liberia'), PhD, Universität Bayreuth, Rechts- und Wirtschaftswissenschaftliche Fakultat, 1986. 254p.

Sylvester Walker, 'An analysis of the American Colonization Society and the founding of Liberia', MA, Fisk University, 1974. 160p.

Rebecca J. N. Ware, 'A historical sketch of the episcopal schools of Grand Cape Mount County', BA, Cuttington College, 1954.

Heather Margaret Warrack-Goldman, 'The nutrition of children in a coastal African (Liberian) food economy', PhD, Cornell University, 1979. 292p.

Moses Kronyahn Weefur, 'A survey of public school finance in Liberia, 1826-1956', MA, Illinois State Normal University, 1957. 82p.

Peter Fowler Weisel, 'Change in traditional agriculture: A study of three towns in northern Liberia', PhD, University of Oregon, 1972. 86p.

Ulrich Weiss, 'Anzahl und Verteilung der Knoten und Würmer bei Kindern Mit Onchokerzose in Liberia und Obervolta' ('Number and distribution of knots and worms in children with onchochercose in Liberia and Upper Volta'), PhD, Universität Hamburg, 1979. 101p.

Karen Weisswange, 'Feindschaft und Verwandtschaft, Konflikt und Kooperation im Zusammenleben von Loma und Mandingo in dem Ort Bokeza in Liberia, Ein Beitrag Zur Sozialstruktur der Loma' ('Enmity and kinship: Conflict and cooperation in the co-existence of the Loma and Mandingo in Bodeza in Liberia; an article on the social structure of the Loma'), MA, Johann Wolfgang Goethe-Universitaet, 1969. 172p.

Robert S. Wetherall, 'The African squadron, 1843-1861', MA, University of Delaware, 1968. 137p.

Irene Theresa Whalen, 'Social and agricultural change in Liberia; the adoption of improved swamp rice among the Kpelle', PhD, Cornell University, 1983. 311p.

Harold Vink Whetstone, 'The Lutheran Mission in Liberia', MA, Hartford Seminary Foundation, Hartford, Connecticut, 1954. 160p.

Evelyn Sophonia White, 'The problems and prospects of service education of teachers in Liberia', EdD, Columbia University, 1978. 228p.

Willie Amzie Whitten, Jr., 'The development of a conceptual model for planning and conducting town meetings with selected tribal adults in Liberia', EdD, Indiana University, 1966. 268p.

Werner Theodor Wickstrom, 'The American Colonization Society and Liberia (An historical study in religious motivation and achievement), 1817-1867', PhD, Hartford Seminary Foundation, 1958. 388p.

Walter Tamu Wiles, 'Analysis of factors influencing the agricultural research delivery system in Liberia', EdD, The Louisiana State University and Agricultural and Mechanical College, 1986. 158p.

Christopher Yula Williams, 'United States relations with Liberia, 1940-1960', PhD, Kent State University, 1976. 189p.

Horatio Weah Williams, 'State formation and political integration in Liberia – 1944-1971', PhD, The University of Chicago, 1986. 277p.

Thomas Nelson Williams, 'How "Ebony" and "Life" magazines reported African political, educational, and socio-economic affairs in 1960 and 1961', MA, Indiana University, 1962. 115p.

Walter L. Williams, 'Black American attitudes toward emigration to Africa, 1877-1900', MA, University of North Carolina, Chapel Hill, 1972. 277p.

Walter L. Williams, 'Black American attitudes toward Africa: the missionary movement, 1877-1900', PhD, University of North Carolina, Chapel Hill, 1974. 332p.

Henry D. Wilson, 'The introduction of rural education in the Liberian hinterland', BA, Cuttington College, 1953.

Lawrence Bertell Wilson, 'The Liberian question and the League of Nations', MA, University of Illinois, 1936. 160p.

Thomasyne Lightfoote Wilson, 'Different patterns of instruction in Liberia: Implications for modernization', PhD, Stanford University, 1971. 326p.

Julie Winch, 'The leaders of Philadelphia's black community, 1787-1848', PhD, Bryn Mawr University, 1982. 230p.

Charles Woiwor, 'Alternative tax regime for the Mifergi Joint Project', MA, Colorado School of Mines, Golden, Colorado, June, 1990. 98p.

Anthony Niblette Wojloh, 'Boundary disputes between Liberia and colonial powers, 1911-1923', PhD, Howard University, 1971. 128p.

Edward Lama Wonkeryor, 'A historical development of the role and function of broadcasting in Liberia', MA, University of South Carolina, 1980. 72p.

Elizabeth Woods, 'The changing patterns in Liberian society', BA, Cuttington College, n.d.

Sue M. Woodson-Marks, 'Social perspectives on contextualization: Witnessing cooperation, conflict and ambiguity in Kpelle funeral discourse', PhD, Brandeis University, Waltham, Massachusetts, 1992. 426p.

Delores Parmer Woodtor, 'Urbanization, community formation and political involvement: A case study of Monrovia, Liberia (Urban West Africa)', PhD, Northwestern University, 1986. 170p.

Mary Gertrude Yancy, 'Developing a reading program for the elementary schools in Liberia, grades 1-4', MA, Illinois State Normal University, 1958. 71p.

**List of Theses and Dissertations**

Walter Ladell Yates, 'The history of the African Methodist Episcopal Zion Church in West Africa, Liberia and Gold Coast (Ghana), 1880-1900', MST, Hartford Seminary Foundation, 1963. 168p.

Walter Ladell Yates, 'The history of the African Methodist Episcopal Zion Church in West Africa, Liberia, Gold Coast (Ghana) and Nigeria, 1900-1939', PhD, Hartford Seminary Foundation, 1967. 398p.

Louise C. Wilson York, 'Science teaching in an underdeveloped country', MA, Wayne State University, 1966.

Levi Zangai-Reeves, 'The Liberian intellectual legacy and organization theory of development administration, 1971-1980: Towards a possibility model of social systems delimitation and para-economy', PhD, University of Southern California, 1984. 448p.

Otto-Gert Zietlow, 'Untersuchungen über den Ablauf des Zahnwechseis bei Liberianischen Schulkindern' ('Investigations about the course of teeth change in Liberian school children'), PhD, Universität Hamburg, 1982. 55p.

# The Country and Its People

1 **Reisebilder aus Liberia.** (Recollections of Liberia.)
Johan Buttikofer. Leiden, Germany, E. J. Brill, 1890. 2 vols. bibliog.

A monumental study of Liberia's fauna and flora, as well as its indigenous peoples. The work was the result of two extended field trips through Liberia's hinterland in 1879-1882 and 1886-1887. Planned by Dr. Hermann Schlegel, Director of the Imperial Zoological Museum in Leiden, the original aim of the expedition was to conduct zoological investigations in Liberia. However, much wider studies were undertaken. The contents of these volumes reveal that significant geographical, ethnographical, and other scientific information was gathered. Volume one carries the subtitle 'pictures of the trip and the general characteristics of the country', and Volume two is subtitled 'the inhabitants of Liberia and the animal world' and includes much information on the political and social conditions of the indigenous peoples of Liberia. An excellent bibliography is included.

2 **Liberia 1970: a pictorial record.**
Monrovia: Department of Information and Cultural Affairs, 1970. 96p.

Published to mark the seventy-fifth birthday of President Tubman, this volume is designed to highlight his achievements since the beginning of his presidency in 1944.

3 **Le Libéria.** (Liberia.)
Louis Dollot. Paris: Presses Universitaires de France, 1981. 128p.
(Que Sais-Je?).

A former French Ambassador to Liberia introduces modern Liberia to a French audience in the famous 'Que sais-je?' series. It breaks no new ground despite the fact that the author witnessed the political upheaval of the 1970s that culminated in the *coup d'état* of 1980. The contents focus on political history, and present a sympathetic coverage of the American Colonization Society's promotion of Liberia as an outpost of the Western world in Africa.

1

4 **Eléments d'une monographie d'une division administrative Libérienne, Grand Bassa County.** (The monographic elements of a Liberian administrative division, Grand Bassa County.)
J. Genevray. Dakar, Senegal: Institut Français d'Afrique Noire (IFAN), 1952. 135p. illus. map. (no. 21).

Describes Grand Bassa County, a region of 9,000 square kilometres spreading along the central coast and reaching deep into the interior. Amongst the topics addressed in this study are the physical setting and climate; the history of the arrival of blacks from the New World, their origins and how they settled; the habitat and anthropometry of the indigenous ethnic groups of the Bassa, the Kru and the Vai; the Liberian administrative system; religion in Liberia; and the Bassa language.

5 **The Liberian flag.**
A. Doris Banks Henries. Monrovia: Published by the author. 1974. 27p.

This national symbol, like the seal and the 1847 constitution, reflects a nineteenth-century concept of Liberia which did not include the political culture of the indigenous African peoples. Although efforts were later made to redress the balance, this book essentially portrays the mid-nineteenth century notion of the country. There is a brief history of the national flag followed by descriptions of the national seal, and the regional or County flags – Montserrado, Grand Bassa, Sinoe (all 1847), Maryland (1857), Grand Cape Mount (1934), Bong, Nimba, Lofa and Grand Gedeh (all 1964). The words and music of the National Anthem, as well as other national hymns are also included.

6 **A land and life remembered: Americo-Liberian folk architecture.**
Svend E. Holsoe, Bernard L. Herman, Max Belcher, Roger P. Kingston.
Athens, Georgia: University of Georgia Press, 1988. 176p.

Contains a photographic essay collaboratively presented by photographer Belcher, the anthropologist Holsoe, the folklorist Herman, and the research associate Kingston. The focus of the work is on the settlement of Arthington, near the Liberian capital. Belcher's captivating photographs are mainly in black-and-white but include four colour photographs of Liberian churches. Central to the study is the contention that settler architecture, imported from America's *ante bellum* South, provides evidence of settler socio-cultural and other forms of domination of Liberian society, which were ended following the 1980 *coup d'état*.

7 **Grand Cape Mount before and after.**
Abeodu Bowen Jones. Monrovia: Republic Press, 1964. 49p.

Gives a brief historical account of the origins and development of this county and major political sub-division which constitutes one of Liberia's original five regions. The chapters cover basic geography; the initial colonization of areas by the Vai and Gola; political development; economic development efforts; the literary and artistic achievements of the Vai and Gola who are indigenous to the county; and educational development. The study was originally published for the Tubman Centre for African Culture in Grand Cape Mount County's capital of Robertsport.

8 **Background to Liberia.**
Monrovia: Ministry of Information, Cultural Affairs and Tourism, 1979.
160p.

This government publication provides an overview of Liberia, and contains basic and
often reasonably reliable information on the land, people, government, social welfare,
infrastructure and amenities, economy, and the major political sub-divisions (counties
and territories) of the country.

9 **Liberia: a country study.**
Edited by Harold D. Nelson. Washington, DC: The American University,
Foreign Area Studies, 1985. 340p. (Area Handbook Series, Department of
the Army, DA Pam 550-38).

Commissioned for the United States Department of the Army, this study examines
Liberia in the years immediately following the coup of 1980. It is essentially a factual
description of Liberia presented in a reference study format and whilst it provides much
information on the armed and security forces, there is little on the United States' military
and other involvement with the Samuel Doe régime. The volume does, however, contain
a number of factual inaccuracies. Of related interest is the more substantial 1972 edition
of the *Area Handbook for Liberia*, by Thomas D. Roberts, Irving Kaplan, Barbara Lent,
Dennis H. Morrissey, Charles M. Townsend, and Neda Franges Walpole which includes
a useful summary of events from July 1964 to September 1971 and background detail
and information on the economy and national security. Each section of the *Handbook*
contains a good bibliography.

10 **Liberia old and new: a study of its social and economic background
with possibilities of development.**
James L. Sibley, Diedrich Westermann. Garden City, New York:
Doubleday, Doran, 1928. 317p.

Sibley travelled to Liberia under the auspices of the American Advisory Committee on
Education and served as education advisor to the government of Liberia. His book
surveys the economic and social conditions in Liberia at this time (ca. 1928), with
emphasis on indigenous cultures and the educational work of missionary societies in the
country. Westermann's contribution centred on the Kpelle culture which he had
experienced at first hand over several years.

11 **Liberia genealogical research.**
Roma Jones Stewart. Chicago: Homeland Publications. 1991. 50p.

The aim of this interesting pamphlet is to encourage genealogical research on Liberia
particularly on the part of African-Americans. As such, Stewart has written a 'How to'
type booklet. The volume is divided into seven sections covering: geography; history
(with an appended reading list); records (including passenger lists, census, birth records,
death records, etc.); genealogical and historical societies (which are listed); record
repositories; various case studies; and 'How to get started'. The author is an Amerian
lawyer who serves as president of the Afro-American Genealogical and Historical
Society of Chicago.

12  **The African republic of Liberia and the Belgian Congo. Based on the observations made and material collected during the Harvard African expedition, 1926-27.**
Edited by Richard P. Strong.   New York: Greenwood Press, 1969. 2 vols. illus.

Originally published in 1930 by Harvard University Press, this is the report of an expedition undertaken in 1926-27 by the Department of Tropical Medicine and the Institute of Tropical Biology and Medicine of Harvard with the encouragement of Harvey S. Firestone who at the time was establishing his rubber venture in Liberia. The purpose of the expedition was to make a biological and medical survey of Liberia, and to conduct a comparative study of other regions including the Belgian Congo. Divided into three parts, the first part describes the geographical and climatic features of Liberia as well as the inhabitants of the coast and the interior and the conditions under which they live. The longer sections in the first volume are medical and pathological investigations of various diseases. Among the items included in volume two is a study of the parasites of wild games and of the relationship of some of these parasites to human disease. 'Special observations made in the Belgian Congo are included, and a comparison between conditions in the two countries is made' (p. 7). Part III includes biological investigations carried on by other members of the expedition with special reference to botany, mammalogy, ornithology, herpetology, helminthology, and entomology.

13  **Africa: the people and politics of an emerging continent.**
Sanford J. Ungar.   New York: Simon & Schuster, 1986. rev. ed. 543p. map. bibliog. (A Touchstone Book.)

A generally fair overview of the continent with emphasis on the economy and politics of its nations, as well as their relations with the United States. There are extensive discussions of Liberia, Nigeria, Kenya and South Africa. Liberia is considered in chapter three – 'Liberia: American stepchild' (p. 87-120) which describes events in Liberia prior to the 1980 military coup d'état, the first eight years of Samuel K. Doe's régime. This chapter is more descriptive than analytical and presents the old image of former slaves enslaving others, and of Liberian society being sharply divided between settlers and natives. The appendix contains a statistical profile of forty-four countries; the bibliographical essay (p. 487-92) contains useful references.

14  **Draft environmental report on Liberia.**
Washington, DC: United States Agency for International Development (USAID), Library of Congress, Science and Technology Division, 1979. 53p.

Sponsored by USAID through the United States National Committee for Man and the Biosphere, this report represented a preliminary review of information available in the United States on Liberia's environmental and natural resources. The topics covered by the report include the nation's physical, demographic, and socio-economic characteristics; renewable and non-renewable resources; parks, reserves, and other protected areas; and environmental problems including deforestation, pollution resulting from mineral exploitation, unregulated urban expansion, inadequate rural water supply and poor sanitation; and a lack of legislative and institutional mechanisms necessary for environmental management. The report contains fifty-nine references and appendices (consisting of demographic, social, and economic data; information about vegetation and endangered animal species; and a biogeographical map).

# Geography and Geology

15 **Historical atlas of Africa.**
Edited by J. F. Ade Ajayi, Michael Crowder. London, New York:
Cambridge University Press, 1985. 72p. bibliog.
The volume contains sixty black-and-white and seventy-two large colour maps
displaying a vast amount of information on the continent's geography, history, politics,
and economics. The product of fifty-seven contributors, the atlas is based on three main
types of maps – 'events' maps (containing information regarding historical events and
offering a frame of reference for the location of towns, battle sites, trade routes, etc.
mentioned in the accompanying text); 'process' maps (providing a visual interpretation
of historical processes); and 'quantitative' maps (which use numerical data to
characterize historical processes or relationships).

16 **Geophysical surveys of Liberia with tectonic and geological
interpretations.**
John C. Behrendt, Cletus S. Wortorson, prepared in co-operation with the
Liberian Geological Survey under the auspices of the Government of
Liberia and the Agency for International Development of the US
Department of State. Washington, DC: Government Printing Office,
1974. 33p. maps. (Geological Survey Professional Paper, no. 810).
To assist in the Liberian government's programme of reconnaissance geologic mapping
of Liberia, 'an aeromagnetic survey and a totalcount gamma-radiation survey were flown
over Liberia in 1967-68. The US Army Topographic Command participated in a gravity
survey with the US Seventy Second Engineering Detachment and provided a gravity
meter'. The present report 'integrates the geologic work with the geophysical data'. The
geological and geophysical interpretations presented in this publication are only
provisional and may be revised as a result of future field investigations.

17 **Planning and development atlas.**
Prepared for the Liberian Ministry of Planning and Economic Affairs,
Monrovia by Deutsche Gesellschaft für technische Zusammenarbeit (gtz),
Eschhorn, Germany: Henning Wocke kg, 1983. 67p. 37 maps.

Contains thirty-seven coloured maps on various topics such as national development
potentials and proposed areas of development; population; languages; natural resources;
elements of infrastructure; sectors of economy; and administrative units. A handbook is
also included, providing basic information on such areas as the natural and physical
conditions; demography and social conditions; economic and political geography; and
political and administrative divisions. A major shortcoming is the study's use of the
dated 1974 census when the 1984 census was published only a year after the study
became available.

18 **Liberia: geographical mosaics of the land and the people.**
K. H. Hasselman.   Lagos, New York: Third Press International, 1979.
287p.

This is a good reference work officially sanctioned by the Liberian government's
Ministry of Information, Cultural Affairs and Tourism. It contains basic information in
the form of narrative 'mosaics' on the economic geography of the country; population
and migration; urban society; and general geographical features.

19 **The climatology of West Africa.**
Derek F. Hayward, Julius S. Oguntoyinbo.   Totowa, New Jersey: Barnes
& Noble, 1987. 271p.

The aim of this book is to provide readers with an understanding of West African
climates, 'what they are like, and why, and the extent to which man is governed by them
and in turn can affect them.' Stressing that little can be sensibly planned for the future
without a knowledge of the environment, the authors assert that like water, soil, gold,
diamonds, or the people themselves, the climate should be regarded as a resource. The
contents include 'Description: the climate and West Africa'; 'Explanation: West African
climatology and meteorology'; and 'Application: applied climatology in West Africa'.
Appendices, a useful glossary of terms, a twenty-three page bibliography, and an index
are also included.

20 **Chiefdom and clan maps of western Liberia.**
Svend E. Holsoe, Warren L. d'Azevedo, John Gay.   *Liberian Studies
Journal*, vol. 1, no. 2 (1969), p. 23-39.

The maps presented here plot, perhaps for the first time, all the Chiefdoms and their
constituent clans for Western Liberia. They include the Vai, Gola, Kpelle, Bandi, and
Loma Chiefdoms. Although the peoples of Western Liberia are in one culture area, there
are so many local variations and there has been so much movement across ethnic
boundaries that many people have redefined themselves with ethnic labels quite different
from those used by their parents. The authors were assisted by Bai T. Moore, Jangaba
Johnson, Thomas Brima, John Kellenu, Margaret Miller, Gerald Currens, and members
of the Order of the Holy Cross, a monastical order of the Episcopal Church.

21  **A new geography of West Africa.**
    Nwadilibe P. Iloeje.    London: Longman, 1972. 201p. index.

The stated purpose of the book is to provide a current text which adequately covers the syllabus for the West African School Certificate. Divided into three parts, it begins with a general study of the historical and physical background of the geography of West Africa. Part two comprises a country by country study with Liberia featured on pages 99-104. In part three the major economic activities discussed in the previous section are selected and viewed in their West African context. A final chapter offers a brief survey of current affairs in the region at the time of publication.

22  **Cultural atlas of Africa.**
    Edited by Jocelyn Murray.    New York: Facts on File, 1981. 240p. maps.
    bibliog.

This very useful atlas for the African continent is divided into 'The physical background'; 'The cultural background'; and brief individual descriptions and country maps of each African nation. Listed in the bibliography (p. 228) is an entry by Bill Siegman, 'Bibliography of Ethnographic Studies in Liberia,' *Rural Africana*, no. 15 (1971) which is of relevance to students of Liberia. Access to the maps and materials is facilitated by a gazetteer and an index.

23  **Clan and Chiefdom maps for the Ma (Mano) and Da (Gio).**
    James Coleman Riddell.    *Liberian Studies Journal*, vol. 4, no. 2 (1971),
    p. 157-63.

The Ma, or Mano, and Dan (Da) are closely related to neighbouring ethnic groups who are largely residents of Nimba County in northcentral Liberia. This article presents two maps intended to delineate the major boundaries for the Ma and Dan. One map portrays the distribution of clans and chiefdoms, which are listed in a separate table, and the principal Mano and Dan towns which are also listed. The other map indicates the extent of the Poro among the Mano. The Dan, however, have no Poro living amongst them. For a discussion of the ambiguity of ethnic labels in northcentral Liberia, see Svend E. Holsoe and J. J. Lauer, 'Who are the Kran/Guer and the Gio/Yacouba? Ethnic identifications along the Liberia-Ivory coast border.' *African Studies Reviews*, vol. 19, no. 1 (1976), p. 139-50.

24  **A new geography of Liberia.**
    Willi Schulze.    London: Longman, 1973. 397p.

Aimed mainly at the general reader and student, this is a basic introduction to the various facets of Liberian geography. Focusing on the Liberia of the Tubman era, the book contains sixty black-and-white plates dispersed throughout the text, sixty-one charts and thirty-five tables.

## 25 Geology of the Buchanan quadrangle, Liberia.

Russell G. Tysdal, prepared under the auspices of the Government of Liberia and the Agency for International Development, US Department of State: Books for Africa Press, 1975. 62p. map. (United States Department of Interior Geological Survey Project Report, Liberian Investigations (IR) LI-82).

Systematic quadrangle mapping of Liberia began in late 1970 when adequate base maps became available. This geological map of the Buchanan quadrangle (located in the south central part of Liberia) was compiled from: data acquired by field mapping, largely undertaken during photointerpretation; from data supplied by colleagues in the co-operative programme between the US and Liberia; and from data supplied by private company geologists.

## 26 A comprehensive geography of West Africa.

Reuben K. Udo. New York: Holmes & Meier, 1978. 304p.

Written as a preparatory guide for the West African school certificate, this study is divided into two parts. Part one considers land rights and use, traders and the organization of local trade, as well as the population and the economy. Part two covers the country studies, with Liberia being featured in chapter twenty-three (p. 188-96). The author claims that 'French-speaking countries and Liberia have been treated in much detail' (p. x). A good reading list and an index are also included.

## 27 Progressive metamorphism of iron-formation and associated rocks in the Wologizi range, Liberia.

Richard W. White, prepared in co-operation with the Liberian Geological Survey, Ministry of Lands and Mines, under the auspices of the Government of Liberia and the Agency for International Development (USAID), United States Department of State. Washington, DC: Government Printing Office, 1973. 50p. map. (Geological Survey Bulletin, 1302).

Part of a larger programme of reconnaissance mapping and mineral exploration, this study was sponsored by the Liberian government and USAID and conducted jointly by the Liberian and the US Geological Surveys. Building upon previous investigations carried out between 1935 and 1966, the study undertook much more detailed technical description of the Wologizi mountain range in an effort to generate geological literature (as opposed to a mere search for high grade iron ore). There are forty-two references cited, including W. H. Newhouse, T. P. Thayer and A. P. Butler, Jr., *Report of the Geological Mission to Liberia, December 1943-May 1944* which was published by the authors in 1945 (139p.).

# Flora and Fauna

28  **West African butterflies and moths.**
John Boorman.  London: Longman, 1970. 79p. bibliog. (West African Nature Handbooks).

A practical handbook with non-technical details, colour photographs and numerous drawings of about 225 of the most common butterflies and moths to be found in West Africa, grouped by family. A useful bibliography is also included.

29  **Small mammals of West Africa.**
A. H. Booth.  London: Longman, 1960. 68p. map. (West African Nature Handbooks).

Presents descriptions of the characteristics and habitats of seventy-six small mammals including insectivora, bats, apes, monkeys and prosimians, pangolins, hares and rodents, civets and mongooses.

30  **West African snakes.**
George S. Cansdale.  London: Longman, 1961. 74p. (West African Nature Handbooks.)

This practical guide, in which the author explains the frequency and social and economic importance of snakes in the region, provides advice on the prevention and treatment of snake bites. The author describes the forty-three most common snakes which are divided into the following groups: the python family; harmless snakes; back-fanged snakes; cobras and mambas; and vipers. Colour illustrations of most species by John Norris Wood provide a means of easy identification. The author also wrote *Animals of West Africa* (London, New York: Longmans, Green, 1960, 3rd ed. 124p.) which was first published in 1946 and was for years the only guide to the more common West African mammals, birds, snakes and insects.

## 31 The useful plants of west tropical Africa.
J. M. Dalziel.    London: Crown Agents, 1937. 612p. bibliog.

This volume, which supplements J. Hutchinson and Dalziel's *Flora of west tropical Africa* (1927), provides a vast amount of information on plant uses in the region. The work contains indexes to vernacular names, common names, scientific names, and a bibliography which amplifies the one contained in the first volume. Dalziel was a Nigerian physician.

## 32 Birds of West African town and garden.
John H. Elgood.    London: Longman, 1960. 66p. (West African Nature Handbooks).

One hundred of the most common West African birds are described in this study and are illustrated with colour paintings for ease of identification. The author was a Visiting Professor of Zoology at the University of Lagos, Nigeria.

## 33 The butterflies of Liberia.
Richard M. Fox, Arthur W. Lindsey, Jr., Harry K. Clench, Lee D. Miller.    Philadelphia: AES at the Academy of Natural Sciences, 1965. 438p. bibliog. (Memoirs of the American Entomological Society, no. 19).

This United States National Science Foundation-funded study of the butterflies of Liberia was researched and written by a team of American scientists. The work is based on the collections of Richard Fox in the Carnegie Museum, and is supplemented by others, such as those of George Naysmith who was a missionary who lived in the Cape Palmas area between 1889 and 1893. The introduction places the subject of the volume in context by briefly describing such basics as climate, biotypes and biogeography. This is followed by description of superfamilies hesperiodea, papilionoidea, Nymphaliodea and Lyceanoidea. Twenty-three pages of useful bibliography and an index complete the study.

## 34 West African trees.
D. Glehill.    London: Longman, 1972. 72p. (West African Nature Handbooks).

Describes sixty-four of the most easily recognizable West African trees and presents illustrations and drawings by Douglas E. Woodall. Scientific and common names are given for each item.

## 35 Large mammals of West Africa.
D. C. D. Happold.    London: Longman, 1973. 105p. map. bibliog. (West African Nature Handbooks).

The volume describes all the larger mammals found in West Africa. Most species are illustrated by colour photographs. The author was once a lecturer in Zoology at the University of Ibadan, Nigeria.

## 36 West African freshwater fish.
Michael Holden, William Reed.    London: Longman, 1972. 68p. bibliog. (West African Nature Handbooks).

Contains descriptions of about eighty of the most common freshwater fish of the region.

37 **The trees of Liberia.**
G. Kunkel. Munich; Basel, Switzerland; Vienna: Landwirtschaftsverlag, 1968. 270p. (German Forestry Mission to Liberia, Report no. 3, Mayerischer).
Provides field notes on trees of the Liberian forests and a field identification key with drawings by M. A. Kunkel.

38 **A collection of small mammals from Mount Coffee, Liberia.**
Gerrit S. Miller, Jr. *Proceedings of The Washington Academy of Science*, vol. 2 (Dec. 28, 1900), p. 631-49.
'In 1897 Mr. R. P. Currie spent about fourteen weeks, February 1 to May 10, as the guest of the New York State Colonization Society, at Mount Coffee, Liberia, where he made extensive collections in the interest of the United States Museum' (p. 631). Mount Coffee on the St. Paul River, about twenty-five miles from Monrovia was where Miller collected twenty-eight species of mammals during his visit. Nine of these were already known but seven were reported as being 'new to science'.

39 **West African lilies and orchids.**
J. K. Morton. London: Longman, 1961. 71p. (West African Nature Handbooks).
This handbook provides summaries of the families of wild flowers, then brief descriptions of lilies; ginger lilies; gladioli; arrowroot lilies; arum lilies; canna lilies; and orchids. Each species is illustrated in colour by Iona Loxton, S. K. Avumtsodo and S. C. Rowles. The volume contains an index.

40 **Medicinal plants of West Africa.**
Bep Oliver-Bever, foreword by G. B. Marini Bettolo, preface by T. A. Lambo. Cambridge, England: Cambridge University Press, 1986. 375p. bibliog.
The study has a pharmacological approach, with chapters on plants affecting the cardiovascular system, the nervous system and hormonal secretions, plants with anti-infective properties and those with oral hypoglycaemic action. The local uses, chemistry and pharmacology of each plant are described within each therapeutic group. The volume has a single combined botanical and general index and an extensive reference section (p. 269-354). Another good source is Edward S. Ayensu's *Medicinal plants of West Africa* (Algonac, Michigan: Reference Publications, 1981, Medicinal Plants of the World Series, no. 2). Some 127 species of medicinal plants are described and numerous local names for the plants are also provided. A bibliography (p. 297-300) and a detailed medicinal index subdivided by medical problems conclude this volume.

41 **Taxonomy of West African flowering plants.**
Omotoye Olorode. London, New York: Longman, 1984. 158p. bibliog.
For the most part this practical illustrated study consists of descriptions of selected angiosperm families, four chapters on dicotyledonous plants and one on monocoty-ledenous plants. There are also preliminary chapters which discuss the science of taxonomy with emphasis on West Africa. A glossary, author citations and keys to groups of plants are also included. Margaret Steentoft Nielsen's *Introduction to the flowering plants of West Africa* (London: University of London, 1965, 246p.) is a very good earlier

study which contains descriptions of the ecology and vegetation of West Africa and which covers over 600 species from 128 families of plants.

### 42 Terrestrial isopods of the family *eubelide* collected in Liberia by Dr. O. F. Cook.

Harriet Richardson. *Smithsonian Miscellaneous Collections*, vol. 4, part 2 (1907), p. 219-47. illus.

This is a study of terrestrial isopods collected in the Mount Coffee and Muhlenburg mission areas of Liberia between 1893 and 1895. Undertaken under the auspices of the New York State Colonization Society, the collection was made by O. F. Cook, custodian of myriapoda in the US Department of Agriculture. The present article is the result of the study of one family of the collection, the *Eubelidae*. 'All the specimens collected represent new species, and a new genus is added to the five genera already known' (p. 212). The author was associated with the division of marine invertebrates at the US National Museum.

### 43 Liberia's wildlife – the time for decision.

Philip T. Robinson, Alexander Peal. *Zoonooz* (Oct. 1981), p. 7-21.

'Despite Liberia's small geographic area, its plant and animal resources are extensive and varied. Yet, within the past fifty years the country's forests have been drastically depleted. The encroachments of hunters, farmers, and road-builders, and miners have produced an 'island effect', dividing once contiguous communities of plants and animals into discreet populations with diminishing prospects of survival. Hence, Liberia is said to be at an environmental crossroads. Presently there are no national parks, nor is there legislation for the protection of wildlife. The current rate of habitat alteration makes the need for conservation measures imperative in the 1980s if Liberia is to avoid irreversible damage to its wildlife' (Abstract). Of related interest is P. T. Robinson, 'Wildlife trends in Liberia and Sierra Leone,' *Oryx* 11 (2-3): 117-122, 1978.

### 44 The bats of West Africa.

D. R. Rosevear. London: Trustees of the British Museum (Natural History), 1965. 418p. map. bibliog.

Contains detailed descriptions of ninety-seven named species and nine subspecies of bats belonging to thirty-one genera in the region. The author provides a general introduction, which is followed by references (p. 352-59), a fold-out map of the region, two colour plates and 232 line drawings.

### 45 A field guide to the birds of West Africa.

William Serle, Gerard J. Morel. London: Collins, 1977. 351p. map.

Covers 'all the birds known to occur in West Africa' (p. 11), with 726 species treated fully and 371 mentioned in brief status notes. Latin, English, Spanish, French and German names are given for most species (p. 295-335), and there is a complete index of scientific names (p. 337-45) and of English names (p. 347-51). In all, 515 species are illustrated, 335 in colour. The authors have each spent more than twenty years in West Africa.

46 **Illustrated key to anopheles mosquitoes of Liberia.**
Charles J. Stojaanovich, Harold George Scott. Atlanta, Georgia: United
States Department of Health, Education and Welfare, Public Health
Service, Communicable Disease Centre, 15, July 1966. 38p.

This is basically an explanatory classification of twelve species of anopheles mosquitoes
found in Liberia. The work includes a map of the biotic regions and climatic areas and
covers the: life cycle of the malaria parasite (*Plasmodium falciparum*); life history of the
malaria parasite (*Plasmodium falciparum*) in man and the anopheles mosquito; the chain
of filariasis transmission; and bionomics. It also incorporates a pictorial key to
microfilariae found in peripheral blood and man and a list of the species referred to in
the text.

# Tourism and Travel Guides

47 **Visitor's and tourist guide to Liberia.**
Monrovia: Liberia Chamber of Commerce, 1987. 72p.

At the time of publication this was a most useful guide. The work includes general information on travel, business, general economic performance, and the then business outlook. The contents include: Liberia in brief; travel formalities; health requirements and health conditions; principal cities, ports, and towns; travel to and from Liberia; travel within Liberia; hotels and restaurants; communications; economy; tourist information; and useful information (resident/work permit, banks, foreign missions in Liberia, etc.).

48 **West Africa: a travel survival kit.**
Alex Newton. Berkeley, California; South Yarra, Victoria, Australia: Lonely Planet Publications, 1988. 460p. maps.

This is a good guidebook and general introduction to sixteen West African countries with useful preliminary information on the region (p. 7-92). Its contents include: 'Facts about the region'; 'Facts for the visitor'; 'Getting there'; 'Getting around'; as well as basic information about each of the countries. Information about Liberia appears on pages 249-66. The author, a former American Peace Corps Volunteer, reflects the realities of the sub-region when he writes: 'Things change – prices go up, schedules change, good places go bad and bad places go bankrupt – nothing stays the same' (p. 4). This is particularly apt for war-ravaged Liberia.

49 **Business traveller's handbook: a guide to Africa.**
Toby Milner. New York: Paddington Press, 1977. 512p.

Milner provides a general overview of the whole continent and then covers each African country in turn, providing economic and business information, as well as practical travel advice on each nation. Liberia is considered on p. 219-27.

50 **Country Profile, Liberia: business travel and security report.**
Tysons Corner, Virginia: Overseas Security Management Incorporated,
1987. 111p.

In the preface to this report, Gordon E. Harvey, President of Overseas Security
Management writes: 'I have long felt that there was a gap in the information available to
corporate security directors and senior executives traveling abroad . . . what has been
needed is a book that covers practical information relating to travel, security, and
temporary work in a country' (p. i). This report has now, of course, been largely
overcome by events but at the time was designed to fill the void as regards Liberia.
Although assessments of political, economic, and 'threat conditions' in the country are
included, the bulk of the report concerns how to visit Liberia safely and comfortably. Its
contents include: visa requirements; embassy and consulate addresses; State Department
travel advisories; political assessment; economic assessment; security threat assessment;
travel information; business information; health security; communications and miscellaneous information.

# Travellers' Accounts and Memoirs

51  **Narrative of a journey to Musardu, the capital of the western Mandingoes.**
Benjamin J. K. Anderson.   London: Frank Cass, 1971. 162p. maps.

This is a nineteenth-century account of an expedition of a Liberian government official into the 'interior' of the state. It originally appeared in two parts although now it is presented in one volume. The first edition of *'Narrative of a journey to Musardu'* appeared in 1870, while the first edition of *'Narrative of the expedition despatched to Musardu by the Liberian government under B. J. K. Anderson in 1874'* appeared in 1912 (as edited by Frederick Starr). This 1971 reprint has a very useful introduction by Humphrey Fisher of London University's School of Oriental and African Studies. Fisher assesses Anderson's work in the context of European colonial explorers, and comments at some length on Anderson's contributions to our knowledge about African slavery, the local history of Bopolo and Musardu (the two main towns which the explorer visited) as well as the expansion of Islam in the area. This reprint edition is indexed and also includes maps.

52  **Journal of a voyage from Boston to the West Coast of Africa, with a full description of the manner of trading with the natives on the Coast.**
Joshua A. Carnes.   New York: Negro Universities Press, 1969. 479p.

Originally published in Boston in 1852, this reprint is the author's account of a trading voyage on the West Coast of Africa. Beyond the mention of a trip 'extending through an extent of country, along the slave coast, of nearly fifteen hundred miles', there is no clear idea of the areas covered by this expedition. Neither is there a table of contents and even though the chapter divisions are indicated, they tend to be misleading. The only guide can be found in captions on the right-hand pages of the text. These include: 'Outward bound view of Boston Harbor'; 'Arrival at Oratana'; 'The peak of Tenneritte'; 'Arrival at the island of Goree'; 'Market in Sierra Leone'; 'Trade along the coast'; 'Village of Bassa'; 'Manufacture of palm oil'. A map, a clear table of contents and an index would have made this travelogue much more user-friendly.

## 53 Monrovia mon amour: a visit to Liberia.

Anthony Daniels. London: John Murray, 1992. 206p.

Presents the travelogue of a London-based British physician who made a visit to Monrovia in the immediate aftermath of the civil war of 1989/90. The contents include: A tug to Monrovia; A brief history of Liberia; University life; The maternity hospital; The All-Liberia Conference; The peace settlement; Field Marshal Brigadier-General Prince Y. Johnson; The Field Marshal at work; Good Friday in Monrovia; The killing fields; The army; The Executive Mansion and Samuel Doe's Ju-ju; and Sierra Leone. Photographs are also included.

## 54 Liberia: land of the pepper bird.

Sidney De La Rue. New York, London: G. P. Putman's Sons; The Knickerbocker Press, 1930. 330p.

The author, an American government official, was once financial advisor to the government of Liberia. The book is an account of his first encounter with Africa and Liberia. The illustrations speak volumes. The frontispiece shows 'A typical village scene in Liberia. Children of both sexes usually go naked'. There are endless references to 'Bozzies' (Loma) and 'Pessis' (Kpelle), with indigenous ethnic groups referred to as 'the African tower of Babel' (chapter 5). According to the author, Liberia of the 1920s had two distinct forms of government, tribal and settler, running concurrently (p. 209).

## 55 Hinterland Liberia.

Etta Donner, translated from the German by Winifred M. Deans.

London, Glasgow: Blackie & Son, 1939. 203p.

The author, a German, first travelled to Liberia in 1934, later making a number of subsequent trips in which he stayed among the Gola, Kpelle, Mano, Dan, Krahn and other indigenous Liberian peoples. Her book is a record of what she learned about these people and the state of the country in 1934-35. This volume about the 'natives' is 'not one in which the customs of strange tribes are systematically recorded but one in which an attempt is made to fathom the thoughts and ideas of these primitive people'. Chapters include: 'Guest of a Mano Chief'; 'Crossing Mount Nimba'; 'Native women'; 'The transmigration of souls'; 'Danane, masks and spirits'; 'Secret societies'; 'Among the Kran people'; 'The law courts'; and 'Merican palaver'.

## 56 A third of a century with George Way Harley in Liberia.

Winifred J. Harley. Newark, Delaware: Liberian Studies Association, 1973. 90p. (Liberian Studies Monograph Series, no. 2).

The author, wife of Methodist American missionary, Dr. George Way Harley (1894-1966) presents her fascinating memoirs of thirty-five years of life and work among the people of Ganta in northern Liberia which began in 1926.

## 57 Native stranger: a black American's journey into the heart of Africa.

Eddy L. Harris. New York: Simon & Schuster, 1992. 315p.

This is the dual quest of a black American for the 'truth' about Africa, and 'how that truth reflects his own notion of self.' To achieve his objective Harris undertook a one-year sojourn through twenty-two African countries, among them Liberia. He finds nothing uplifting. Perhaps the problem is that Harris' search took him to the wrong places and he recounted the wrong situations. There is no historical perspective and no evidence of real contact with ordinary Africans. Instead, the author seems to be preoccupied with travel difficulties both in terms of the inadequacy of transportation as well as the frustrations of the bureaucracies encountered. Chapter seven – 'Jungles of love and lunacy' – focuses on travels through the Ivory Coast and Liberia (p. 219-62).

## 58   Le Libéria intime. (Inside Liberia.)
M. H. Lelong.   Algiers: Edition Baconnier, 1946. 233p. maps.

This account of a journey taken in 1944 by a French colonialist from N'Zérékoré at the French Guinean/Liberian border to Monrovia is more than just an ordinary travelogue. Lelong presents an interesting intimate picture of Liberia through the medium of a journal that attempts to capture the spirit of the people and describes the author's experiences on his travels into and out of Liberia. Part one, 'Journey by star' (N'Zérékoré – Monrovia) considers the people encountered and events experienced on the trip from Guinea through the Liberian interior to the beaches of Monrovia. This is followed, 'for reasons of practical order' by a special account of the author's observations in the capital city. Entitled 'Monrovia, capitale pour rire' (Monrovia, laughing capital), the highlights include: 'Pius Sunday'; 'Walk through Krutown'; 'Portrait of politicians'; the 'Colony of foreigners'; 'Goodbye to President Barclay'; 'When Liberia inaugurates a President' (Tubman's first inauguration in 1944). Part two, 'The Route of Cola nut' (Journal of the return from Monrovia to Guinea) concludes the book.

## 59   Thinking through the times.
K. Moses Nagbe.   Monrovia: Pen-Tina Publications, Herald Publishing, 1991. 86p.

Presents the reflections of a Liberian journalist upon his experiences during the civil war of 1989-90. In the preface he addressed his readers thus: 'If you are a stranger to the war I recount, you may not be a total stranger to war. Relive whichever you may have experienced and let us together moan the presence of this heinous shadow of strife trailing human beings.'

## 60   Liberia: the Americo-African republic. Being some impression of the climate, resources, and people, resulting from personal observations and experiences in West Africa.
Thomas McCants Stewart.   New York: Edward O. Jenkins' Sons, 1886. 107p.

This study, with an introduction by G. W. Samson, former president of Columbia University, Washington, DC, provides background information on such topics as the founding of Liberia, climate, and natural resources. The more interesting part of the book focuses on people – native customs and manners, the 'Kroo' (Kru) and 'Vey' (Vai), the 'Americo-Africans', and 'relation of Liberians and natives'. With respect to the latter the author points out the problems of the unequal relationship, and suggests that some enlightened leadership was already effecting improvements. Stewart felt that Liberia had a claim on America because it was a quasi-colony of the latter (p. 100). He was in the mainstream of the black intellectuals of his time which saw Liberia's primary purpose as one of civilizing and Christianizing the country, and then the rest of the African continent, with the ultimate goal of establishing a 'government of Africans, for Africans and by Africans, which shall be an inestimable blessing to all mankind' (p. 107). The author, a lawyer by profession, became an Associate Justice of the Supreme Court of Liberia and a major social commentator.

## 61 Adventure and observations on the West Coast of Africa and its islands.

Charles W. Thomas. New York: Derby & Jackson, 1860. 479p.

A 'History and descriptive sketches of Madeira, Canary, Biafra and Cape Verde Islands; their climate, inhabitants and productions; accounts of places, peoples, customs, trade and missionary operations'. A description of early Liberia can be found on p. 123-74. The author was a clergyman who gathered information for the study between 1855 and 1857 when he served with the United States sloop-of-war *Jamestown*, then a flagship of the African squadron of the US Navy. A major aim of the study was to correct 'prevailing errors respecting the colonies of civilized blacks, and the state of Christian missions on the West Coast' of Africa (p. vi).

## 62 Seven days to Lomaland.

Esther Sietmann Warner. Cambridge, Massachusetts: Riverside Press, 1954. 269p.

Recounts the impressions of a sympathetic American visitor to hinterland Liberia who spent some time among the Loma people. Of interest as well is the author's *New Song in a Strange Land* (Riverside Press, 1948. 302p.) and *Trial by Sassawood* (London: Victor Gollancz Ltd., 1955, 254p.), in both of which she recounts and reflects on her experiences on visits to interior Liberia.

## 63 The crossing fee – a story of life in Liberia.

Esther Sietmann Warner. Boston, Massachusetts: Houghton Mifflin, 1968. 304p.

This seems to be the latest of Warner's travelogues on Liberia, following *New song in a strange land* (1948) and *Seven days to Lomaland* (1954). Presented in two parts – 'Discovery' and 'Return', the story is essentially about Liberia undergoing social change, perhaps most notably in the 1960s. The focus, as in the earlier works, remains on the indigenous peoples, particularly the Mano, whom she had visited. She writes in the afterword: 'What interests me is not so much what they can learn from us (Westerners) in the way of techniques, sanitation, etc., as what we can learn from them. We can learn laughter, we can learn to really listen with our entire person, we can learn how to enjoy ourselves and one another. We can be radiant with the joy which tingles through the body when the mind is delighting in imaginative thought. We can discover the poetry in daily life. These are the gifts I have from the country people of Liberia. This book has been written to thank them'.

# History

## General

64 **A thousand years of West African history: a handbook for teachers and students.**
Edited by J. F. A. Ajayi, Ian Espie, foreword by K. O. Dike. New York: Humanities, 1972. 2nd ed. 549p. maps. bibliog.
First published in 1965, this volume contains twenty-five essays, a broad list of sixty topics for further study and a bibliography. Articles relevant to Liberian studies include 'Peoples of the Windward coast, AD 1000-1800' by Christopher Fyfe; 'Portuguese and Dutch in West Africa before 1800'; 'West African Trade, AD 1000-1800' by Christopher Fyfe; and 'Sierra Leone and Liberia in the nineteenth century' by Hollis R. Lynch.

65 **The role of the military in the history of Liberia, 1822-1947.**
Harrison Oladunjoye Akingbade. PhD thesis, Howard University, Washington, DC, 1977. 349p.
This is the only known major historical study of the Liberian military and its political activities during the nineteenth and early twentieth centuries. The emphasis is on the use of military personnel in the political administration of rural regions.

66 **A history of colonization of the Western coast of Africa.**
Archibald Alexander. New York: Negro Universities Press, 1969. 603p.
Perhaps the best of the apologies of the back-to-Africa idea which the American Colonization society represented, this treatise consists of thirty-nine chapters, thirty-four of them devoted to events in Africa. These events begin with the 1818 American mission of exploration to Liberia, and continue through the white administration of the early Liberian settlement which ended with the drowning of Governor Thomas Buchanan at Bassa Cove in 1842. The author resolves all of the social contradictions in early Liberia in favour of the emigrants.

67 **A tribal reaction to nationalism.**
Warren L. d'Azevedo. *Liberian Studies Journal*, Part I, vol. 1, no. 2 (1969), p. 1-22; Part II, vol. 2, no. 1 (1969), p. 43-63; Part III, vol. 2, no. 2 (1970), p. 99-115; Part IV, vol. 3, no. 1 (1970/71), p. 1-19.

This four-part series is the result of an investigation conducted by the author in Western Liberia into the role of the Gola people of that region in certain historical and structural processes affecting the internal development of the Liberian state. Seeking to establish the inadequacy of the view that polities indigenous to the Liberia area were simply 'awkwardly overwhelmed' by the state, d'Azevedo advances evidence 'that the dynamics of Gola subjugation and eventual co-operative involvement in the emerging Liberian nation must be understood not only in terms of specific features of Gola and colonial (Liberian) social organization, but also in terms of regional historical events prior to colonial occupation and during the long period of struggle on the part of the newcomers to establish cultural and political jurisdiction over a portion of the West African coast' (Part I, p. 4). The study suggests this manner of viewing Gola reaction to nationalism in Liberia may well be applicable to the other ethnic groups indigenous to the Liberia area. The author, an American anthropologist, is one of a small number of western pioneers to have studied 'hinterland' Liberia since the Second World War.

68 **Yankee traders, old coasters, and African middlemen: a history of American legitimate trade with West Africa in the nineteenth century.**
George E. Brooks, Jr. Boston, Massachusetts: Boston University Press, 1970. 370p. bibliog. (African Research Studies, no. 11).

Describes the growth and organization of legitimate American trade from the 1790s to the 1870s, and relates American commerce to that of European, African, and other traders. An extensive bibliography is also included.

69 **Western Africa to c. 1860 AD: a provisional historical schema based on climate periods.**
George E. Brooks, Jr. Bloomington, Indiana: Indiana University Press, 1985, 213p. (African Studies Program Working Papers Series, No. 1).

Asserts that climate changes in the last two millennia have been a major factor in the history of West African states. Using archaeological and biological data, Brooks suggests that 'the periodic shift from wet to dry periods, and the consequent shifting boundaries of desert, sahel, and savannah, have affected the rise and fall of states, the spread of language, culture and political institutions, and commercial relations'. A significant portion of the latter half of the book discusses the effects of climate on trade, movements of peoples and the development of institutions in the area now known as Liberia.

70 **Liberia: a century of survival, 1847-1947.**
Raymond Leslie Buell. Philadelphia: University of Pennsylvania Press, 1947; New York: Kraus Reprint, 1969. 140p.

A prominent American observer of the Liberian scene assesses, with a critical eye, the country and its prospects on the occasion of its one hundredth anniversary, in 1947. He advocates a Liberian rehabilitation programme with committed American involvement, and radical action to narrow the gap between 'the governing élite and the Liberian people.'

71 **Sovereignty for sale: the origins and evolution of the Panamanian and Liberian flags of convenience.**
Rodney P. Carlisle. Annapolis, Maryland: Naval Institute Press, 1980. 278p.

With emphasis on Panama and Liberia, this is an historical account of 'flags of convenience' or the 'open registry system' whereby vessels are registered in one country and have ownership in another. The book chronicles and analyses how these two countries attracted so many, largely American, vessels that they became maritime powers, as measured in national registered tonnage. By the late 1960s Liberia had by far overtaken Panama because of an aggressive American-administered Liberian registry. Policy issues concerning the locus of 'control' of these vessels in the event of a military crisis are also explored.

72 **A brief history of Monserrado County.**
Monrovia: Department of Information and Cultural Affairs, 1965. [n.p.].

This booklet was prepared by a special committee of the Department of Information and Cultural Affairs on the occasion of the seventieth birthday celebrations of President W. V. S. Tubman of Liberia. The committee was composed of Liberian writers including E. Reginald Townsend, A. Doris Banks Henries, Bai T. Moore, and S. Jangaba M. Johnson. The book includes biographies of some Liberian writers, among them Edward Wilmot Blyden, Benjamin J. K. Anderson, Abayomi Karnaga, Alexander Crummell, Hilary Teague and Henry Johnson.

73 **The United States and Africa: a history.**
Peter Duignan, Lewis H. Gann. Cambridge, England: Cambridge University Press, 1984. 450p.

This study traces the reciprocal relationships between North America and Africa over a period of some four centuries. The authors highlight America's impact on Africa through her missionaries, traders, prospectors, miners, educators, soldiers of fortune, scientists and others, as well as Africa's impact on America through trade and immigration (both enforced and voluntary). The influence of Africans on the arts, agriculture and other facets of American life is also considered. Naturally, Liberia figures prominently.

74 **Preliminary report on an archaeological survey of Liberia.**
Creighton Gabel, Robert Borden, Susan White. *Liberian Studies Journal*, vol. 5, no. 2 (1972-74), p. 87-105.

This is an archaeological survey of Liberia undertaken under the auspices of the United States Educational and Cultural Foundation in Liberia. The preliminary findings reported by the authors include the following: that the Liberian coast was most likely to have been inhabited before 'recent' centuries; that it was probably reached by Stone Age hunters through areas of high forest; and that the location of late Iron Age ceramic sites along the western coast is of enormous significance. The article is studded with illustrations of archaeological interest. The authors were associated with the Anthropology Department and African Studies Centre of Boston University. Of related interest are J. Atherton's 'Archaeology in Liberia: Problems and Possibilities' (*West African Archaeological Newsletter*, XI, 1969, p. 19-21), and K. Orr, 'An introduction to the archaeology of Liberia' (*Liberian Studies Journal*, IV, 1971-72, p. 55-79).

75 **African and American values: Liberia and West Africa.**
Katherine Harris. Lanham, Maryland: University Press of America, 1984. 101p.

Presents an account of the impact of American values on the West African settlement which eventually became the Liberian state. This slim volume focuses on the period to 1837, but unfortunately includes much that is irrelevant to the subject. Fascinating topics are introduced for discussion but are not fully analysed including the American values of capitalist production, the plantation economy, individualism, notions of private property, Western Christianity and religious superiority, and racism.

76 **Liberia.**
Sir Harry Hamilton Johnston. New York: Negro Universities Press, 1969. 2 vols.

Originally published in London by Dodd and Mead in 1906, this early overview of Liberian history contains twenty-four biological drawings, twenty-two maps, and 402 black-and-white illustrations. The author, a British colonial administrator and Africanist, presents the story of Liberia as 'an attempt to establish a civilized Negro State in the West African forest,' and considers it to be a 'somewhat paltry atonement' by Britain and the United States 'for the wrong-doing of the slave trade'. The first volume, which begins with an annotated bibliography of Liberia, covers the history of pre-Liberia, the founding of Liberia, and the political history of the Liberian state. It also provides basic information about the settler population, commerce, geography, climate and minerals. The second volume consists of information on the flora and fauna of Liberia. Chapters twenty-seven to thirty-two consider the origins, and history, folklore and languages of the indigenous peoples who then numbered some two million. There is a useful index at the end of the second volume.

77 **From slaves to palm kernels: a history of the Galinhas country, West Africa, 1730–1890.**
Adam Jones. Wiesbaden, Germany: Franz Steiner Verlag,1983. 220p.

This work is essentially an economic (trade) history of the 'Galinhas Country' which includes the chiefdoms of Kpaka, Peri-Massaquoi and Soro-Gbema, and has a total area of 1,700 square miles, located between the Moa and Mano Rivers. The study also contains numerous maps and plates and the names of many villages and peoples. The Galinhas were ceded by local rulers to the Liberian state in the 1850s. Annexed by the British to their colony of Sierra Leone in 1885, it is currently part of southern Sierra Leone.

78 **The origins of modern African thought: its development in West Africa during the nineteenth and twentieth centuries.**
Robert W. July. New York: Praeger, 1967. 512p.

This important study of the precursors to inter-war and post-Second World War pan-Africanist and nationalist thought and action highlights the significant contributions of Liberia and Liberians to the development of these theories, including the impact of the West on the modern West African. Among Liberian personalities highlighted are: the statesman, Hilary Teague; the cleric, Alexander Crummell; the scholar, Edward W. Blyden; and the journalist, John Payne Jackson.

79 **A history of the African people.**
Robert W. July. New York: Charles Scribner's Sons, 1974. 713p. 4th ed. 1980.

First published in 1970, this thematic history primarily of sub-Saharan Africa was written with the perspective of the African peoples in view. Its two principal parts cover ancient and modern African respectively. Specific treatment of Liberia includes 'Liberia and the tribulations of independence (p. 414-6), and 'Liberia and African nationalism' (p. 520-24). The author, a respected American historian, has both taught and travelled widely in Africa.

80 **History of Liberia.**
Abayomi Karnga. Liverpool, England: D. H. Tyte & Co., 1926. 72p.

This is an unusual and refreshing account of Liberia's history by a Liberian. Karnga's brief study has two parts: part one 'From the conquest of the Golas to the founding of the Empire Republic' covers the period from prehistory to the repatriation of African-Americans to Africa; and part two 'Founding of the Empire Republic' starts with the colonial settlements and considers developments up to, and including, the early administration of President C. D. B. King (1920-30). The author's analysis of Liberia's indigenous and western experiences is remarkable.

81 **Growth of the Liberian state: an analysis of its historiography.**
Clarence Ernest Zamba Liberty. PhD thesis, Stanford University, Stanford, Connecticut, 1977. 320p.

Presents an historiographical analysis of the 'paramountcy' of emigrant ethnicity in Liberian life. In so doing, the author breaks new ground in the study of the history of the Liberian state. The work contains valuable surveys of the major works of leading European and American analysts of the Liberian experience.

82 **History of Liberia.**
John Hanson Thomas McPherson. New York: Johnson Reprint Corp. 1973. 61p.

Originally published in 1891 by the Johns Hopkins University Press, Baltimore, Maryland, as the ninth series of the Johns Hopkins University Studies in Historical and Political Sciences, this is an abridged version of a doctoral thesis presented by the author at the same institution. Among the questions considered in the introduction are those relating to the capacity of the black man for self-government, the perception of Liberia as America's sole attempt to establish a 'colonial enterprise' in Africa, and the suggestion that Liberia's success as a black state would have powerful consequences for America's black population. The contents include: 'The colonization idea'; 'The colonization movement'; Maryland in Liberia'; 'The Republic of Liberia'; and 'The historical significance of colonization'.

83 **The Cambridge history of Africa.**
General editors Roland Oliver, J. D. Fage. Cambridge, England: Cambridge University, 1975-86. 8 vols. maps. bibliog.

This study covers the continent from prehistoric times onwards and contains substantial material on West Africa in each volume as well as detailed maps and bibliographies. The periods covered are: vol. one 'From the earliest times to c. 500 BC' (1982. 1157p.); vol.

two 'From c. 500 BC to AD 1050' (1979. 700p.); vol. three 'From c. 1050 to c. 1600' (1977. 816p.); vol. four 'From c. 1600 to 1790' (1975. 752p.); vol. five 'From c. 1790 to c. 1870' (1977. 816p.); vol. six 'From c. 1870 to c. 1905' (1985, 956p.); vol. seven 'From 1905 to 1940' (1986. 1063p.); and vol. eight 'From 1940 to c. 1975' (1984. 1011p.). For specific coverage of Liberia see vol. five, chapter five.

## 84 Black exodus: black nationalist and back-to-Africa movements, 1890-1910.
Edwin S. Redkey. New Haven, Connecticut: Yale University Press, 1969. 319p.

A moving account of the work of the southern black American cleric, Bishop Henry McNeal Turner (1834-1915). Turner, along with thousands of others, as part of a response to the conditions of blacks in the United States, encouraged ordinary blacks to consider emigrating to Liberia. Converted to the cause of repatriation by Alexander Crummell, Turner devoted a great deal of his energy and resources to the effort but with little result due to unfavourable circumstances on both sides of the Atlantic. In the end it appears that the movement faltered in the United States through lack of support from black intellectuals.

## 85 General history of Africa.
UNESCO International Scientific Committee for the Drafting of a General History of Africa. Paris: UNESCO; London: Heinemann; London; Berkeley, California: University of California, 1981- . 8 vols. maps. bibliog.

When completed, this series will represent a comprehensive history of Africa, written by Africans. The societies of 'pre-Liberia' are highlighted in the following articles, 'The pre-history of West Africa' (vol. 1); 'West Africa before the seventh century' (vol. 2); 'Liberia and Ethiopia, 1880-1914: the survival of two African states' and 'Ethiopia and Liberia, 1914-1935: two independent states in the colonial era' (both vol. 8).

## 86 Liberia: a nineteenth and twentieth century miracle.
Ernest Jerome Yancy. Tel Aviv, Israel: Nateev Publishing House, 1971. 304p.

Written from essentially the same perspective as that adopted by the early African-American pioneers of the Liberian state, this book presents the history of Liberia as a heroic struggle by settler-Liberians to persevere in the face of the unrelenting hostility from the 'natives of the land' and an outside, Western world that could not countenance 'members of the dark race' as 'sufficiently adapted for a civilized, democratic government, and a consequent threat to colonial ambitions in Africa'. The author was a former Liberian Minister for Education who had also been Ambassador to Israel. Of related interest is Yancy's *Historical lights of Liberia's yesterday and today* (Xenia, Ohio: Aldine Publishing Co., 1934).

# The nineteenth century

**87 Black spokesmen and activists: The Liberian elites in the nineteenth century.**
Monday Benson Akpan. *The Calabar Historical Journal*, vol. 1, no. 1 (June 1976), p. 89-144.

The author identifies two societies in Liberia, traditional and modern, each with its own élite. The paper focuses on the modern élites of nineteenth-century Liberia, 'recruited predominantly from the Americo-Liberians' or New World settlers. Akpan categorizes them as political leaders, government administrators, military leaders, economic leaders, educators and clergymen, and professionals including physicians and lawyers and discusses their characteristics, their 'cosmology', their perception of Africa, their relationship to European activities in Africa and their views on pan-Africanism.

**88 History of the American colony in Liberia, from December 1821 to 1823.**
Jehudi Ashmun. Washington, DC: Way & Gideon, 1826. 42p.

Ashmun, a white American, played an important role in the founding of the Liberian state and provided pioneering leadership. This booklet details the major events and problems as the early settlement took root.

**89 The American colonization society and the creation of the Liberian state: an historical perspective, 1822-1900.**
Amos Jones Beyan. Lanham, Maryland: University Press of America, 1991. 207p.

This book is devoted to a study of the impact of nineteenth-century American values on an African society. While contributing importantly to an understanding of Liberian settler heritage, Beyan also discusses how that heritage encountered the native African culture, and how the two experiences together with the added factor of the world economy shaped Liberia's national institutions. Particular emphasis is placed on the American-influenced settler heritage. The first two chapters consider the origins of the American Colonization Society and the nature of pre-Liberian society. The remaining four chapters investigate the establishment and development of Liberia up until 1900.

**90 La République de Libéria.** (The Republic of Liberia.)
Pierre Bourzeix. Paris: Typographie de la Revue Diplomatique, 1887. 88p. illus.

The author, a French Roman Catholic Priest of the Apostolic Missionary of the Congregation of the Holy Spirit and of the Sacred Heart of Mary, presents to his French audience an account of 'the only free and independent state among the savage tribes of the African continent' (p. 88). The motive for writing the book seems to be one of soliciting funds for the construction in Liberia of schools, churches and hospitals in furtherance of the work of the Roman Catholic Mission in the country. The three major divisions of the study are entitled: 'overview of the political history of Liberia, from its origins to the declaration of independence, and from its independence to the present (December 1885)'; 'overview of the economy of Liberia'; and 'overview of the moral situation of Liberia (including the 'Liberian character' and a historical glimpse of the status of religion in Liberia)'.

91 **Maryland in Africa, the Maryland State Colonization Society, 1831-1857.**
Penelope Campbell.   Urbana, Illinois: University of Illinois Press, 1971. 264p.

Marylanders who were critical of the national organization, the American Colonization Society which was founded in 1816, founded the Maryland State Colonization Society in 1831 and sponsored a separate colony along the coast of West Africa called Maryland in Liberia. The history of the establishment of the Maryland society in America and the colony in Africa in 1834 is recounted up to, and including, the merger of the colony with the republic of Liberia in 1857.

92 **Self-determination in colonial Liberia.**
Rodney P. Carlisle.   *Negro History Bulletin*, Washington, DC, April 1973, p. 77-83.

This article links the 'convergence of white supremacist motivations behind the American Colonization Society with [the] emergence of Afro-American nationalism to eventual Liberian independence.' The author considers both black initiatives which were supportive of the emigrationist movement and the opposition of black emigrationist-nationalists to the colonization society.

93 **Liberia: history of the first African Republic.**
C. Abayomi Cassell.   New York: Fountainhead Publishers, 1970. 457p.

This is not a balanced account of the history of the Liberian state for it focuses on the external origins of the modern Liberia and makes little effort to relate the external to the internal circumstances. If there is a primary value to the book, it is that it considers an important aspect of the political history of the country during the nineteenth century from the point of view of a Liberian who was a part of the political establishment. That it relegates 'Tribal life in Liberia' to an appendix is indicative of the limited perspective the author brought to the study. The volume covers the period from 'the landing of the pioneers on Providence Island, Liberia, 1822, until 1900, the year of the first inauguration of President Coleman'. The author, now deceased, left in manuscript form a second volume covering the period 1900 to 1952.

94 **Americans in black Africa up to 1865.**
Clarence Clemens Clendenen, Peter Duignan.   Stanford, California: Stanford University, 1964. 109p. bibliog. (Hoover Institution Studies, no. 5).

The second in a series of three studies on United States activities in Africa prior to 1865, this work provides a simple outline of American involvement without considering African reactions to American merchants, missionaries, and explorers. The study is a synthesis of historical scholarship, mostly from printed sources, though there is ample use of theses, private papers, missionary reports and government dispatches. The contents include: American traders; missionaries and colonization societies; and explorers and frontiersmen. There is also a useful bibliography.

95 **Americans in Africa, 1865-1900.**
Clarence Clemens Clendenen, Robert Collins, Peter Duignan. Stanford, California: Stanford University, 1966. 130p. bibliog. (Hoover Institution Studies, no. 17).

This is the third publication in a series covering American activities in Africa. Largely narrative, with little interpretation, its contents include: 'The vanishing flag' (post-American Civil War activities); 'The lamb and wolves' (American-Liberian relations and Liberia's difficulties with European colonial powers); 'Neutrality and philanthropy'; 'Traders and soldiers of misfortune'; 'Miners and adventurers'; and 'Capitalists and men of God'. The study also contains a good bibliography.

96 **Un état nègre: la République de Libéria.** (A black state: the Republic of Liberia.)
Maurice Delafosse. Bulletin du Comité de l'Afrique Française, Renseignements Coloniaux, no. 9 (Notice geogr. Hist. Econ. et Ethnog.). 1900. 31p.

Written essentially from a pro-colonialist viewpoint, the main text of the work is divided into eleven sections. The historical section briefly outlines developments in Liberia from 1822 to 1900 and emphasizes the continuity of policy from colonial leaders to the republican leaders. The section also contains the first modern attempt to sociologically define the composition of the emigrant community and to place it in a comparable West African setting.

97 **A history of the State of Maryland in Liberia.**
Ernest Eastman. Monrovia: Bureau of Information, Department of State, 1956. 108p.

The first settlement of New World blacks in Liberia was in 1822 at Cape Mesurado (now Monrovia), but there were other independent settlements, among them the state of Maryland at Cape Palmas sponsored by the Maryland State Colonization Society of the United States. This Maryland in Africa was settled in 1833 and formally annexed to the Republic of Liberia in 1857. The author, a career official of the Liberian government, presents here a well-documented history of Maryland in Liberia. It chronicles: the origins of colonization societies in America, including the Maryland society; the journey back to Africa of the Maryland settlers; the vicissitudes of colonial settlement in Cape Palmas (Maryland in Africa); and the circumstances that led the Maryland colony into union with Liberia.

98 **Africa and the American flag.**
Andrew H. Foote. New York: Negro Universities Press, 1969 (reprinted). 390p.

Originally published in 1854 by a US naval officer, this work focuses largely on the role of the US Navy on the West coast of Africa prior to the Liberian colonial settlement, as well as the part played by the navy (The American Flag) in the years that followed the first settlement. Some of the American vessels involved included the US Sloop-of-war *Cyane*, the Schooner *Alligator*, the *John Adams*, the Schooner *Porpoise*, the *Shark*, and the *Mary Carver*. In recording the many and varied activities in which US vessels were involved, the author did so with a view to underscoring the responsibility undertaken by US-flagged vessels to protect Americans and their commerce.

## 99 American involvement in Africa south of the Sahara, 1800-1860.
Lawrence C. Howard. New York: Garland, 1988. 347p.

This book develops two major themes, the first being that the US had a variety of political, economic and ideological connections with Africa between 1800 and 1860, and that after this period US involvement in Africa was not as strong until after the Second World War. The second theme is the author's characterization of US involvement in the establishment of Liberia as a facet of American imperialism. Though American historians have appeared reluctant to use the term 'imperialism' to define the US experience in Liberia during this period, the author contends that the US manifested ideological, economic and political interest on a scale not dissimilar to Britain's in the same areas in the first half of the nineteenth century. Particularly lacking in the book is an assessment of the role of American missionaries and some analysis of US relations with European nations as they affected Africa.

## 100 Free negro labor and property holding in Virginia, 1830-1860.
Luther Porter Jackson. New York: D. Appleton-Century Company, 1942. 270p.

Focuses on free black property owners and entrepreneurs in Virginia between 1830 and 1860 when, in spite of legal strictures, the overall favourable economic conditions made it possible for important advances to be made by the free blacks. Second only to the State of Maryland in the number of resident free blacks (47,348 in 1830 and 58,042 in 1860), Virginia was important for Liberia because it was a significant centre of the back-to-Africa colonization movement. Indeed, a number of Virginia's relatively prosperous free black residents emigrated there and became a part of the early black leadership. Perhaps the most outstanding was Joseph Jenkins Roberts, once a resident of Petersburg, Virginia, who became Liberia's first president in 1848. Roberts, along with his mother Amelia, was among those persons with considerable property who journeyed to Liberia to avail themselves of greater freedom and the commercial opportunities which West Africa then promised. Other free black Virginians who emigrated included: Joseph Sheppard, Colson Waring, William Nelson Colson (a successful barber), Colin Teague, and the Rev. Lott Carey.

## 101 The Virginia history of African colonization.
Philip Slaughter. Freeport, New York: Book For Libraries Press, 1970. 116p.

First published in 1855 in Richmond, Virginia, by Macfarlane and Fergusson, this study details both the history of the Virginia State Colonization Society and its relationship to the 'national' American Society for the Colonization of the Free People of Colour. The contents include: 'Introduction: Africa in America'; 'History of African colonization from its first suggestion by Thomas Jefferson in 1776 . . . to its full development in the American Colonization Society at Washington, DC in 1817'; 'The agency of President Monroe in the plantation of Liberia . . .'; 'Era of local societies in Virginia . . .'; 'Richmond auxiliary changed into independent State Society, 15th December 1828'; and 'Rise of Northern Abolitionism'. Chapters 6-14 are largely historical, consisting of a chronological compilation of documents. The concluding chapters are: 'Africa and America'; 'The geography of (coastal) Liberia'; and 'Testimony of eye witnesses of Liberia'.

102  **Sojourners in search of freedom: the settlement of Liberia by Black Americans.**
James Wesley Smith.   Lanham, Maryland: University Press of America, 1987. 228p.

The book 'concentrates on those black Americans who settled Liberia early in the nineteenth century. . . It examines the motives of these settlers for immigrating, depicts the role they played in the colonization and development of the colony, and relates the hardships, sufferings, and privations they experienced in the process'. The volume contains a bibliography, which lists original archive sources but fails, almost completely, to cite modern publications.

103  **The African colonization movement, 1816-1865.**
P. J. Staundenraus.   New York: Columbia University Press, 1961. 323p. bibliog.

This work does consider the settlement of Liberia but its main achievement is in providing an exhaustive study of American social thought regarding slavery and colonization. The author's principal source materials were the archives of the American Colonization Society which consist of several hundred volumes held by the Manuscript Division of the Library of Congress. A detailed bibliography and a bibliographical essay are also included.

104  **Facts and opinions touching the real origin, character, and influence of the American Colonization Society: views of Wilberforce, Clarkson, and others, and opinions of the free people of color of the United States.**
Giles Badger Stebbins.   New York: Negro Universities Press, 1969. 224p.

The original preface to this book (first published in 1855 by John P. Jewett, Boston), written by William Jay, stated that colonization was 'intimately connected with the security of the slave holders and the permanency of human bondage' (p. iii). The stated purpose of the book is 'to bring together an array of facts in regard to the real character and influence of the ACS and its auxiliaries. . .' (p. 5). These facts reveal, according to the author, that the whole purpose of the resettlement movement was to rid the United States of the unwanted free people of colour whilst maintaining the institution of slavery.

105  **Settler politics in the nineteenth century: the case of Sinoe County, Liberia.**
Mary Jo Sullivan.   Boston, Massachusetts: African Studies Centre, Boston University, 1980. 24p. (Working Papers in African Studies, no. 33).

This working paper is an abstract of the author's doctoral thesis ('Settlers in Sinoe County, Liberia, and their relations with the Kru, c. 1835-1920'; Boston University, Massachusetts, 1978). It addresses the political economy of nineteenth-century Sinoe County, and its impact on the relations between settler-Liberians and Kru-Liberians. Sullivan argues that 'Sinoe settler presence and interests complicated and often hindered national policy toward the Kru Coast' (p. 1).

106 **Libéria: histoire de la fondation d'un état nègre libre.** (Liberia: history of the founding of a free negro state.)
Henri Emmanuel Wanwermans. Brussels: Institut National De Géographie, 1985. 271p.

Presents a sympathetic interpretation of the history of the Liberian state between 1822 and 1884. Events are chronicled in such a way as to demonstrate the ability of the Westernized black to govern himself in accordance with a Western system of representative government. The contents include: 'Questions of human rights'; 'The American committee'; 'Geographical description of the Grain Coast'; 'Beginning of the Colony (1820-1828)'; 'Colonial government (1828-1847)'; 'Free Negro state (1847-1871)'; 'Boundaries question'; and 'Mores, customs, commerce, industry'. There are two maps and appendices are also included.

107 **Slaves no more: letters from Liberia, 1833-1869.**
Edited by Bell I. Wiley. Lexington, Kentucky: University Press of Kentucky, 1980. 349p.

This collection of 273 letters, with annotations, written by former slaves who had emigrated from America and settled in Liberia, to their former masters, offers interesting glimpses into life in the Liberian settlements between 1833 and 1869.

# Slavery

108 **Slave testimony: two centuries of letters, speeches, interviews and autobiographies.**
Edited by John W. Blassingame. Baton Rouge, Louisiana: Louisiana State University Press, 1977. 777p.

This is the largest collection of annotated and authenticated accounts of slaves published in a single volume. The slaves speak here for themselves and discuss their living conditions and how they coped or rebelled. 'These wide-ranging documents together with annotations, notes, an index, dozens of illustrations, and an incisive introduction, form a volume of unusual scope and character'. The sections which particularly relate to Liberia include: agriculture in Liberia (p. 62, 101, 104-108, 112); churches in Liberia (p. 104-10); education in Liberia (p. 102, 108); letters from Liberia (p. 18, 61-65, 97-108, 110-12); and living conditions in Liberia (p. 62-64, 97-100, 102-103, 112, 557-58). The author is Professor of History at Yale University.

109 **A slaver's log book *or* twenty years residence in Africa.**
Theophilus Conneau, with an introduction by Mabel M. Smythe. Englewood Cliffs, New Jersey: Prentice-Hall, 1976. 370p.

Presents Conneau's original manuscript written in 1853. Conneau was an illegal slaver born in 1808 in Italy of French parents and raised in the US. He carried out his evidently illegal slaving activities between 1820 and 1846 and his writings include his meetings with some of the American founders of Liberia, notably James Hall of the Maryland, or Cape Palmas, settlement.

## 110  The Atlantic slave trade: a census.

Philip D. Curtin.  Madison, Wisconsin: University of Wisconsin Press, 1969. 338p. bibliog.

The aim of Curtin's work is to measure and describe the slave trade, and to synthesize existing information. His conclusion is that around ten million slaves were imported into the Americas between 1451 and 1870. However, it is believed that his figures may vary approximately twenty per cent from the actual totals. For a review of the literature since 1969, see Paul Lovejoy, 'Volume of the slave trade', *Journal of African History*, vol. 23, no. 4 (1982), p. 473-501.

## 111  The United States and the African slave trade 1619–1862.

Peter Duignan, Clarence Clendenen.  Stanford, California: Hoover Institution Press, 1963. 72p.

This monograph, which is not intended as a history of the slave trade, seeks to show that the slave trade was an important economic and cultural factor in the formative years of the United States, and that the slave trade profoundly affected the relations of the United States with the European powers.

## 112  The Atlantic Slave Trade: effects on economics, societies, and peoples in Africa, the Americas, and Europe.

Edited by Joseph E. Inikori, Stanley L. Engerman.  Durham, North Carolina; London: Duke University Press, 1992. 412p.

Presents a collection of papers from a conference entitled: 'The Atlantic slave trade: who gained and who lost?' sponsored by the Institute for African and African-American studies of the University of Rochester in October 1988. The editors divide the issue into three areas: the social cost in Africa of forced migration; Atlantic slavery and the rise of the Western World; and Atlantic slavery, the world of the slaves, and their enduring legacies. Among the numerous papers are Patrick Manning's 'The slave trade: the formal demography of a global system'; Johannes Postma's 'The dispersal of African slaves in the West by Dutch slave traders, 1630-1803'; and Seymour Drescher's 'The ending of the slave trade and the evolution of European scientific racism'.

## 113  The African nexus: black Americans perspective on the European partitioning of Africa, 1880-1920.

Sylvia M. Jacobs.  Westport, Connecticut; London: Greenwood Press, 1981. 311p.

'The study seeks to assess the extent and possible impact of the views and attitudes of black Americans on the European partitioning of Africa during the late nineteenth and early twentieth centuries'. In chapter 10, 'Liberia: Struggle against European Domination, 1880-1914', the author recounts the threat that British and French colonialism and German ambition in Africa posed to Liberian independence, the attitude of ambivalence of the United States, and the diplomatic manoeuvres of Liberian officials. The general study surveys how one segment of the black community in America ('literate and articulate blacks') viewed the partitioning of Africa by European powers. Such views 'generally varied from tacit approval to partial rejection' (p. 274).

114 **Transformations in slavery: a history of slavery in Africa.**
Paul E. Lovejoy. New York: Cambridge University Press, 1983. 352p.

This pioneering work provides clear information about various forms of slavery within Africa and their relationship to economic contact with the outside world. It details how slaves were acquired, transferred from one owner to another within and outside Africa, and how they were eventually liberated prior to the colonization of Africa.

115 **Black cargo: a history of the Atlantic slave trade, 1518–1865.**
Daniel P. Mannix, in collaboration with Malcolm Cowley. New York: Viking Press, 1962. 306p. map.

This is a well-written and well-documented account of the transatlantic slave trade. The first general history of the trade to be written in recent times, it uses diaries, business records, and testimonies, to document a story of greed, violence and incredible callousness. The book claims that 'the importation of Negro slaves from Africa to the two Americas was a gigantic commercial operation that cost between thirty and forty million lives, helped finance the English and French industrial revolutions, and gave rise to the American plantation system, maritime trade, and the civil war; it inflicted wounds on Africa – and on America – which are still unstaunched'.

116 **'Dear master', letters of a slave family.**
Edited by Randall M. Miller. Ithaca, New York: Cornell University Press, 1978. 281p.

Presents a unique collection of letters written by members of a Virginia slave family over a thirty-year period and spanning two continents. Organized into two categories – 1834-1861 (The Peyton Skipwith family, initially of Virginia), and 1847-1865 (The George Skipwith family, formerly of Alabama), the letters are useful additions to a growing body of primary sources from the African-American experience which include Bell Wiley's *Slaves no more: letters from Liberia*; Lexington, Kentucky: University Press of Kentucky, 1980. 349p. (see item no. 107).

117 **The Dutch in the Atlantic slave trade, 1600-1815.**
Johannes M. Postma. New York: Cambridge University Press, 1989. 442p.

Based primarily on Dutch archival material, the book examines Dutch involvement in the Atlantic slave trade between the seventeenth and early nineteenth centuries.

118 **Slavery and the rise of the Atlantic system.**
Edited by Barbara L. Solow. New York: Cambridge University Press, 1991. 350p.

These essays attempt to place slavery in the context of modern history, describing the role it played in bonding the economies bordering the Atlantic, its impact on Africa, and the empires of Portugal, the Netherlands, France, and Britain.

# The twentieth century

119 **Indirect rule and the emergence of the 'Big Chief' in Liberia's central province, 1918-1944.**
Martin Ford. Bremen, Germany: Liberia Working Group, 1992. 88p.
(Liberia Working Group Paper, no. 7).

The author presents a case study of how the rule of the Liberian state in the hinterland (Central Province) 'transformed leadership among the local Dan and Mano from 1918 to 1940' (p. 2). Characterizing governmental authority in the Central Province as 'indirect rule', Ford is concerned about both the motives and the effects of this approach. Overall the policy was pursued on the basis that the interior was 'a reserve of wealth for Liberian officialdom, from which the indigenous population gained virtually nothing in return', with no regard for 'traditional' authority since the indigenous leadership was reshaped to fit the needs of a narrowly-conceived state.

120 **Unknown Liberia.**
Harry J. Greenwall, Roland Wild. London: Hutchinson, 1936. 279p. illus.

This account of Liberia by two English authors was written in the aftermath of the crisis occasioned by the charges made in the early 1930s of slavery and forced labour. With the co-operation of Liberian authorities the authors travelled extensively in the country, including the hinterland. The conclusion they came to was that Liberia should be mandated to Germany in order to protect the Negro Republic 'in its freedom', and to facilitate Germany's return to the League of Nations so that world peace would be preserved. The underlying aim of this suggestion was to remove the condition of darkness and despair that prevailed in the country and replace it by a future 'lightened by hope'. The authors are careful to deflect the blame from the leaders of Liberia: 'It is not their own fault, because all through their history the Liberians have been the tools of white people. They who practice slavery were first slaves' (p. 276). It is apparently because of this that Liberian Secretary of State, Gabriel Dennis, judged the study more objective than most (p. 5).

121 **Lighting up Liberia.**
Arthur Ingram Hayman, Harold Preece. New York: Creative Age Press, 1943. 279p.

Focuses on the social and political conditions during the administration of President Edwin Barclay (1930-1944) and is highly critical of a perceived settler hegemony that excluded an indigenous majority from political participation. Chapter nineteen argues vigorously in favour of 'making Liberia safe for democracy', and makes continuous pleas for the United States to be more meaningfully concerned about conditions in Liberia. As Barclay's term was ending and William V. S. Tubman's (1944-1971) was on the horizon, the authors called for the removal of the property qualification for voting as an important measure to bring democracy to Liberia (p. 270).

122 **Black Zion: the return of Afro-Americans and West Indians to Africa.**
David Jenkins.   London: Wildwood House, 1975. 285p.

Black Zion, the author writes, 'is the ideal held by millions of blacks in America and the Caribbeans of returning to the land from which their forefathers were wrenched'. In attempting to show what happened to those who actually returned in the post 1787 period, returnees to Sierra Leone and Liberia, respectively, figure prominently in this study. The author interviewed 100 people in Ghana, Sierra Leone and Liberia during the first half of 1973; 'Their reactions ranged from complete desolation to almost complete contentment'. The author's objective in recording this range of reactions was to illustrate the differences between people's expectations of Africa and the *de facto* situation.

123 **Bitter Canaan: the story of the negro republic.**
Charles S. Johnson, with introductory essay by John Stanfield.   New Brunswick, New Jersey: Transaction Books, 1987. 256p.

Hidden in the archives at Fisk University until recently, this classic is a historical-sociological exposé of Liberian society. Written in 1930 and revised in 1948, it seeks to demonstrate how social, economic and political forces shaped the Liberian nation. John Stanfield of Yale University has written an insightful introductory essay in which he clarifies Johnson's account of 'how a Liberian nationality evolved'. He asserts that Johnson's 'critical study of American corporate intervention in Liberian society in the twentieth century has the flair of contemporary political analysis'.

124 **The Republic of Liberia.**
Abeodu Bowen Jones.   In: *History of West Africa, vol. 2.*   Edited by J. F. Ade Ajayi, Michael Crowder.   New York: Columbia University Press, 1973, p. 308-43.

This account of the political history of Liberia is presented in an abridged form. It makes an effort to integrate the history of the pre-Liberian state period with that of the modern state.

125 **The republic of Liberia: being a general description of the negro republic, with its history, commerce, agriculture, flora, fauna, and present methods of administration.**
Reginald Charles Faulke Maugham.   New York: Negro Universities Press, 1969. 299p. illus. map.

This volume was originally published in 1920 by George Allen and Unwin, London. The author, a former British Consul General in Monrovia, presents his perspective on Liberia as it was in 1918. The contents include: geography and general description; history of early immigrants; founding of the republic; the national administration in 1918; the economic condition; flora and fauna; the natives; 'slavery-missions and religious institutions – schools and education – immigration'; climate; health; and the author's concluding remarks.

126 **United States and Liberia: the slavery crisis, 1929-1935.**
Parthenia E. Norris.    PhD thesis, Indiana University, Bloomington,
Indiana, 1961. 279p. (order no. 61-4472).

Analyses the tangled relationship between the United States and Liberia which grew out
of accusations by American travellers and the League of Nations that the government of
Liberia was engaged in practices akin to slavery toward some of its indigenous citizens.
The crisis, which led to the resignation of President C. D. B. King in 1930, and a full
League of Nations investigation (the Christy Commission), is given a more systematic
treatment in Ibrahim Sundiata's *Black scandal: America and the Liberian labor crisis,
1929-1936* (Cambridge, Massachusetts: Institute for the Study of Human Knowledge,
1980). (*See* item no. 417).

127 **The black republic: Liberia, its political and social conditions today.**
Henry Fenwick Reeve.    New York: Negro Universities Press, 1963.
207p.

Originally published in 1923 by H. F. & G. Witherly, London, this is an account of
Liberia by a British colonial official. The study is based on several visits to Liberia by
Reeve and is 'fortified by inquiries from all classes of the Liberian community', as well
as by published accounts notably those of Sir Harry Johnston and Frederick Starr. It
indicts the Liberian leadership for incompetency and dishonesty, particularly as regards
its hinterland administration.

128 **Liberia: description, history and problems.**
Frederick Starr.    Chicago: University of Chicago Press, 1913. 277p.
(African Studies Monograph, no. 14).

Interprets the Liberian State as a miniature mirror-image of the American nation
complete with a political machine and a corrupt electoral process. Its flaws were deemed
to be of a generic nature 'largely inherent in (the form) of government . . . due to the
descent of the Americo-Liberians from American slaves'. It is the 'problems' mentioned
in the title that constitute the bulk of the book, around sixty per cent of the pages. The
tone is paternalistic, advocating close US-Liberia relations with emphasis on 'kinship'
ties.

# Military rule and civil war (1980–94)

129 **Violation of the law of armed conflict: Liberia.**
Africa Rights Monitor.    *Africa Today*, vol. 37, no. 2 (2nd quarter, 1990).
p. 82–84.

Briefly outlines those traditional aspects of the 'law of war' which relate to modern
human rights and looks for the existence of basic humanitarian principles in the conduct
of those engaged in the Liberian Civil War.

130 **Liberia under military rule.**
Similih Henry Cordor. Monrovia: Liberian Literary & Educational
Publications, 1980. 103p.

Presents an eyewitness, journalistic analysis combined with historical and political
observations. The work provides insights into the socio-political condition of Liberia just
before the 1980 military coup and chronicles the main events of the first five months of
military rule.

131 **A short history of the first Liberian republic.**
Joseph Saye Guannu. Pompano Beach, Florida: Exposition Press of
Florida, 1985. 152p.

Asserting that on April 12, 1980 the course of Liberian history was radically changed,
Guannu sets out to answer two questions: why did a new order emerge; and what should
the new order do to ensure endurance, stability and development. His book seeks to
provide the answers.

132 **Liberia: reconstruction and unity for the coming decade.**
Edited by Abraham L. James. Philadelphia: University of
Pennsylvania, 1991. 139p.

These are the proceedings of a conference on the reconstruction and unity of Liberia
held between January 4-6, 1991 at the University of Pennsylvania. It sought to address
the needs of Liberia following the devastating civil war which began in December 1989.
The keynote speech was delivered by J. Rudolph Grimes who was Liberia's Secretary of
State, 1960-71. Papers included: Emmet A. Dennis 'Health and reconstruction in
Liberia'; Gordon C. Thomasson, 'Flumo forges a cutlass in the 1981 Year of the
Disabled'; Similih Cordor, 'Reconciliation and healing for a new Liberia'; Burgess Carr,
'Justice, reconciliation and human community in a new Liberia'; Corann Phelps-
Okorodudu, 'Reconstruction through education'; C. William Allen, 'Liberia: the role of
human communication and press freedom in reconstruction'; Flumo Stephens,
'Economic recovery for Liberia'; Al-Hassan Conteh, 'Demographics of the Liberian
Civil War'; David Jallah, 'Independence of the Judiciary'; George K. Kieh, 'The
military and post-Civil War Liberia'; Abraham L. James, 'Liberia: the quest for
leadership for a new era'; D. Elwood Dunn, 'Reflections on a foreign policy for post-
Civil War Liberia'; and Beverlee Bruce, 'Liberia, African-American relations'.

133 **The Africans.**
David Lamb. London: Bodley Head; New York: Random House, 1983.
363p. map. bibliog.

*The Africans* is an interesting portrait of the continent from the perspective of the author,
formerly bureau chief for the *Los Angeles Times* in Nairobi. The section specifically on
Liberia (p. 123-32) is a vivid account of the *coup d'état* of 1980, the pre-execution
'trial', and the execution, on June 22, 1980, of thirteen senior officials of the government
of assassinated President William R. Tolbert, Jr. Lamb apparently witnessed the June 22
executions. He makes this rather perceptive observation: 'The shortcomings that resulted
in Tolbert's murder and Doe's ascendance exist in every African country, usually far
more acutely than they did in Liberia' (p. 132). A statistical profile of Africa and a short
bibliography (p. 349-51) conclude the volume.

134 **Liberia.**
Gail B. Stewart.   New York: Crestwood House, Macmillan, 1992. 48p.
(Places in the News).

This is an interesting presentation of the Liberian tragedy and Civil War aimed at young people. Crestwood House's series on *Places in the News* aims to look behind the headlines and explore global conflict areas. Like others in this collection, Stewart's *Liberia* explains in simple, clear language the historical background behind the conflict and shows how these changes are affecting the lives of the people involved in them. The contents includes: Liberia in the news; the land of the free; sinking into Civil War; Liberia's future; and facts about Liberia. Another recent work, which deals specifically with the Civil War, is James Youboty's *Liberian Civil War: a graphic account* (Philadelphia, Pennsylvania: African Publishing Company, 1994. 650p.). Called by one commentator 'a bone-chilling and suspenseful true-life story', this is a journalistic account of many of the heretofore obscure details of the events of the civil war in Liberia. Graphic in its language and supported by almost two hundred equally graphic photographs, this is perhaps the first of what one suspects will be several other accounts of the Liberian tragedy.

135 **The Liberian crisis and ECOMOG: a bold attempt at regional peace keeping.**
Edited by Margaret A. Vogt.   Lagos: Gabumo Publishing, 1992. 451p.

This is a Nigerian government-sanctioned account of the involvement of the Economic Community of West African States in the Liberian Civil War. It attempts to document 'the debate on the deployment of ECOMOG (the peace-keeping force), situating the analysis in its historical and international contexts' (p. 4). In the foreword the Nigerian military leader, General Ibrahim Babangida, expresses the hope that the 'ECOMOG regional peace-keeping model' will serve, when modified and adapted, to meet 'the challenges of peace-keeping and conflict resolution in other parts of the world' (p. vi). The contents include: 'The internationalization of the Liberian crisis and its effects on West Africa'; 'The problems and challenges of peace-making: from peace-keeping to peace enforcement'; and 'perceptions of the ECOMOG peace initiative'. The opening sketch of Liberia's history leaves much to be desired given the often dated sources employed by the contributors. Indeed, the first two chapters, 'Brief history of Liberia' and 'Historical background to the Liberian crisis' are laden with inaccuracies: for example, the 'last census' is said to have been conducted in 1974 (instead of 1984); and the country is still presented as administratively divided into nine countries when in fact there are thirteen. The editor is Senior Research Fellow at the Nigerian Institute of International Affairs.

136 **Liberia military dictatorship: a fiasco 'revolution'.**
Edward Lama Wonkeryor.   Chicago: Struggler's Community Press, 1985. 251p.

The report of a journalist on the military dictatorship in Liberia between 1980 and 1985, written from the perspective of an eyewitness and with the zeal of someone directly affected by the régime's brutalities. The author strongly believes that the cause of genuine political reform in Liberia has been betrayed. He calls Samuel Doe's departure from this 'noble cause' of reform a 'fiasco'.

**The role of the military in the history of Liberia, 1822-1947.**
*See* item no. 65.

# Historical Biographies

**137   This is Liberia: a brief history of this land of contradictions with biographies of its founders and builders.**
Stanley A. Davis.   New York: William-Frederick Press, 1953. 152p.

The author, an American of West Indian origin, visited Liberia in 1951, documenting his impressions of the country. Davis was troubled by the contradictions he encountered in a country founded as a refuge from oppression and yet engaged in oppression of another variety. Yet he remains hopeful that the oppression by settler-Liberians will end and that the natives will rise ('dry bones will yet rise and march'). Amongst the settler leaders profiled are Presidents of Liberia; the explorer Benjamin J. K. Anderson; the Pan-Africanist Edward Wilmot Blyden; the scholar and cleric Alexander Crummell; and the cleric Samuel David Ferguson. The indigenous Liberian founders and builders profiled include Chief Boatswan; Bob Gray; Vice-President Henry Too Wesley; the Physician Thomas N. F. Lewis; Daybe Nimne; Jah Maley; Toweh of Bowquella; and Sie Nma Teke. In all there are eleven 'American' and fourteen 'African-born builders' profiled.

**138   Reflections of an African nationalist.**
T. O. Dosumu-Johnson.   New York: Vantage Press, 1980. 301p.

The author, a very moderate African nationalist, who was a Liberian diplomat for more than three decades, reflects both upon his diplomatic experiences and his life prior to entering government service. He represented the Tubman and Tolbert governments of Liberia, and was a close friend of Ghanian president, Kwame Nkrumah, and the Nigerian president, Nnamdi Azikiwe.

**139   Alexander Crummell, an apostle of negro culture.**
William Henry Ferris.   Washington, DC: American Academy, 1920. 16p.

An early and interesting biography of Dr. Crummell, a nineteenth-century Liberian cleric, scholar and writer. More recent book-length biographies of Crummell include those of Gregory U. Rigsby (*Alexander Crummell: pioneer in nineteenth century pan-African thought.* Westport, Connecticut: Greenwood, 1987. 249p.), and Wilson Moses (*Alexander Crummell: a study of civilization and discontent.* Oxford: Oxford University Press, 1989. 352p.).

140 **Edward Blyden and African nationalism.**
M. Yu Frenkel, translated from the Russian by E. Bessmertnaya.
Moscow: USSR Africa Institute, Academy of Sciences, 1978. 139p.

An appraisal of the life and work of the Liberian nationalist and Pan-Africanist, Edward
Wilmot Blyden. The author is a Russian scholar whose primary interest seems to be to
uncover the indigenous source of African socialism. The study credits Blyden as being
the 'first ideologist of Pan-Africanism'.

141 **Selected works of Dr. Edward Wilmot Blyden: statesman, politician,
linguist, educator and great pan-Africanist (1832-1912).**
Edited by Willie A. Givens.   Cape Mount, Liberia: Tubman Center of
African Culture, 1976. 319p.

This study makes a major contribution to our understanding of the importance of the life
and work of Edward Wilmot Blyden. Givens draws upon *The African Repository and
Colonial Journal*, and its successor, as well as the works of Blyden's major biographer,
Hollis R. Lynch (1967), and a number of other creditable sources. By reproducing these
documentary texts the author lets Blyden 'speak' for himself. This work compliments
Lynch's *Black spokesman* (1971).

142 **Life of Jehudi Ashmun, late colonial agent in Liberia.**
Ralph Randolph Gurley.   New York: Negro Universities Press, 1969.
393p.

Originally published in 1835 by James C. Dunn, this is the biography of one of the white
agents of colonial Liberia. The appendix contains extracts from his journal and other
writings, with a brief sketch of the life of Lott Carey, a black colonial agent.

143 **Paul Cuffe: black American and the African return.**
Sheldon H. Harris.   New York: Simon & Schuster, 1972. 288p.

An important interpretative biography of this wealthy African-American (1759-1817)
who was interested in establishing colonies of free black Americans in Africa. He
devoted his fortune and his life to achieving his vision, but died before its realization.
The American Colonization Society (ACS) sought to bring his work to fruition but the
politics and racism of American society led it in directions that diverged drastically from
Cuffe's original aims.

144 **Presidents of the first African Republic.**
A. Doris Banks Henries.   London: Macmillan, 1963. 102p.

Contains sketches of the lives of all the Presidents of Liberia from the first, Joseph
Jenkins Roberts, to the eighteenth, William V. S. Tubman. The sketches are largely
laudatory, and Tubman's is the most extensive. An introduction precedes the sketches.

145 **The life of Joseph Jenkins Roberts (1809-1876) and his inaugural
addresses.**
A. Doris Banks Henries.   London: Macmillan, 1964. 155p.

This is a glowing account of the life and work of the first president of Liberia. Henries
writes that Roberts 'started life as a worker on a flat-boat, and became a successful
merchant in Africa, a High Sheriff in a pioneer community constantly fighting the slave

trade, a Vice-Governor of the Liberian Commonwealth, and finally, the highest office of all, President of the Liberian Republic' (p. v). The first part of the work provides a biography of Roberts, whilst the second part contains his 'inaugural addresses'.

## 146 I came, I saw, I worked.
A. Doris Banks Henries. London: Cassell, 1977. 90p.

An autobiography of the author (1918-81) detailing her life and work at the University of Liberia, Ministry of Education, and international organizations up until 1977. Also highlighted are her missionary, literary, and political experiences in Liberia in collaboration with her husband, Richard A. Henries, who was speaker of the Liberian House of Representatives for many years prior to his execution in 1980. The author, an African-American, became a naturalized Liberian and was a prolific writer before her departure from the country in the wake of the 1980 *coup d'état*. She died in the United States in 1981.

## 147 Blyden of Liberia: an account of the life and labors of Edward Wilmot Blyden as recorded in letters and in print.
Edith Holden. New York: Vantage Press, 1966. 1,040p.

Edward Wilmot Blyden was Liberia's foremost nineteenth-century scholar. This volume is essentially a source book for the study of Blyden, and contains a particularly useful and extensive bibliography of Blyden's works (including unpublished manuscripts). Holden was the granddaughter of the Rev. John Knox, who played an important role in Blyden's life.

## 148 James Milton Turner and the promise of America: the public life of a post-civil war black leader.
Gary R. Kremer. Columbia, Missouri: University of Missouri Press, 1991. 245p.

An interesting biography of an élitist black American leader who became America's first black diplomat to Liberia. He served as US Minister Resident between 1871 and 1878 and saw his role, as did Alexander Crummell, as one of a 'potential civilizer' of indigenous Africans. He advocated Christianity as the means to 'debarbarize and benefit' thousands 'whose intellects are today debased by the destructive potency of heathenish superstition' (p. 58-59).

## 149 Harvey Firestone: free man of enterprise.
Alfred Lief. New York: McGraw-Hill, 1951. 324p.

A sympathetic biography of Harvey Firestone, Snr. (1868-1938) who established the Firestone rubber empire in Liberia in 1926. Allan Nevins writes in the foreword: 'By farsighted planning, Firestone built first a strong local industry in the Ohio town of Akron, then a national business, and finally an international structure with factories on all continents and vast rubber plantations in Liberia' (p. vii). 'Firestone Enters Liberia' (chapter sixteen) considers the early relationship between the American entrepreneur and the Liberian government.

150 **Black spokesman: selected published writings of Edward Wilmot Blyden.**
Edited by Hollis R. Lynch.   London: Frank Cass, 1971. 354p.

Lynch, the foremost biographer of Blyden, presents here both works and reprints of the writings of this pioneer pan-Africanist. Most of these works had hitherto been available only in specialist libraries. They include various aspects of continental and diaspora African life – history, institutions, culture, political and social thought and eminent personalities. As Liberia was Blyden's home for almost all of his working life, the bulk of the material relates specifically to Liberia. There is an introduction by the editor, and the collection is grouped under seven headings, namely: Afro-America and Africa; Liberia – its role and history; Africa – its history and culture; race and the African personality; education – its nature and purpose for Africa; Islam and West Africa; and European Imperialism in West Africa.

151 **Golah boy in America.**
Bai T. Moore.   Richmond, Virginia: Quality Printing Co., 1937. 27p.

This is a brief autobiographical essay blended with a description of Liberian traditional life – especially among the Gola people. The booklet was written in the hope that funds generated from the sale would assist the author in his study of medicine in the United States. Moore actually took a first degree in Biology but distinguished himself as a literary figure in Liberia.

152 **Alexander Crummell: a study of civilization and discontent.**
Wilson Jeremiah Moses.   New York: Oxford University Press, 1989. 380p.

An intellectual biography of a major black historical figure who, though born in the United States, spent twenty years of his life working in Liberia. Moses portrays Crummell as a synthesis of Victorian intellectual, American evangelist, Liberian nationalist and African-American leader.

153 **Destiny and race: selected writings, 1840-1898: Alexander Crummell.**
Edited by Wilson Jeremiah Moses.   Amherst, Massachusetts: University of Massachusetts Press, 1992. 306p.

Contains 'a concise, albeit representative, selection of Crummell's published and unpublished writings' edited by an expert in this field. The work includes an introduction by Moses and an essay on Crummell by W. E. B. DuBois. The main text is divided into 'Materials of Biographical Interest' (of relevance are: 'Report from Buchanan, Liberia, on a journey to St. Andrew's church'; and 'Report from Caldwell, Liberia, on a journey through the Dey and Vai countries'); 'Sermons Revealing the Theological Basis of Crummell's Social Theories ('The Episcopal Church in Liberia: on laying the corner stone at St. Andrew's' is directly related to Liberia); and Statements of Social and Political Ideology (An item on Liberia is 'The progress and prospects of the Republic of Liberia').

154 **Liberian odyssey 'by hammock and surfboat': the autobiography of F. A. Price.**
Frederick A. Price. New York: Pageant Press, 1954. 260p. illus.

This is an account of Christian mission work in Liberia during most of the first half of the twentieth century. The author, who became a naturalized Liberian, went there in 1904 for the Board of Missions of the Methodist Episcopal Church of the United States, subsequently becoming Liberia's Consul General in New York in 1956. He relates his experiences gained as he carried out his mission work over a wide area of coastal and hinterland Liberia. Publications of comparable interests relative to missionary enterprise in Liberia include: *Adventure with the Kru in West Africa*, by Walter B. Williams and Maude W. Williams (New York: Vantage Press, 1955. 146p. illus.) which is an account of Methodist missionary work on the 'Kru Coast' from 1909 to 1933; and *The Lutheran mission in Liberia* by Harold V. Whetston (New York: Board of Foreign Missions of the United Lutheran Church in America, 1955. 255p. illus.)

155 **Who's who in Africa: leaders for the 1990s.**
Alan Rake. Metuchen, New Jersey: Scarecrow Press, 1992. 447p.

This is 'an attempt to provide pen portraits of the most prominent political figures in Africa South of the Sahara. It concentrates on those in power, those recently in office, and those most likely to succeed . . .' (p. v). Arranged by countries in alphabetical order, the work features Liberians such as guerilla leader Prince Yormie Johnson (p. 175-77), Interim President Amos Sawyer (p. 177-79), and guerilla leader Charles Taylor (p. 179-82). There is an alphabetical index containing name, country and page number of the individual profiled. The author is Managing Editor of *New African*, London.

156 **Liberia past and present.**
Nathaniel R. Richardson. London: Diplomatic Press & Publishing Company, 1959. 348p.

This work largely consists of historical sketches, together with a compilation of state papers, photographs and biographies of some of Liberia's leading political and social leaders who held power prior to the end of the 1950s.

157 **Alexander Crummell: pioneer in nineteenth century Pan-African thought.**
Gregory U. Rigsby. New York: Greenwood Press, 1987. 231p.

Presents a biography of Alexander Crummell (1819-98), a major figure in African-American history who spent twenty years of his fruitful life in Liberia as a citizen. Rigsby's is an intellectual biography of sorts since he has focused his study on the nature and evolution of Crummell's pan-African thinking, and not the wide array of concerns with which his subject was involved.

158 **Tolbert of Liberia.**
Wilton Sankawulo. London: Ardon Press, 1979. 192p.

A semi-official biography of President William Richard Tolbert, Jr. (1913-80) written by an assistant minister in the President's office as Liberia prepared to host the annual meeting of the Organization of African Unity in July 1979. The preface is written by Guinean President Ahmed Sékou Touré, and the book largely chronicles the life and work of the President drawing on family and official government sources. Of related interest is *His Challenge is mankind: William R. Tolbert, a political portrait* by Robert A. Smith, with an introduction by President Siaka A. Stevens of Sierra Leone (Monrovia: Providence Publications, 1972. 268p).

## 159  The symbol of Liberia: the memoirs of C. L. Simpson.

C. L. Simpson.   London: Diplomatic Press & Publishing Co., 1961. 293p.

This is the autobiography and political memoirs of a major Liberian political figure who served as Vice-President (1944-52) and Ambassador to the United States and to Britain (1952-60). With a Vai-Liberian mother and a father from settler stock, he sought to portray himself as symbolizing the two cultural streams of Liberia. A candidate for the presidency in 1944 when president Tubman won his first term, Simpson's evident ambition was never realized since Tubman dominated the scene and Simpson died two years before Tubman in 1969.

## 160  William V. S. Tubman: the life and work of an African statesman.

Robert A. Smith.   Monrovia: Providence Publications, 1966. 184p.

The author purports to have written a 'preliminary sketch' of the life and work of President Tubman. In fact, what we are presented with is a full-blown political biography written by an admirer mid-way through the President's fifth term of office. With no effort made to provide perspective, Tubman is portrayed as the leader who brought about national unity and unprecendented material development to Liberia. Smith has written other laudatory studies on Tubman's presidency such as *We are obligated: an interpretive analysis of twenty-five years of progressive leadership* (Hamburg, Germany: Hanseatische Druckanstalt, 1969. 206p.) and *Meet the President* (Monrovia: Providence Publications, 1968. 78p.).

## 161  Paul Cuffe: black entrepreneur and pan-Africanist.

Lamont D. Thomas.   Urbana, Illinois: Chicago: University of Illinois Press, 1986. 188p.

A biography of this important African-American with particular emphasis on the relationship between his life and work and the origins of the ACS (American Colonization Society) which sponsored the founding of Liberia. The major themes that shaped the ACS are outlined here; the establishment of legitimate trade links to West Africa and the evangelization of Africa by African-Americans. Cuffe was himself able to send only one group to Africa (Sierra Leone), but he set the stage for the national movement embodied in the ACS. When the society was formed in 1816, it was to Cuffe that they turned for advice. Prior to Cuffe's death southerners began to be included in the ACS, which led to a reshaping of the society to reflect the southern antagonism to the presence of free blacks in southern communities. The society's characterization of free blacks as an evil which should be excised from the nation led northern blacks, for the most part, to turn against emigration. Cuffe died before the storm broke, but was not likely to have supported emigration under those circumstances.

162 **The Presidents of Liberia: a biographical sketch for students, containing biographies of the presidents and some of the leaders in the making of the republic.**
Thomas H. B. Walker.    Jackson, Florida: Chadwyck-Healey, 1915. 92p.

Provides brief biographical information, often placed in the context of political events, about the first fourteen of Liberia's twenty presidents – Joseph Jenkins Roberts (1848-1856), to Daniel Edward Howard (1912-1920). This work is available on microfiche from Chadwyck-Healy Inc., 1101 King St., Alexandria, Virginia 22314, USA.

163 **Writings and papers of Fatima Massaquoi Fahnbulleh.**
Filmed in Liberia, Oct. 1973. One reel of film, about 900 pages.
West Falmouth, Massachusetts: Africa Imprint Library Services.

Contains facsimile reproductions of the private papers of Madam Fahnbullah, a Liberian educator of Vai ethnicity who once served as Dean of Liberia College. Among the works included in this collection is 'Bush to boulevards: the autobiography of a Vai nobleman', filmed from the original manuscript. There are also proverbs, miscellaneous studies, the 'national oration' (Independence Anniversary Address to the nation) of 1921 delivered by Momolu Massaquoi, father of Fatima and a former Liberian consul general in Germany. A few of the more important papers from the Institute of African Studies, University of Liberia, of which Madam Fahnbulleh was founder and director, are also included.

# Population and Demography

### 164 The changing geography of West Africa.
Kathleen M. Baker. In: *The changing geography of Africa and the Middle East*. Edited by Graham P. Chapman, Kathleen M. Baker. London, New York: Routledge, 1992, p. 80-113.

This is a good analysis of the 'geography of change' in the West Africa sub-region. 'For nearly all of these countries the doubling time (sic.) for the population is less than thirty years ... rates of urbanization are high, and increasing education and the media are changing the political awareness and expectations of these populations'. The principal topics addressed in the chapter include: 'Images of West Africa, past and present'; 'Population and peoples'; 'Nations caught in economic traps'; 'Economic entrapment, government inexperience and political turmoil'; 'Urban expansion: population increments unmatched by resources'; 'The industrial sector in West Africa'; and 'Agriculture and causes and effects of environmental degradation'. The author is Lecturer in Geography at London University's School of Oriental and African Studies.

### 165 Liberia demographic and health survey 1986.
Dorothy Chieh-Johnson, Anne R. Cross, Ann A. Way, M. Jeremiah Sullivan. Monrovia: Bureau of Statistics, Ministry of Planning and Economic Affairs; Institute for Resource Development/Westinghouse, Columbia, Maryland, USA. February 1988. 117p.

The Liberia Demographic and Health Survey (LDHS) was a national-level survey conducted between February and July 1986, covering a sample of 5,239 women aged 15 to 49. The purpose of the survey was to provide planners and policymakers with data regarding fertility, family planning, and maternal and child health. A secondary objective was to collect baseline information for the Southeastern Region Primary Health Care Project. The contents includes: 'Marriage and exposure to the risk of pregnancy'; 'Fertility'; 'Contraceptive knowledge and use'; 'Fertility preferences'; and 'Mortality and health'. Useful appendices and a page of references complete the work.

166 **Liberia: 1962 census of population.**
Monrovia: Department of Planning and Economic Affairs, 1968. 440p.
This is a government publication containing population data as of April 1962. It provides information about such matters as the age of the population, the number of males and females, places of birth, citizenship, marital status, the number and size of households, ethnic population, school attendance, educational attainment, the economic activities of the people, industry and occupational status.

167 **Liberia: the effects of population factors on social and economic development.**
The Futures Group. Resources for the Awareness of Population Impacts on Development (RAPID), 1983. 94p.
This United States Agency for International Development-funded analysis is intended to assist the planning process in Liberia by examining the effects of population growth on the labour force, child dependency and new job requirements; production and consumption of rice; urbanization; education; and health. Contents include population dynamics, how Liberia's population characteristics will affect national objectives, and effects of population programmes.

168 **The population of Liberia.**
Abel Z. Massalee. Paris: Comité Internationale de Coordination de Recherches Nationales en Démographie, 1974. 56p.
This publication contains basic statistics concerning the Liberian population for the year 1974.

169 **1984 Population and Housing Census: summary population results in graphic presentation PC-1.**
Monrovia: Republic of Liberia: Ministry of Planning and Economic Affairs, 1986. 26p.
This summary of the 1984 population and housing census not only depicts the spatial distribution of the population by political subdivisions but also includes illustrations, graphs and other visual aids to increase understanding of the information collated. Also included are the population estimates for 1986 by counties and territories which have been calculated using the 'linear extrapolation method'. The figures show that 'the average annual population growth rate for Liberia has been constant from the first census of 1962 to 1974 and from 1974 to 1984 [it] has been slightly over three per cent'.

170 **National policy on population for social and economic development.**
Monrovia: Republic of Liberia, National Population Commission, (NPC), 1987. 24p.
This publication, which was the product of a collaborative research exercise, was designed to aid the development planning process in Liberia. It attempts to formulate a national policy on population that seeks the incorporation of population variables into national development plans as a 'first step towards ensuring the welfare and meaningful existence of the Liberian people' (p. 11). Parts one to three of the document provide general background information on the policy declaration while sections four to eight cover the declaration itself. Financial support for the study was provided by the government of Liberia, the Futures Group, Rapid II Project, and the Pathfinder Fund.

# Major Population Groups

## General

171 **African resistance in Liberia: the Vai and the Gola-Bandi.**
Monday B. Akpan. Bremen, Germany: Liberia Working Group Papers
No. 2, 1988. 68p.

Contains two contributions which cover the resistance of the Gola and Bandi between
1905-19, and of the Vai between 1825-82, respectively, to the expansion of the Liberian
State into their traditional domains.

172 **Tribe and chiefdom on the windward coast.**
Warren L. d'Azevedo. *Liberian Studies Journal*, vol. 14, no. 2 (1989),
p. 90-116.

First published in *Rural Africana* (no. 15, 1971, p. 10-29), the author examines 'the
relevance of the concepts of 'tribe' and 'chiefdom' as they have been utilized in
ethnographic investigation of Liberian peoples'. He concludes that 'the accumulating
evidence suggests that these concepts have been applied in such a way as to seriously
restrict our recognition of crucial social and historical realities that have characterized
the actual situation in the region for centuries' (p. 112). D'Azevedo, an American
anthropologist, is one of the modern pioneers of Liberian studies.

173 **Kolonial Völkerkunde: Wiener Beiträge zur Kulturgeschichte und Linguistik.** (Colonial anthropology: contributions to cultural history and linguistics from Vienna.)
Edited by Herman Baumann. Germany: Verlag Berger, Horn, N/D, 1944. 351p.

The book highlights selected regions and peoples of Africa and reviews the state of European ethnographic research in Africa. In the first chapter Etta Becker-Donner describes the Krahn and Grebo of Liberia. Among the topics considered in this volume are: settlement conditions; house construction and their interiors; agriculture; cattle breeding; clothing; jewellery; tattooing; tooth mutilation; hairstyles; craftmanship; blacksmiths; hide manufacturing; techniques of weaving; ceramics; musical instruments; carving; art; dance; music; poetry; marriage; birth; name-giving; education and work; circumcision; divorce; government; and religion.

174 **Peuples de la Forêt de Guinée.** (People of the Guinean Forest.)
Jacques Germain. Paris: Académies des Sciences d'Outre Mer, 1987. 380p.

Presents an ethnographic study of three groups – the Kono, Kpelle, and Mano – who live in an area which straddles Liberia's border. Based on notes taken by the author while a colonial administrator in Guinea for sixteen months in 1946-1947, it is written with an evident colonial bias. Nonetheless, this work provides important information on the pre-colonial conditions experienced by these peoples.

175 **Die Völkerstämme im Norden von Liberia. (The tribes of northern Liberia. Results of an exploration expedition commissioned by the Saxon State Exploration Institute of Ethnology in Leipzig in the years 1928 and 1929.)**
Paul Germann. Leipzig, Germany: R. Voigtlanders Publication House, 1933. (Ethnography and Ethnology, Publications of the Saxon State Exploration Institute for Ethnology in Leipzig, vol. 2. Edited by Professor Otto Rech).

Focuses on the Kissi, Bandi and Loma peoples of northern Liberia, describing almost every aspect of the lives of each of the three groups. Germann examines the lives of the peoples, their clothing and jewellery, communities, homes and building materials, economy, agriculture and hunting, arts, dance, music, slavery and forms of government. The work is richly illustrated with photographs and drawings.

176 **Mission dans l'est Libérien: résultats démographiques, ethnologiques et anthropométriques.** (An expedition to eastern Liberia: demographic, ethnological and anthropometric results.)
Bohumil Holas, P. L. Dekeyser. Dakar, Senegal: Institut Français d'Afrique Noire 1952. 566p. illus. (IFAN, no. 14).

This is a report of the first research venture outside French colonial territory by IFAN (Institut Français d'Afrique Noire). The study is divided into eight parts which provide demographic details of the ethnic regions of eastern Liberia visited by the group and which consider such subjects as: physical anthropology; linguistics; religion and magic; and arts and crafts. Part six contains a comprehensive bibliography covering material in

English, French, German and other languages; part seven provides a subject and place name index; and part eight consists of thirty-nine plates of ethnological interest.

177 **Stateless societies in the history of West Africa.**
Robin Horton. In: *History of West Africa.* Edited by J. F. A. Ajayi, Michael Crowder. New York: Columbia University, 1976. 2nd ed. vol: 1, p. 72-113. bibliog.

Horton describes the problems associated with writing a history of stateless societies (indigenous polities lacking centralized authority), their present-day distribution, their social organization and systems, and their relation to the nation. Liberian examples of stateless groups include the Kissi, the Dan and the Kru.

178 **Note sur deux peuplades de la frontière Libérienne, les Kissi et les Toma.** (Notes on two peoples of the Liberian border, the Kissi and the Loma.)
H. Neele. *L'Anthropologie*, no. xxiv (1913), p. 445-75.

This article is an ethnographical study of these two peoples. The work is divided into two parts dealing with the Kissi and the Loma, respectively. Part one, 'The Kissi' considers the geography of the area in which these people live, and examines their anthropological characteristics, their industries, their money (including the famous 'Kissi penny'), their mythology and legends and their interesting history. The Kissi are thought to have fled to the area from Fouta where they had been persecuted by the Dialonke. Taking refuge in the forest, they took the name Kissi which means 'saved'. The second part 'The Loma' considers the people's geographical location and discusses their anthropological characteristics, their art and their government which is very similar to that of the Kissi. The Loma chiefs have a very strong authority. Often of Mandingo origin, they are aided by a kind of council of elders.

179 **The Kwa speaking peoples of Liberia.**
Niamey, Niger: Organization of African Unity, Centre for Linguistic and Historical Studies by Oral Tradition, 1977. 91p.

Provides brief profiles of each of the following Kwa-speaking peoples: Grebo; Krahn; and Kru (each by Moulai Z. Reeves); and Bassa (by Joseph M. N. Gbadyu). The work also includes an oral history research questionnaire (p. 76-91) prepared by Abeodu B. Jones.

180 **Tribes of the Liberian hinterland.**
George Schwab. Cambridge, Massachusetts: Peabody Museum, 1947. 545p. (PM Papers, no. 31).

Conducted under the auspices of the Peabody Museum, this monumental work on the ethnic groups of the northern regions of Liberia was undertaken by an amateur anthropologist and his wife. Schwab had spent some fifty years as a missionary in the Cameroons. The work contains additional material supplied by George Way Harley who also served as a missionary for many years among some of the people considered in this study. More than twenty ethnic groups were covered, and basic data on their economy, social system, religious beliefs and material culture is provided. There are appendices on languages, a glossary, and a substantial section of illustrations relating to artifacts and physical anthropology.

181  **Liberia, facing mount Nimba: a documentary history of the United Nimba Citizens' Council (UNICCO).**
Nya Kwaiwon Taryor.  Clinton, New York: Strugglers' Community Press, 1991. 310p.

Although the book concentrates on the activities of UNICCO, an association for Liberians of Nimba origin now living in the US, it also focuses on the people of Nimba County, the Mano (Mah), Dan, and Mandingo, and considers their mythological, political and economic histories along with their relationships with the wider Liberia.

# Bassa

182  **The Bassaman and the expansion of the Liberian state: 1847-1912.**
Joseph M. N. Gbadyu.  In: *Anthology of Liberian literature*. Monrovia: Society of Liberian Authors, 1974, p. 135-57.

In this interesting article the author, a distinguished Bassa-Liberian journalist, attempts to highlight the origins of the Bassa ethnic group. He considers Bassa history and culture with reference to their early contacts with European traders in the pre-Liberia period, as well as their encounters with New World blacks which culminated in the establishment of the Liberian state. Gbadyu combines both oral history and historical accounts in his work.

183  **My people, the Bassa tribe.**
Abba G. Karnga.  Pasadena, California: World-wide Missions, 1975. 109p.

The author, a Bassa-Liberian Christian Minister, describes the way of life and the 'major customs of the Bassa people' (q.v.). The book's contents include: 'The Bassa people – where they live'; 'Marriage customs'; 'Traditional education'; 'Means of communication'; 'Wise sayings of the Bassa Tribe'; 'Tribal identity, its significance'; 'Religious beliefs'; 'Music in Bassa life'; and 'Burial and funeral of a chief'.

184  **Ethnographic survey of southeastern Liberia – report on the Bassa.**
William C. Siegmann.  Robertsport, Liberia: The Tubman Centre of African Culture, 1969. 41p. map.

A general survey of Bassa ethnography including language and linguistic affiliation, ecology and economics. The work covers such subjects as family and lineage organization, community and settlement patterns, history, political organization, social stratification, life cycles, sodality (secret society, bush school . . .), and religion.

# Belle

185   **The traditional history and folklore of the Belle tribe.**
S. Jangaba M. Johnson.   *Liberian Studies Journal*, vol. 1, no. 2(1969),
p. 45-73.

A profile of the Belle ethnic group by a veteran Liberian scholar. The Belle's traditional location is Lofa county in northeastern Liberia, and they are considered the oldest of Lofa county's ethnic groups. Among the topics addressed are issues of origins, tribal government, Belle judicial practices, inter-tribal relations, inter-tribal wars, religion, cultural societies, domestic life and economics, marriage customs and funeral practices.

# Dan (Da, Dahn)

186   **Die Dan, ein Bauernvolk im westafrikanischen Urwald; Ergebnis
dreier völkerkundlicher Expeditionen im Hinterlande Liberias, 1949/
50, 1952/53, 1955/56.** (The Dan: an agricultural people in the west
African jungle – the result of three research expeditions to the hinterland
of Liberia, 1949/50, 1952/53, 1955/56.)
Hans Himmelheber, Ulrike Himmelheber.   Stuttgart: W. Kohlhammer,
1958. 256p. illus.

An important record of three of the six expeditions by Hans Himmelheber (the principal author, an ethnologist, physician and art expert – see his *Negerkunst und Negerkünstler*) all among the Dan (Dahn) of Nimba county. Of related interest is Ulrike Himmelheber's *Schwarze Schwester: von Mensch zu Mensch in Afrika. Mit 45 aufnahmen der Verfasserin* [Black Sister: from human to human in Africa with 45 pictures by the writer], (Bremen, Germany: C. Schunemann, 1957. 213p. illus. maps). Concerns about women's affairs led Ulrike to produce a second volume. Both books contain useful photographs.

# Dei (Dey)

187   **The tribes of the Western Province and the Denwoin (Dei) people.**
Bai T. Moore.   Monrovia: Bureau of Folkways, Interior Department,
Monrovia, Liberia, 1955. 83p.

A pioneer government-sponsored survey of the indigenous peoples of the Western Province (Bandi, Belle, Gola, Kissi, Kpelle, Loma, Mandingo and Mende), and the Denwoin or Dei people. According to the author, the original Dei country was located between the Lofa and St. Paul Rivers, extending from the Atlantic Ocean twenty miles inland. Though Moore asserts that the Dei were absorbed by the Gola, Vai and

Mandingo (p. 57), he then proceeds to consider the 'Structure and types of Dei villages' (chapter 4); 'Kinship and other ties' (chapter 5); and 'Dei cultural societies' (chapter 6).

# Gbande (Bandi)

### 188  The Gbandes: a people of the Liberian hinterland.
Benjamin C. Dennis.   Chicago: Nelson-Hall, 1972. 333p.

This is one of the few ethnographic studies to be written by a social scientist who is also an African. In this case a Mende-Liberian writes about the Bandi (Gbande) culture with which he was closely associated throughout his early life. Drawing on his own experiences and his knowledge of certain spheres of Bandi life, including thoughts and values, which would largely be unavailable to an outside observer, Dennis provides useful accounts of domestic life, glimpses into Bandi attitudes and their relationships among neighbours, and information on the socialization of children.

### 189  Tales from Bandiland.
Barnabas Saji Ndebe.   Newark, Delaware: Liberian Studies Association in America, Inc., 1974. 292p.

This is a collection of fifteen Liberian folktales presented in both the original Bandi language and English.

# Gola

### 190  Continuity and integration in Gola society.
Warren Leonard d'Azevedo.   PhD Thesis, Northeastern University, Evanston, Illinois, 1962. 302p.

This benchmark study of hinterland Liberia analyses sociocultural continuity and integration which was imposed as a result of the historical circumstances of the Gola people of Liberia. It suggests that the integration of Gola society may be characterized by a dynamic relationship between two sets of principles in the Gola world view expressed through crucial institutions: 'The first is derived from the ritualized model of ideal social relations embodied in the structure and function of the secret societies, and provides a common cultural orientation and ultimate reference point for all Gola sub-groups. The second involves the opportunistic values manifested most directly in the structures of administrative authority of Chiefdoms, but which also permeate all levels of Gola social organization as guides to personal and local-group behavior in the pursuits of competitive ends' (Abstract).

191 **Uses of the past in Gola discourse.**
Warren Leonard d'Azevedo. *Journal of African History*, vol. 3, no. 1 (1962), p. 11-34.

Contends that the Gola sense of history is compartmentalized and variable locally/ regionally as a phenomenon, and is undergoing continual change. 'The earlier impact of Sudanic and Muslim culture, the migration of a heterogenous population into the region, and the shifting foci of political power among the various inter-tribal societies, were predisposing conditions which were effective for many centuries. It is in this context and in these terms that a concept of history may be characterized for the Gola people' (p. 33).

192 **Gola of Liberia.**
Warren Leonard d'Azevedo. New Haven, Connecticut: Human Relations Area Files, 1972. 2 vols.

These volumes contain valuable descriptive ethnographic material concerning the Gola peoples of Liberia which stemmed from research carried out between January and June 1967. A major series of interviews was conducted and the responses obtained from the local informants is included. In addition, the volumes provide background information and vernacular terms for concepts of social organization and aggression. A brief annotated bibliography is also provided (p. 442-443).

193 **The traditional history and folklore of the Gola tribe in Liberia.**
S. Jangaba M. Johnson. Monrovia: Bureau of Folklore, Department of the Interior, 1961. 2 vols.

These two volumes by a prominent Liberian folklorist deal with the oral or traditional history of the Gola and the contemporary social, economic, and political circumstances that this group experiences. Johnson studies the Gola either by chiefdoms and clans, or by the political subdivisions designed by the Liberian government. This work is particularly useful for the information it provides about the indigenous religions, marriage, and family customs of the Gola and also for the light it sheds on the Liberian government's administration of the Gola region. It also considers the Gola's problematic relationship with the government and discusses the Gola war of 1918. The author travelled widely in Gola territory and lived among the Gola people.

# Grebo

194 **Ethnographic survey of southeastern Liberia: the Grebo-speaking peoples.**
Ronald J. Kurtz, assisted by H. J. Tarplah, B. Reiser, G. McWilliams, C. Nyema, Peter Tweh, C. Browne, and J. Tarpeh. Philadelphia: Institute for Liberian Studies, 1985. 267p. (Liberian Studies Monograph Series, no. 7).

Presents the results of research carried out by an American anthropologist concerning nineteen Grebo-speaking ethnic groups and one Wee (Krahn)-speaking group. Basic ethnographical information is provided for each of the sub-groups of Grebo ethnicity.

195 **The traditional history and folklore of the Glebo tribe of Liberia.**
S. Jangaba M. Johnson. Monrovia, Liberia: Bureau of Folklore,
Department of the Interior, 1955. 194p.

Studies the Glebo (Grebo) ethnic group in Maryland County in eastern Liberia and
provides significant data on their history and their position in the early 1950s. Attention
is paid to the story of the origin and migration of the Grebo peoples, the indigenous
family, their religious and political systems, as well as the interaction and conflicts
between the group and the Liberian government, especially during the nineteenth
century when this region was being integrated into the modern Liberian state.
Appendices providing the names of Grebo leaders, and information about the activities
of Christian missionaries among the Grebo are also included.

196 **Civilized women: gender and prestige in southeastern Liberia.**
Mary H. Moran. Ithaca, New York: Cornell University Press, 1990.
189p.

This anthropological study focuses on the 'connections between cultural construction of
gender and other means of social ranking' among the Glebo (Grebo) of southeastern
Liberia. Asserting that the civilized and native (settler/indigene) dichotomy split Grebo
society as it does Liberian society in general – unlike the situation in other West African
countries where divisions are created by ethnicity or regionalism – the author
demonstrates how the Grebo have transferred this dichotomy into other gender and age-
based systems of 'prestige allocation'.

# Kissi

197 **A segmentary society between colonial frontiers; the Kissi of Liberia,
Sierra Leone and Guinea, 1892-1913.**
Andreas W. Massing. *Liberian Studies Journal*, vol. 9, no. 2
(1980-81), p. 1-12.

The article explores the segmentary Kissi people in the context of how they encountered
and reacted to such centrally-organized political units as chiefdoms and territorial states,
including the Liberian state. It ends with a 'tentative' list of Kissi chiefs as confirmed, or
appointed by, the Liberian government following the establishment of Liberian rule in
the early part of the twentieth century.

198 **Les gens du riz: Kissi de haute-Guinée Française.** (The rice people:
the Kissi of Upper French Guinea.)
Denise Paulme. Paris: Plon, 1954. 232p.

Describes in detail the social, economic, and political institutions of the Kissi ethnic
group found in Guinea, Sierra Leone, and Liberia. As the title suggests, rice is a staple in
the diet of this people. Of related interest is André Schaeffner's *Les Kissi: Une société
noire et ses instruments de musique* (see item no. 199).

199 **Les Kissi: une société noire et ses instruments de musique.** (The Kissi: a black society and its musical instruments.)
André Schaeffner. Paris: Herman et Cie, 1951. 95p. (Actualités Scientifiques et Industrielles, no. 1139. *L'Homme*, Cahier d'Éthnologie, de Géographie et de Linguistique, no. 2).

Drawing upon research carried out among the Loma and other neighbours of the Kissi, the author describes both the musical instruments of the Kissi and then attempts to compare them with their eastern and southeastern neighbours. However, in the course of studying musical instruments, the author reveals a society in the process of 'reconsolidation'. The Kissi, according to Schaeffner, 'give signs less of people who have given up than a people restoring self-consciousness. They were attempting to reassemble the fragments of a past that was and was not theirs'. At the time when this research was carried out the Kissi were distributed throughout the Guinea forest, Liberia and Sierra Leone. Among the instruments described are the wooden drum, string and air instruments, trumpet, bells and calabash gourd.

# Kpelle

200 **Village of curers and assassins: on the production of Fala Kpelle cosmological categories.**
Beryl L. Bellman. The Hague: Mouton, 1975. 196p.

This study attempts to posit and describe the actual methodology native Fala Kpelle speakers use to understand, or interpret, the subjective meanings of each other's talk.

201 **Women and marriage in Kpelle Society.**
Caroline H. Bledsoe. Stanford, California: Stanford University Press, 1980. 217p.

The product of field research carried out between 1973 and 1974 among the Kpelle of Fuama Chiefdom in Liberia, this study analyses Kpelle marital patterns in order to determine the power-seeking and power-maintenance strategies of men and women. Bledsoe identifies the underlying social network of the traditional Kpelle agrarian economy as a 'wealth-in-people' system, in which men and old persons of both sexes have legal rights as regards women and the young. The institution of marriage is presented as probably the most influential social institution, maintaining the Kpelle 'wealth-in-people' system. Unfortunately, modern economic trends – the growing sale of land once available for traditional agriculture and the impact of the money economy – are eroding the traditional social structure.

202 **Full respect: Kpelle children in adaptation.**
Gerald M. Erchak. New Haven, Connecticut: Human Relations Area Files, 1977. 225p.

Describes and analyses the context in which Kpelle-Liberian children learn. While focusing on socialization and enculturation, the author provides what he considers relevant data on Kpelle technology and their economy, kinship, political organization, and ideology. An important conclusion is that the learning environment is shaped by the

Kpelle agricultural economy which he defines as a basic cultural characteristic. However, given the effect of change, or Westernization, on that context, he goes further to advance the idea of 'a sociological vacuum' in which learning is expected to take place. Kpelle children are seen as handicapped in this new setting and are likely to remain so until education is made less Western and more related to Kpelle culture.

## 203 The Kpelle of Liberia: a study of political change in the Liberian interior.

Richard Melvin Fulton. PhD thesis, University of Connecticut, Storrs, Connecticut, 1969. 285p.

Explores the political development of Liberia's largest ethnic group. Fulton divides his work into three parts: the political system of the Kpelle before 'pacification' by the Liberian state; the process of 'pacification'; and the contemporary (late 1960s) efforts to incorporate Kpelle institutions within the Liberian state.

## 204 Red dust on green leaves.

John Gay. Thompson, Connecticut: InterCulture Associates, 1972. 240p.

This is a novel by an American missionary scholar who spent more than fourteen years living and working at Cuttington College, located in the heartland of Liberia's Kpelle community. The book focuses on two Kpelle twin boys growing up in their traditional society. The boys are torn between the traditions of their isolated civilization and the attractions of taking part in the nation-making process in Liberia. *Red Dust* becomes a chronicle of Kpelle society divided by the strength of tradition and the attractions of modernization.

## 205 The brightening shadow.

John Gay, with the editorial advice of John Kellemu. Chicago: Intercultural Press, 1980. 280p.

As a sequel to *Red dust on green leaves* (q.v.), this fictional account provides, in general terms, a picture of life among Kpelle-Liberians in the recent past, including ritual practices, family relations, agricultural practices, city life, and conflicts occasioned by the clash of Western and traditional practices.

## 206 The Kpelle of Liberia.

James L. Gibbs, Jr. In: *Peoples of Africa.* Edited by James L. Gibbs, Jr. New York: Holt, Rinehart & Winston, 1965, p. 197-240.

The Kpelle people constitute the largest of Liberia's many ethnic communities. Gibbs profiles this 'polycephalous associational' group, and pays particular attention to their: economy; community and territorial organization; life cycle; stratification; political organization; tribal societies; law; religion; ethos; and the impact of change. The author is a leading black American anthropologist, now a Professor at Stanford University.

207 **Kinship and territory in the history of a Kpelle Chiefdom (Liberia).**
William P. Murphy, Caroline H. Bledsoe. In: *The African frontier, the reproduction of the traditional African societies.* Edited by Igor Kopytoff. Bloomington, Indiana: Indiana University Press, 1987, p. 121-47.

This paper is based on the 'widespread notion' that in the societies of sub-Saharan Africa the 'first occupation of a territory legitimizes the first comers and their descendants, as landowners who allocate land to later arrivals and have special claims to their allegiance'. A closely-related notion is that 'marriage and kinship ties between first comers and late comer groups also structure their relations'. Against this backdrop anthropologists Murphy and Bledsoe postulate 'that kinship and territory are cultural constructs expressed in a code of categories, beliefs, values, and symbols'. They provide an overview of Kpelle society, and examine the Kpelle semantics of kinship and territory with case illustrations of how the derived meanings are politically managed (p. 123).

208 **Let the inside be sweet: the interpretation of music event among the *Kpelle* of Liberia.**
Ruth M. Stone. Bloomington, Indiana: Indiana University Press, 1982. 180p.

Stone is concerned with the dynamics of symbols and metaphors in social relations, and in this study focuses on the 'concept of music event' among the Kpelle and emphasizes the connections between musical performance and the structure of Kpelle society.

209 **Officers and elders: a study of contemporary Kpelle political cognition.**
Michele M. Teitelbaum. PhD thesis, Rutgers University, New Brunswick, New Jersey, 1977. 163p.

Explores contemporary notions of political authority among Liberians of Kpelle ethnicity who reside in the town of Kakata, Liberia.

210 **Old age, midwifery and good talk: paths to power in West African gerontocracy.**
Michele Teitelbaum. In: *Aging and cultural diversity: new directions and annotated bibliography.* Edited by Heather Strange, Michele M. Teitelbaum (et al.). South Hadley, Massachusetts: Bergin & Garvey Publishers, 1987, p. 39-60.

This anthropological study focuses on 'the relationship of power to a multiplicity of attributes associated with old age'. Based on field research conducted among the Jokwele Kpelle peoples of Liberia in the mid-1970s, the author seeks to explain the Kpelle theory about how old people acquire power, and suggests the relevance of the discussion 'to generalizations that have been made about the aged in non-industrial societies' (p. 40).

211 **Secret medicines, magic and rites of the Kpelle tribe in Liberia.**
William E. Welmers. *Southwestern Journal of Anthropology*, vol. 5 (1949), p. 208-43.

Describes, with little detailed explanation, certain features of Kpelle life in the 1940s. The topics discussed include: proprietorship and medicine; therapeutic and prophylactic medicine; poison and black magic; power over natural events; fortune telling; ordeals; and tribal secret societies. A brief conclusion states that 'the tribal organization of the Kpelle people appears to be based on two pillars – the material affairs controlled by the landowners, and the non-material or "medicine" affairs controlled by the medicine men' (p. 242). The study focuses primarily on the non-material or 'medicine' aspects of Kpelle organization, using the 'material' or legal aspects, such as the economy, land tenure, political organization and administration only where the two 'pillars' are combined in the secret societies (p. 243).

212 **Die Kpelle: ein Negerstamm in Liberia.** (The Kpelle: a black tribe in Liberia.)
Diedrich Westermann. Göttingen, Germany: 1921. 552p.

One of the early detailed ethnographies of the Kpelle of Liberia, this includes highly specific descriptions of family, village, and chiefdoms, as well as the institutions of the Poro and Sande.

# Krahn (Wee)

213 **A social survey of Grand Gedeh County, Liberia.**
Svend E. Holsoe. University of Delaware. Newark, Delaware: Institute for Liberian Studies, 1979. 80p. maps.

This USAID-funded project was designed to scientifically collect basic social data on Grand Gedeh County as a prerequisite for undertaking a development programme in the area. For the first time ever, according to the author, all officially-recognized districts were identified and located enabling researchers to ascertain the number of people who officially fell within the jurisdiction of each village. As a result of these investigations, it was possible to map the whole county demographically.

214 **Ethnographic survey of southeastern Liberia: the Liberian Kran and the Sapo.**
Gunter Schroder, Dieter Seibel. Newark, Delaware: Published for the Tubman Center of African Culture by the Liberian Studies Association in America, 1974. 161p. maps. bibliog.

This brief study of the ethnic groups in Grand Gedeh County, details such features as demography, political organization, historical background, and the family life of the Krahn and the Sapo.

# Kru

215 **Les Kroumen de la côte occidentale d'Afrique.** (The Kru of West Africa.)
Christine Behrens. Talence, France: Centre d'Études de Géographie Tropicale, 1974. 243p. (Travaux et Documents de Géographie Tropicale, no. 18).

Traces and documents the evolution of 'Kru' maritime activities on the West African coast from the historical and contemporary anthropological angles, respectively. It is based on field work carried out in south western Ivory Coast in 1970.

216 **Structural continuity in the development of an urban Kru community.**
Lawrence B. Breitborde. *Urban Anthropology*, vol. 8, no. 2 (1979), p. 111-30.

Examines the role of traditional rural-based social structural principles in the organization of the urban Kru community of Monrovia.

217 **The Kru mariner in the nineteenth century: an historical compendium.**
George E. Brooks, Jr. Newark, Delaware: Institute for Liberian Studies, 1972. 121p. (Liberian Studies Monograph Series, no. 1).

The first known published monograph on the Kru, this work consists of two parts: the Kru and their employment on European trading ships in African waters in the nineteenth century; and efforts at ascertaining the origins of the Kru, their ethnic identity and geographical boundaries. The study provides useful, well-documented data about these people and contains a good bibliography.

218 **Ethnohistorical studies on the Kru coast.**
Ronald W. Davis. Philadelphia: Institute for Liberian Studies, 1976. 217p. (Liberian Studies Monograph Series, no. 5).

The author of this work, an American anthropologist, attempts an historical sketch of the Kru coast (south of the river Cestos) during the 150 years prior to effective Liberian government control of the area which occurred at the turn of the last century.

219 **Tribe and class in Monrovia.**
Merran Fraenkel. London: Oxford University Press for International African Institute, 1964. 244p.

Although the research for this study was conducted in the 1950s, this work is nevertheless still a very useful account of the structure of Monrovian society and the process of social mobility. Ample documentation is provided on the persistence of rural values and institutions amid rapid social change in an urban setting. Of related interest is Fraenkel's 'Social change on the Kru Coast of Liberia', *Africa*, no. 34 (1966), p. 154-72, which considers cultural change in the rural setting and the conflicts and differences which can arise between 'Westernized' and 'non-Westernized' indigenous people.

220 **The economic anthropology of the Kru (West Africa).**
Andreas Massing. Wiesbaden, Germany: Franz Steiner Verlag, 1980.
281p.
Considers the cultural characteristics of the 'Kru' linguistic area (a delimitation of the 'Kru culture area'), and analyses agricultural practice in the region with a view to testing the rationality of resource allocation in the Kru indigenous economy.

# Loma

221 **The sacred forest: the fetishist and magic rites of the Toma.**
Pierre-Dominique Gaisseau, translated from the French by Alan Ross.
London: Weidenfeld & Nicolson, 1954. 199p.
A record of the experiences and impressions of four Frenchmen who spent several months attempting to live the life of the Toma (the French word for the Loma people). Travelling through Loma country in Guinea and parts of Liberia, the author and his three colleagues claim to have been initiated into Loma secret society as a means of facilitating investigation of 'the moral code of the Toma' with a view to understanding their traditions. 'Three fetishers consented to let us watch and film their secret ceremonies, obliging us to undergo ritual tests. Others, however, annoyed by this sacrilege, invoked ancestral laws to arouse the Toma tribe against us' (p. 11). It is questionable whether any information of real value was acquired in the course of this 'investigation' by people who were not professional ethnologists.

222 **Culture and psychosis among the Loma tribe of Liberia, West Africa.**
Jay Hamilton Nolan. PhD thesis, Stanford University, California, 1972.
276p.
Nolan describes and analyses twenty-three Loma-Liberian individuals in an attempt to understand the manner in which the Loma culture relates to psychosis in its ethnographic setting. Among the study's findings is the suggestion of 'some promising possibilities in the cross cultural study of how societies manage crisis situations and provide for positive, or negative, crisis resolution experiences'.

# Mano

223 **Native African medicine; with special reference to its practice in the Mano tribe of Liberia.**
George Way Harley. Cambridge, Massachusetts: Harvard University Press, 1941. 294p. bibliog.
Examines the Mano people and their medicine, including such topics as their beliefs concerning the treatment of disease, and the relationship between medicine and their

secret societies. Harley, an experienced missionary doctor, concludes with an exposition and definition of fetishism. Of related interest, is Harley's *Masks as agents of social control in northeastern Liberia* (New York: Kraus Reprint, 1968. 45p. originally published by the Peabody Museum of Harvard University, vol. 32, no. 2, 1950).

224 **Anthropological study of masks as teaching aids in the enculturation of Mano children.**
Pearl Eileene Primus. PhD thesis, New York University, Washington Square, New York, 1978. 234p.

An anthropological study which explores masks as learning aids in youth enculturation among the Mano of Liberia, and suggests their wider use as teaching aids in the development of the creative arts.

225 **Labour migration and rural agriculture among the Gbannah Mano of Liberia.**
James Coleman Riddell. PhD thesis, University of Oregon, Eugene, Oregon, 1970. 158p.

Considers the involvement of male Mano-Liberians in the modern Liberian economy with reference to Mano labour migration and the attendant adjustment in village social infrastructure. One conclusion of the study is that as a consequence of the migration of Gbannah males to the Firestone plantation in Harbel from 1926 onwards, 'planning functions traditionally undertaken by males are now assumed by the wives of migrants, and the domestic groups of the Gbannah towns are now engaged in cash cropping in addition to subsistence farming'.

# Mende

226 **The conceptualization of family-size goals among the Mende in Sierra Leone and the Vai in Liberia.**
S. Momolu Getaweh. PhD thesis, Boston University, Massachusetts, 1978. 419p.

The two parts of this study contain an investigation of the conceptualization of family-size limitation, independent of external influence, among the Mende and the Vai and an exploration of the impact of family planning techniques. The following conclusions are drawn: that educational achievement need not necessarily determine reproductive behaviour; that the size of the family for these two ethnic groups is determined less by the number of offspring than by the number of dependants; and that religious persuasion does not influence the choices made in planning a family.

227 **The Mende of Sierra Leone: a West African people in transition.**
Kenneth L. Little. Routledge & Kegan Paul, 1951. 307p.

This seminal study of the Mende of Sierra Leone highlights their traditional culture, social organization and kinship, religion and medicine, modern methods of government, and modern social trends.

# Mandingo (Manding)

**228 Manding: focus on an African civilization.**
Edited by Guy Atkins. London: Published by the Centre for African Studies, School of Oriental and African Studies, University of London, 1973. 33p.

This publication is the product of a symposium organized collaboratively by the School of Oriental and African Studies and the Société des Africanistes, which included an international conference on Manding Studies (30 June to 3 July 1972) held in London under the Presidency of Senegal's poet-president, Leopold Sedar Senghor. The contents of this booklet includes: 'The people and their language' by David Dalby; 'Social organization' by Robert Launay; 'History and religion' by Herman Bell; 'Arts and craft' by John B. Donne; 'Music' by Winifred Dalby; 'Oral literature' by Gordon Innes; and 'Francophone literature' by Gerald Moore. This volume on the Manding, some of whom inhabit Liberia, also includes a bibliography. Of related interest is Carleton Taylor Hodge's *Papers on the Manding*, (Indiana University Publication, African Series, vol. 3, 1971. 307p.)

**229 Manding voluntary associations in Monrovia.**
Tim Geysbeek. *Liberia-Forum*, no. 6, vol. 4 (1988), p. 45-64.

The stated purpose of the article is 'to identify the different types of Manding associations in Monrovia, offer a hypothesis that accounts for the formation of Manding associations, and evaluate the importance of these associations in the Manding community' (p. 45). The author identifies Mandings in Monrovia as originating either from elsewhere in Liberia, or from Guinea. They both form voluntary associations 'to exploit the opportunities that are perceived to exist in Monrovia and to reinforce traditional customs and values.' (p. 56).

**230 The Manding in Western Liberia.**
Svend E. Holsoe. *Liberian Studies Journal*, vol. 7, no. 1 (1976-77), p. 1-12.

This article summarizes the interrelationship of the peoples of western Liberia with the Manding. Beginning with 'early history', it traces Manding origins in Liberia, their relations with the Vai and the Gola, their conflict and co-operative relations with the Liberian central government, as well as their more recent efforts to fully participate in the life of the Liberian nation.

# Vai

**231 Negro culture in West Africa.**
George Washington Ellis. New York: Neale Publishing, 1914. 290p.

This interesting sociological study of the Vai covers: physical aspects; economy; politics and government; religious life and practice; moral standards; proverbs; folklore and stories; language; and culture. The work also contains a conclusion, as well as fifty stories and 114 proverbs. The author, a black American, was acclaimed to be comparable with Edward Wilmot Blyden and Alexander Crummell, and his book as having a definite mission 'as a scientific investigation, as a contribution to social problems, as a basis for political action'.

232 **The Vai and their kinsfolk.**
H. Boakai Freeman. *The Negro History Bulletin*, vol. 16 (1952),
p. 51-63.

Discusses the history and culture of the Vai and related ethnic groups. Among the topics discussed are land tenure, religion, domestic slavery, marital customs, social life and literature. The Vai language is also examined.

233 **The cassava-leaf people: an ethnohistorical study of the Vai people with a particular emphasis on the Tewo chiefdom.**
Svend E. Holsoe. PhD thesis, Boston University, Boston,
Massachusetts, 1967. 298p.

Examines the culture and social structure of the Vai, emphasizing their political and economic systems. The author's aim is to place the history of the Vai and the social structural modifications that have taken place over the ages in their proper context.

234 **Africa.**
John Ogilby. London: Tho. Johnson, 1670. 413p.

This is an early geographical study of Africa. The section on Liberia includes a detailed description of the history and lifestyle of the Vai people of Cape Mount, Liberia. One source considers the entire book to be a translation of Olifert Dapper's *Naukeurige beschrijvinge der Afrikaensche Gewesten* (1668). (See Svend E. Holsoe, *A study guide for Liberia, development program*, African Studies Center, Boston University, October, 1967, p. 7).

# Repatriate (New World Blacks)

235 **The Americo-Liberian ruling class and other myths: a critique of political science in the Liberian context.**
Carl Patrick Burrowes. Philadephia: Temple University, Institute of African and African-American Affairs, 1989. 77p. (Occasional Paper, no. 3, spring 1989).

This is an important attempt to question a hypothesis which passes for conventional wisdom in Liberian studies: that the emigrant-Liberians have constructed a ruling class which has oppressed the indigenous inhabitants. Focusing on three works: Liebenow's *Liberia: the evolution of privilege* (Ithaca, New York: Cornell University Press, 1969. 247p.); Fahnbulleh's *The diplomacy of prejudice* (1985); and Hlope's *Class, ethnicity and politics in Liberia* (Washington, DC: University Press of America, 1979. 336p.), Burrowes challenges the basic common assumptions in all of these works, placing them in the context of what he terms as epistemological problems 'of historicism, essentialism and Eurocentrism' (p. 71). He argues that 'Liberianist political science needs stricter standards of conceptualization and data verification if it is to deliver on the promise that is inherent in its name' (p. 75). Topics discussed include: the uses and misuses of ethnicity; the state and other instruments of power; the Americo-Liberian ruling class; and Eurocentrism and the privileging of Westerners.

236 **Immigrants to Liberia, 1865 to 1904: an alphabetical listing.**
Peter J. Murdza, Jr.   Newark, Delaware: University of Delaware, Department of Anthropology, 1975. 76p. (Liberian Studies Research Working Paper, no. 4).

The second in a series, this compilation covers the period 1865-1904 and includes 4,093 individuals who left the United States for Liberia. Excluded are the 346 blacks who migrated in 1865 from Barbados under the sponsorship of the American Colonization Society. Murdza begins with a useful introduction that attempts to provide historical context and explain the listings.

237 **The making of the Americo-Liberian community: a study of politics and society in nineteenth-century Liberia.**
James Thomas Sabin.   PhD Thesis, Columbia University, Morningside Heights, New York, 1974. 300p.

Based primarily on archival sources in the United States and Europe, this study makes the claim that as the nineteenth-century New World Black settlement in Liberia began to expand beyond its original locus at Cape Mesurado after 1821, a unique socio-economic system was established. Its features included 'an urban community in which family connections were keys to economic and social progress. Physical labour was held in disdain, and [indigenous] African "pawns" or apprentices did much of the menial labour'. There is little analysis of the dynamics of the interaction between settlers and indigenes in the nineteenth-century context within which the settler community was embedded and shaped.

238 **Behold the promised land: a history of Afro-American settler society in nineteenth century Liberia.**
Tom W. Shick.   Baltimore, Maryland: Johns Hopkins University Press, 1980. 208p.

This is one of several studies on the majority of the Liberian settler population (i.e. those from the United States). Shick seeks to present a social history of the earliest settlers as they made the transition from life in America to life in Africa. His essential theme is that these 'Americo-Liberians' (called 'élites') created a distinctive society with a 'settler standard'. This society was as much a part of Afro-American history as it was African history. Notwithstanding this, the author does little to demonstrate the blend of experiences, American and African, that one would expect to constitute this society. Instead, he attempts, with little success, to write a 'complete' history of the 'Americo-Liberian Republic'.

239 **Emigrants to Liberia, 1820 to 1843: an alphabetical listing.**
Tom W. Shick.   Newark, Delaware: University of Delaware, Department of Anthropology, 1971. 111p. (Liberian Studies Research Working Paper, no. 2).

Provides an alphabetical list of emigrants sent to Liberia during this period by the American Colonization Society and similar organizations. Each ship that arrived in

Liberia is listed along with basic information on each passenger including details of age, occupation and level of literacy etc.

240 **Ebony kinship: Americo-Liberians, Sierra Leonean Creoles and the indigenous African population, 1820-1900.**
Kula Okoro Uche.   PhD thesis, Howard University, Washington, DC, 1974. 298p.

In his analysis of the relationship between the indigenous and settler groups in Liberia and Sierra Leone, respectively, the author contends that the emigrant groups genuinely sought to make common cause with the indigenous groups. For Liberia in particular, the view taken here is in opposition to the 'black colonialism' school of thought.

# Language

**241  A sociolinguistic study of language attitudes among tertiary Liberian bilinguals and their attained proficiency in ESL.**
Robert H. Brown.   PhD dissertation, University of Essex, Colchester, England, 1989. 388p. (Order no. DA51A.0151.B-88505).

Analyses the results gained from a survey of some 200 students. Among the findings is the revelation 'that the respondents do have positive language attitudes, and that the choice of a language may be influenced by such factors as the setting, the interlocutors and the topic. It is suggested that the evidence provided by the responses highlights the need for a bilingual education in Liberia.'

**242  The phonology and morphology of Kisi.**
George Tucker Childs.   PhD thesis, University of California, Berkeley, California, 1988. 404p. (UMI order no. DA8902054).

This is a description of the phonology and morphology of the Kisi language (part of the southern branch of the West Atlantic family of African languages) spoken in parts of Liberia, Sierra Leone and Guinea.

**243  Language and history in Africa.**
Edited by David Dalby.   London: Frank Cass, 1970. 159p.

The idea for this volume of collected papers stemmed from a seminar held at the School of Oriental and African studies at London University in the 1960s. This work is basically a historical interpretation of the contemporary languages of Africa which aims at establishing 'a dialogue between comparative linguists and historians on the one hand, and social anthropologists and socio-linguists on the other'. The sections which deal with Liberia include David Dalby's 'The historical problem of the indigenous scripts of West Africa and Surinam' (p. 109-19) in which he focuses on the scripts of the Vai, Mende, Loma, Kpelle, Bassa and Gola of Liberia; and Charles S. Bird's 'The development of Mandekan (Manding): a study of the role of extra-linguistic facts in linguistic change' (p. 146-59). Liberia is highlighted as part of the 'Mandekan extensions', i.e., the extension of the Mandingo or Mandingo ethnic or language group.

## 244 The languages of Africa.

Joseph H. Greenberg. Bloomington, Indiana: Indiana University, 1970. 3rd ed. 180p. 5 maps. index. bibliog. (Research Center for the Language Sciences, Indiana University, publication no. 25).

The volume contains a 'complete genetic classification of the languages of Africa'. The author classified 730 languages into the following language groups: Niger-Congo; Afroasiatic; Khosian; Chari-Nile; Nilo-Saharan; and Niger-Kordofania. An enumeration of the membership of the Niger-Congo language groups shows the Liberian indigenous languages under the sub-family of *West Atlantic* (Kissi, Gola), *Mande* (Mande, Gbandi, Loma, Kpelle, Vai, Malinke), and *Kwa* (Grebo, Bassa, Dei, Kru).

## 245 A Grebo-English dictionary.

Gordon Innes. Cambridge, England: Cambridge University Press in Association with the West African Languages Survey and the Institute of African Studies, Ibadan, Nigeria, 1967. 131p. (West African Language Monograph Series, no. 6. Edited by Joseph H. Greenberg and John Spencer).

Although it draws upon earlier studies of the grammatical and lexicographical work of the Grebo language, the material in this dictionary was collected during work undertaken by the author in London, aided by a presumably Grebo assistant, J. Y. Dennis (a researcher at the School of Oriental and African Studies from 1955-57). Earlier works of related interest include J. L. Wilson, *A brief grammatical analysis of the Grebo language* (Cape Palmas, 1938); John Payne, *Dictionary of the Grebo language* (Philadelphia, 1967); J. G. Auer *Elements of the Gedebo language* (Stuttgart, 1870); and F. Muller *Die Sprachen Basa, Grebo and Kru* (Bassa, Grebo and Kru languages) (Vienna, 1977).

## 246 The languages of Africa.

Frederick William Hugh Migeod. Freeport, New York: Books For Libraries Press, 1972. 2 vols. map. (Black Heritage Library Collection).

First published in 1911 by a transport officer in the colonial Gold Coast, volume one includes preliminary remarks on languages and a tabular statement of grammatical rules in thirty-three languages (including Mandingo and Mende, spoken in Liberia). Volume two includes 'Vai writing and literature' (p. 266-81); and includes the works of Momulu Massaquoi such as 'The Vai people and their syllabic writing' (African Society's Journal, July 1911), and of the Rev. S. W. Koelle of the Church Missionary Society of Freetown, Sierra Leone.

## 247 An introduction to Liberian English.

John Victor Singler (assisted by J. Gbehwalahyee Mason, David K. Peewee, Lucia T. Massalee, and J. Boima Barclay, Jr.). East Lansing, Michigan: Peace Corps/Michigan State University, African Studies Center, 1981. 261p.

'Liberian English' is a broad term encompassing the many varieties of English spoken by Liberians. It has been shaped by pre-Liberian Portuguese and English contacts, West African coastal pidgin speakers, New World emigrants, indigenous Liberian languages, West African varieties of English, and ongoing American ties with Liberia. This study is divided into two parts. Part one discusses Liberian English, and in particular, its history, varieties and variations within it, its pronunciation and its grammar. Part two uses

Liberian English to describe aspects of contemporary Liberian culture (p. vii). A ninety-minute cassette accompanying the text is also available.

248 **Copula variation in Liberian settler English and American black English.**
John Victor Singler. In: *Verb phrase patterns in Black English and Creole.* Edited by Walter F. Edwards, Donald Winford. Detroit, Michigan: Wayne State University Press, 1991. p. 129-64.
This comparative study of language patterns involves the English spoken by semi-literate descendants of Liberian settlers and 'American Black English'. On the Liberian side the study examines copulas, or connections in settler English, and is based on interviews with three settler descendants, respectively from Farmersville (Sinoe County), Fortsville (Bassa County), and Robertsport (Cape Mount County).

249 **Languages of West Africa.**
Diedrich Westermann, M. A. Bryan. Folkestone, England: Dawsons of Pall Mall for the International African Institute, 1970. rev. ed. 277p. map. bibliog.
This important volume surveys the languages of West Africa or the 'area extending from the Atlantic coast at the Senegal River eastward to the Lake Chad region'. First published in 1952, it includes a map showing language locations, among them the West Atlantic, the Mande, the Kru, and the Kwa language groups. The various languages are described and estimates of the number of speakers are given. This revised edition has an extensive bibliography by D. W. Arnott of London University's School of Oriental and African Studies (p. 203-63) which supplements the original (p. 178-201).

**Liberia.**
*See* item no. 76.

**A bibliography of the Vai language and script.**
*See* item no. 654.

# Religion

### 250 The status of Muslims in Sierra Leone and Liberia.

Mohammed Alpha Bah. *Journal Institute of Muslim Minority Affairs*, vol. 12, no. 2 (July 1991), p. 464-81.

Considers the introduction of Islam to Liberia and Sierra Leone and surveys its dispersion patterns in both countries. The majority of the article is given over to a discussion of 'the predominant economic role of Muslim communities in the two states in contrast to their limited political power, especially in the area of leadership'. A postscript highlights religious and ethnic factors in the Liberian civil war of 1989/90 as they related to Liberians of the Islamic faith who seem also to be predominantly of Mandingo (Mandinka) ethnicity.

### 251 Christianity, Islam and the negro race.

Edward Wilmot Blyden. Edinburgh: Edinburgh University Press, 1967. 407p.

Originally published in London in 1888 by W. B. Whittingham and Co., Printer, 'The Charterhouse Press', this collection of writings focuses on problems of race and religion. The author, a West-Indian born Liberian scholar and statesman, was widely acknowledged to be the 'first African personality'. A major objective of the work was to emphasize the role of the black Christian and the black Muslim in the redemption of Africa, each being free from the 'disease of European casuistry' (p. xi). Among the articles included are those entitled: 'Christian missions in West Africa'; 'Ethiopia stretching out her hands unto God (Africa's Service to the World)'; 'Mohammedanism in West Africa'; 'Islam and race distinction'; and 'Sierra Leone and Liberia'.

### 252 Ten years episcopacy: a reflection.

George Daniel Browne. Sandpoint, Idaho: St. Agnes' Episcopal Vicarage USA, 1980. 95p.

Browne, a bishop of the Episcopal Church in Liberia, chronicles his first ten years as chief pastor of the Liberian Episcopalians. Highlights of this work include Church-State relations and the role of the Church in education in Liberia. Browne died in 1993.

253 **The growth of Christianity in the Liberian environment.**
John Walter Cason.   PhD thesis, Columbia University, New York, 1962. 551p.

Addressing the pattern of Christian development in Liberia, this study raises questions about the quality of Christian growth, 'a growth which gives direction to the whole'. It seeks to approach this topic in Liberia 'both as an isolated study in Church history and an example of a way in which the Christian faith may become indigenous in Africa' (p. 3). All of the 'mainstream' Christian denominations represented in Liberia in the early 1960s are surveyed. They include Baptists, Episcopalians, Presbyterians, Lutherans, Roman Catholics and Seventh Day Adventists.

254 **The future of Africa: being addresses, sermons, etc. delivered in the republic of Liberia.**
Alexander Crummell.   New York: Negro Universities Press, 1969. 354p.

Originally published in 1862 by Charles Scribner, the contents include: 'The English language and Liberia'; 'The duty of a rising Christian state to contribute to the world's well-being and civilization'; 'The progress of civilization along the West Coast of Africa'; 'The progress and prospects of the Republic of Liberia'; 'God and the Nation'; 'The fitness of the Gospel for its own work'; 'Address on laying the cornerstone of St. Mark's hospital, Cape Palmas'; 'The relations and duty of free colored men in America to Africa'; 'Hope for Africa'; and 'The Negro race not under a curse'. The author's stated purposes for the publication were 'to show that the children of Africa have been called, in the Divine Providence, to meet the demands of civilization, of commerce, and of nationality; and that they are beginning to embark on the great work of civilization . . . and to the solemn responsibility of establishing the Christian faith amid the rude forms of paganism' (p. 4).

255 **Sisters, servants, or saviors? National Baptist women missionaries in Liberia in the 1920s.**
Jeannine Delombard.   *International Journal of African Historical Studies* (Boston, Massachusetts), vol. 24, no. 2 (1991), p. 323-47.

The author contends that the African-American women who were posted to Liberia as missionaries for the National Baptist Convention USA, not only expounded, but also experienced a sisters/servants/saviour metamorphosis as their role changed over the years. Delombard examines these women's opinions and beliefs as expressed in the official organ of the NBCs Foreign Mission Board, *The Mission Herald*. She considers how their contributions to the *Herald* reflected their attitudes about the African people and culture that surrounded them and also how they revealed their ambivalent sense of their own spiritual and cultural role in the Liberian context.

256 **A history of the Episcopal Church in Liberia, 1821-1980.**
D. Elwood Dunn.   Metuchen, New Jersey: Scarecrow Press, 1992. 503p. illus.

This study, which includes a preface by the Episcopal Bishop of Liberia, George D. Browne (1933-1993), provides: an important discussion of the role of the Christian missions in the evolution of modern Africa; an historical account of the work in Liberia of the Episcopal Church of the United States; and a glimpse into the social history of Liberia. In seven chapters covering the period 1821-1980, using primary archival sources and interviews, the author considers the factors which led the American Church to extend its missionary enterprise to Liberia, how it was established in the area, and how it came to be shaped by the peoples and cultures of the region, even as it left its controversial cultural imprint on the land. The Church set in motion a complex interaction involving the indigenous peoples of the area, foreign missionaries (who were mostly white), and Westernized blacks from the New World. That interaction, under the political direction of the Liberian state, has been significant in shaping the Liberian national character.

257 **Christianity in independent Africa.**
Edited by Edward Fashole-Luke, Richard Gray, Adrian Hastings, Godwin Tasie. Ibadan, Nigeria: Ibadan University Press; London: Rex Collins, 1978. 630p.

This study is the product of a research programme conducted over two years at seminars and conferences in eight universities and ecumenical centres in Africa, the United States and Britain. It seeks to address the state of the Christian church in independent Africa. The authors consider this question in the context of its wider cultural significance in Africa and beyond. Attention is also paid to the continuing interaction between Christianity and African traditional religions, as well as the extent to which developments within Islam in Africa illuminate the Christian experience. Part one addresses religious and secular structures, and part two is entitled 'Traditional religion and Christianity: continuities and conflicts'.

258 **Lott Carey, first black missionary to Africa.**
Leroy Fitts. Valley Forge, Pennsylvania: Judson Press, 1978. 159p.

Lott Carey (1780-1828) was born a slave in America and emigrated to Liberia in 1821 where he established the first Church, the Providence Baptist Church, in Monrovia. He later became a colonial official. Fitts provides an interesting biography of Carey, and considers his life and work from his formative years in the American state of Virginia through to his pioneering missionary enterprise in Liberia, and its impact on subsequent black American missionary endeavours. The influence of Christian missions on Liberia is largely considered in a nineteenth-century context.

259 **The planting of Christianity in Africa.**
C. P. Groves. London: Lutterworth Press, 1964. 330p. (The Planting of Christianity in Africa, vol. 1, to 1840).

This chronological history is the first of a four-volume series which presents 'in perspective within the limits of a simple narrative the various attempts to plant Christianity in Africa'. Of particular interest is chapter twelve, which expresses 'West African hopes' for establishing Christianity and discusses 'the American colonization of Liberia' and the role of Christian missions in the early Liberian settlement. Liberia is discussed intermittently throughout the remaining volumes.

260 **The Presbyterian mission to Liberia, 1832-1900.**
Eva Naomi Hodgson. PhD thesis, Columbia University, New York, 1980. 386p. (University Microfilm Order no. AAD82-22405).

The abstract of this dissertation asserts that 'the nineteenth century was a period of aggressive Christian missions. The Presbyterian Church (USA) represented many of the influential members of the American society. When, therefore, it undertook a mission to

Africans on the West Coast of Africa where, according to the American Colonization Society, there were to be settlements of free Blacks who would convert and civilize Africans, it should have succeeded. It did not. This study examines the reasons for that failure'.

### 261 Catholic missionaries and Liberia: a study of Christian enterprise in West Africa, 1842-1950.
Edmund M. Hogan.   Cork, Ireland: Cork University Press, 1981. 268p.

Using rare Catholic archival material held in Paris, Rome, and Ireland, Hogan recounts the 'ups and downs' of the Roman Catholic Church in their attempts to establish a foothold in Liberia. Although he discusses the endeavours of the missionary-sending bodies of the Church and the relationship between the Church in Liberia and the government, he fails to consider the response of the Liberian people to the missionary effort. The social framework portrayed in the study is essentially that of pre-World War Two Liberia.

### 262 Muslim penetration into French Guinea, Sierra Leone, and Liberia before 1850.
James Franklin Hopewell.   PhD thesis, Columbia University, New York, 1958. 187p.

The author claims that 'Muslim allegiance has periodically been gained among West African peoples who live a considerable distance from an organized Muslim state. An agency in their conversion has frequently been the Muhammadan trader, whose value to a village's economy has secured his welcome in areas that normally would be hostile to a political or religious intrusion'. This thesis documents the considerable evidence which shows that the merchants were instrumental in the spread of Islam prior to 1850 in Guinea, Sierra Leone and Liberia. After this date the part played by the merchants has to be considered in conjunction with other important influences such as the *jihads* of Umar Samory and European colonial activity.

### 263 Black Americans and the missionary movement in Africa.
Edited by Sylvia M. Jacobs.   Westport, Connecticut: Greenwood Press, 1982. 255p.

This is a good collection of essays which 'discuss the role of black Americans in the American Protestant mission movement in Africa before 1960, including the rise of mission sentiment among Afro-Americans and the various types of mission activities in which they were engaged'. Although the entire book is relevant for students of Liberia, Tom W. Shick's article 'Rhetoric and reality: colonization and Afro-American missionaries in early nineteenth century Liberia' (p. 45-62) is of particular interest.

### 264 Living in two worlds: the Wanda Jones story.
Wanda Jones with Sandra P. Aldrich.   Grand Rapids, Michigan: Zondervan Books, 1988. 164p.

A biography of Wanda Jones, the wife of the African-American evangelist, Howard O. Jones, which recounts their Christian ministry. Howard, who was the first black evangelist on the crusade staff of American evangelist, Billy Graham, served for many years in Liberia with ELWA (Eternal Love Winning Africa), a movement affiliated to the Sudan Interior Mission.

265 **Born to lose, bound to win: the amazing story of Mother Eliza Davis George.**

Lorry Lutz. Irvine, California: Harvest House Publishers, 1980. 194p.

This is the story of the life and work of an extraordinary black American who spent more than half a century evangelizing and educating throughout the whole of Liberia. When she was nearly 100 years old she was forced to return to the United States against her will in order to receive medical treatment. She left behind her a legacy of accomplishments that included the Bible Industrial Academy (BIA) [now the Liberia Baptist boarding school], the National Baptist Mission (ten churches associated with the National Baptist Mission Board of the US), the Liberian Baptists organization in Sinoe county (some fifty churches), and the Independent Churches of Africa (with some 100 churches). The author states that 'seldom has any woman packed so much incredible adventure for God into 100 years of thrills and sorrows, conquests and heartbreaks'. Mother George celebrated her 100th birthday on 20 January 1979 and died on 8 March of the same year.

266 **Alexander Crummell (1819-1898) and the creation of an African-American church in Liberia.**

John R. Oldfield. Lewiston, New York: Edwin Mellen Press, 1990. 165p.

The title of the author's doctoral thesis *The life and work of Alexander Crummell, 1819-1898*, which inspired this book is a more accurate description of the book's contents than the implied focus on the church in Liberia suggested by the subtitle. The thesis, like the book itself, is an overview and assessment of Crummell's life and work in America, the land of his birth, in England, Liberia, and finally in America again where in his later years he created the American Negro Academy and founded St. Luke's Episcopal Church in Washington, DC. Though there are interesting highlights on Crummell's life and work in Liberia (chapters six and seven), his desire to create an African-American church in Liberia is not the main focus of the book.

267 **Sketches in ebony and ivory.**

Walter Henry Overs. Hartford, Connecticut: Church Missions Publishing, 1924. 24p.

Contains biographical sketches of three Liberian, and three white, American churchmen by an American missionary bishop of the Episcopal Church in Liberia. The three Liberians are T. Momolu Gardiner (Bishop Suffragan of Liberia), Albert Momolu Massaquoi (diplomat), and Henry Too Wesley (the first indigenous vice-president of Liberia, 1924-28).

268 **Voice under every palm.**

Jane Reed, Jim Grant. New York: Zondervan, 1970. 150p. illus.

This is a description of the work of the ELWA (Eternal Love Winning Africa) missionary radio station in Liberia.

269 **Revelation of the religions.**
J. Samuel Reeves.   Monrovia: Sabanoh Printing Press, 1990. 110p.

A Liberian Baptist clergyman considers three groups of religions – Christianity, Islam, and African traditional religions – as practised in Liberia in particular and on the continent of Africa generally.

270 **Mission possible: world missions in the 1980s.**
Marian Schindler, Robert Schindler.   Wheaton, Illinois: Victor Books, 1984. 168p.

An American medical missionary and his wife recount thirteen years of service in Liberia with the Sudan Interior Mission. Working under the auspices of the Eternal Love Winning Africa (ELWA), Robert Schindler founded the ELWA hospital, an important medical facility in Monrovia.

271 **Day dawn in Africa.**
Anna M. Scott.   New York: Negro Universities Press, 1969. 314p.

This narrative description of the work of the Episcopal Mission of the United States in Cape Palmas (Liberia) during its first two decades beginning in 1836 is written from the perspective of a nineteenth-century Western missionary.

272 **Ellen of Kakata.**
Dorothy E. Scott, Ethel Trice.   Pentecostal Assemblies of the World, 1985. 138p.

This saga of Ellen Moore Hopkins is told in typical traditional Western missionary style. It recounts the dramatic story of an African girl who: worked her way from the jungle to the hearts of the American people; received an education in the States; and who returned to her native land and dedicated her life to aiding suffering humanity. In fact, Mrs. Hopkins spent thirty-five productive years of her life working in the areas of religion, health, education and social welfare in Kakata, Liberia, largely under the auspices of the Samuel Grimes Memorial Maternity and Child Welfare Center (of The Pentecostal Assemblies of the World), which she founded. The work is available from Ethel Trice, 7421 Meridian Hills Court, #D, Indianapolis, IN 46260, USA.

273 **The cultural policies of religious change: a study of the Sonoyea Kpelle in Liberia.**
Randolph Stakeman.   Lewiston, New York: Edwin Mellen Press, 1986. 255p. index.

This study illustrates various aspects of religious and cultural change and is based primarily on American Lutheran missionary accounts and apparently extensive interviews with the first generation of the Sonoyea Kpelle to be influenced by Christianity.

274 **Impact of the African tradition on African Christianity.**
Nya Kwiawon Taryor, Sr.   Chicago, Illinois: Strugglers' Community Press, 1984. 309p.

Based on the author's doctoral thesis, this book purports to provide 'a historical survey of the planting of Christianity in Africa and the contributions of Africans to the growth, development and spread of the Faith', while discussing 'the major contribution of ... independent churches [in Africa] to Christianity in Africa and what African cultural practices they have incorporated into Christianity'. It is written with a view to rendering the Christian faith more meaningful for the African. The author is a Liberian Methodist clergyman and former Dean of the Gbarnga School of Theology in Liberia.

275 **Religion and politics in Liberia.**
Nya Kwaiwon Taryor. Clinton, New York: Strugglers' Community Press, 1989. 45p.

The two articles that constitute this pamphlet are entitled 'Religion in Liberia' and 'A call for freedom, justice and democracy: the Liberian case'.

276 **Traditional theism in African creation myths with the Bassa (Liberian) Djuankadju as central theme.**
Robert Gbatiae Tikpor. (Doctor of Sacred Theology thesis). Rome: Pontifical University of St. Thomas Aquinas, 1981. 451p.

This thesis aims to search for an 'authentic African theological foundation' which existed before the spread of Christianity in what became Liberia. He claims that religious and theological wisdom spring from indigenous creation 'myths'. Tikpor examines the Djuankadju myth which emanates from the Bassa people. He writes of this myth 'we have not only the creation of Gleypoh the Supreme creator, but also a 'fall from grace', a redemption, a struggle to regain a paradise lost' (p. 20). The rest of the study is then devoted to decoding this myth, the central issue becoming: 'If God created man and wills his salvation ... how did our ancestors who did not live to hear Abraham's faith, or Christ's redemptive act, fare in God's plan for salvation?' (p. 27). The author asserts that 'the nations outside Israel were prepared for the salvation that was to come from God, and that the gentile myth represented by the Djuankadju was part and parcel of God's plan for humankind – independent of the Judeo-Christian and Islamic traditions'.

277 **Islam in West Africa.**
J. Spencer Trimingham. Oxford: Clarendon, 1964. 262p. map. bibliog.

Based on scholarly sources and observations throughout West Africa the author seeks 'to assess what has been the result of the impact of Islam, the way it influences African society, and, conversely, the way the African community moulds the Islam it receives. ... At the same time it (the book) embraces more than the actual study of Islam in West Africa since it is concerned with the way Africans assimilated it, the degree to which it fulfills their religious aspirations, and, where these cannot find expression in Islam, in what directions they are fulfilled' (preface to the 1959 edition). Liberia figures particularly on pages 3 and 19 and on page 233, which details 'statistics of religious allegiance'. The historical background to this subject is described in the author's *A history of Islam in West Africa* (London: Oxford University Press, 1962. 262p.).

278 **The American Colonization Society and Liberia: an historical study in religious motivation and achievement, 1817-1867.**
Werner T. Wickstrom. PhD thesis, the Hartford Seminary Foundation, Hartford, Connecticut. 1958. 338p. (UMI order no. 62-3064).

Whilst recognizing that there was a mixture of motives underpinning the creation and activities of the ACS, the author contends that the religious motive was dominant.

Moreover, he asserts that the Christian faith made a vital contribution to the establishment and shaping of the character of the Liberian nation.

279 **Black Americans and the evangelization of Africa, 1877-1900.**
Walter L. Williams. Madison, Wisconsin: University of Wisconsin Press, 1982. 259p.

The book examines 'the activities, experience, cultural conflicts, and leadership of the black missionary movement before 1900'. The first part of the study describes the development of the mission sentiment among Black Americans, while the second part discusses Black American mission thought on Africa. Appendix D carries a list of Black American missionaries in Liberia, from 1877 to 1900 (p. 184-86).

280 **God's impatience in Liberia.**
Joseph Conrad Wold. Grand Rapids, Michigan: Eerdmans, 1968. 226p.

An American Christian missionary attempts to explain the limited impact of the Christian Church in Liberia, and to suggest how this might be remedied. 'Slow growth', he writes, 'is a serious but curable disease. Its needless continuance surely tests God's patience.' (p. 10). Though lacking in analysis of the situation faced by missions in the 1960s, this book does set forth the empirical views of one mission theorist and practitioner. The author draws upon the experiences of Liberians of Loma ethnicity as they were introduced to the Christian faith.

281 **The history of the African Methodist Episcopal Zion Church in West Africa, Liberia, Gold Coast (Ghana) and Nigeria, 1900-1939.**
Walter L. Yates. PhD thesis, Hartford Seminary Foundation, Hartford, Connecticut 1967. 398p. (UMI order no. 68-7262).

An historical account of the establishment and development of the work of the AME Zion Church in Liberia, Ghana and Nigeria. Particularly noteworthy is the section which covers the period when the nation's leaders had to face charges of encouraging slavery and forced labour.

**A third of a century with George Way Harley in Liberia.**
*See* item no. 56.

# Social Conditions and Welfare

## General

282 **Urban situation analysis in Liberia.**
E. Ofori Akyea.   Monrovia: UNICEF, University of Liberia, June 1986.
55p.
This study was undertaken by UNICEF in collaboration with the Regional Planning
Programme of the University of Liberia, and others, with a view to examining the
problem of rapid urbanization especially as it affects the new arrivals to the cities from
the rural areas. The work covers: patterns of urban growth; consequences of urban
growth; the urban poor; strategies and prospects; and the role played by UNICEF in the
urban situation. The study includes a number of statistical tables and other illustrations.

283 **Country report: development assistance programs of US non-profit
organizations in Liberia.**
New York: American Council of Voluntary Agencies for Foreign
Service, Technical Assistance Information Clearing House, June 1976.
25p.
A description of the assistance programmes for Liberia, including thirty-three set up by
American organizations. The report covers voluntary agencies, missions and other non-
profit organizations which provide the Liberian people with material assistance in
several areas including medicine and public health, education and food production. This
is one of a series of periodically revised country reports of TAICH which are available
from TAICH, 200 Park Avenue South, New York, NY 10003, USA.

284 **The language of secrecy: symbols and metaphor in Poro ritual.**
Beryl L. Bellman. New Brunswick, New Jersey: Rutgers University
Press, 1984. 164p.

This book aims to make a contribution to the general theory of secrecy and the sociology
of knowledge by firstly analysing 'secrets within context where secrecy is a major
organizing principle of daily social life, with a view to examining forms and variety of
secrecy in order to isolate secrecy as a phenomenon'; and secondly offering an
'investigation of the Poro initiations as a ritual process'. It then analyses the symbols
and metaphors used in order to provide a detailed account of ritual secrecy drawn from a
complex of societies associated with a major secret society, Poro, and its female
counterpart, Sande, in areas of West Africa that include Liberia, southern Sierra Leone,
and parts of Guinea and the Ivory Coast.

285 **On the category civilized in Liberia and elsewhere.**
David Brown. *Journal of Modern African Studies* (London), vol. 20,
no. 2 (June 1982), p. 287-303.

The author examines the historical and social significance of the term 'civilization' in
the Liberian context and elsewhere in Africa as a term with distinctive class
implications.

286 **Facing the realities of the Liberian nation: problems and prospects
of a West African society.**
Similih M. Cordor (formerly S. Henry Cordor). Iowa City, Iowa:
International Writing Program at the University of Iowa, 1980. 89p.

In this important social critique, Cordor presents his personal perceptions of Liberia's
contemporary social, economic, cultural, and political problems, with particular
reference to freedom of expression, socio-political activism, national unification and
integration, national development programmes, and the rise of radical and intellectual
movements.

287 **A study of the social situation in Liberia.**
Monrovia: Department of Planning and Economic Affairs, 1970. 126p.

This government publication contains results obtained from field visits throughout the
country by three members of the Social Planning Division of the Department of
Planning and Economic Affairs under the leadership of D. Franklin Neal. Hailed as 'the
first of its kind in Liberia', it covers such subjects as: the general level of income and
consumption; land ownership and rights; tribal land laws; employment and working
conditions; housing conditions (social conditions of the population); and social policy
institutions and services. Appendices include lists of hospitals and clinics in Liberia,
dentists and doctors in the country, tribal schools, and social welfare organization and
institutions. There is also an appendix indicating the distribution of modern schools.

288 **Notes on the Poro in Liberia.**
George Way Harley. New York: Kraus Reprint Corporation, 1968. 39p.
map. bibliog. (Paper of the Peabody Museum of American Archaeology
and Ethnology, Harvard University, vol. 19, no. 2, 1941).

Harley, a missionary doctor who gave many years of service in hinterland Liberia
presents his observations of this male sodality found among several ethnic groups in

Central and Western Liberia. He provides information on the distribution of the Poro in the country, and details about its operation and social functions among the various peoples. Illustrations, a distribution map, and a good bibliography are also included.

289 **Eine verborgene Dimension gesellschaftlicher Wirklichkeit: Anmerkungen zur Geschichte und Bedeutung der Geheimbünde Poro und Sande in Liberia.** (A hidden dimension of social reality: observations on the history and importance of the secret groups Poro and Sande in Liberia.)
Gunter Schroder.   Bremen, West Germany: Liberia Working Group, 1988. 84p. (no. 6).

An overview which presents facts, theories and hypotheses about the Poro and the Sande institutions, and their changing fortunes in Liberian society.

290 **Conference on social research in Liberia (papers presented: August 1969).**
Stanford, California: Stanford University, Committee on African Studies, 1969. various paginations.

Contains a collection of important papers on various aspects of Liberian social studies. The contents include, James C. Borg, 'Language and Tribe among government school students in Monrovia: A preliminary report'; Jeannette P. Carter, 'The rural Loma and Monrovia: ties with an urban center'; John Gay and Michael Cole, 'Occasion for use of a Kpelle classification system'; C. E. Zamba Liberty, 'The decline of the Dey'; Martin Lowenkopf, 'Political modernization and institutional development in Liberia'; John P. O'Grady, 'Hospital use among the Kpelle of Liberia'; James C. Riddel, 'Mano labor migration and cash-cropping'; Dieter H. Seibel, 'Achievement and ascription in Liberia: a comparative view'; and 'Traditional cooperative among the Kpelle'. The collection is available from Stanford University.

291 **Model and ideology: dimensions of being civilized in Liberia.**
Elizabeth Tonkin.   In: *The structure of folk medicine.*   Edited by Ladislav Holy, Milan Stuchlik.   London: Academic Press, 1981. p. 305-30.

'Civilized' and 'Kwi', words considered salient by most commentators on Liberia, are used by the author in her discussion of settler-indigenous relations in Liberia. This discursive history touches on such issues as cultural assimilation, the fluidity of ethnic identities, and the changing nature of social cleavages and political unions which have typified the Liberian experience. The study contributes considerably to delineating what is, in fact, a complex social reality, rather than a simple settler-indigenous social divide.

# Health

292 **Proximate determinants of child mortality in Liberia.**
Omar B. Ahman, Isaac W. Eberstein, David F. Sly.   *Journal of Biosocial Science*, vol. 23, no. 3 (July 1991), p. 313-26.

Examines the effects of maternal socio-demographic characteristics and environmental quality on child survival in the context of such variables as breastfeeding and pre-natal care. The authors employ a linear structural equation theory to examine infant and child survival based on a weighted sample of 5,180 Liberian children aged between 0 and 5 years old.

### 293 The transmission dynamics of onchocerciasis on the Firestone Rubber Plantation, Harbel, Liberia.

Victor Kevin Barbiero. PhD thesis, Johns Hopkins University, Baltimore, Maryland, 1982.

This thesis analyses and quantifies the factors contributing to the transmission of onchocerciasis, a 'blinding disease' caused by parasites living under the skin. The study concludes that the Harbel area is one of high onchocerciasis transmission and therefore a significant public health problem on the Firestone plantation. Recommendations are advanced to reduce the spread of the disease.

### 294 Biological control and fauna assessment of *Anopheles gambiae* vector of malaria breeding in rice fields in Liberia, West Africa.

Fatorma Kormo Bolay. PhD thesis, Johns Hopkins University, Baltimore, Maryland, 1989. 199p. (UMI order no. Da8923660).

Investigates larval mosquito species and their reproduction through four cycles of rice cultivation at the Central Agriculture Research Institute in Bong County, Liberia.

### 295 Clinical features of Lassa fever in Liberia.

John D. Frame. *Review of Infectious Diseases*, vol. 2, supplement 4 (May-June 1989), p. S783-S789.

The author, who is associated with the Division of Tropical Medicine at Columbia University, New York, examines 213 cases of Lassa fever which had been diagnosed by virus isolation and seroconversion at the Curran Lutheran Hospital in Zorzor over a six-year period between July 1980 and April 1986. He provides statistical data for the death rates of various groups such as pregnant women, those who had recently given birth, and children under twelve. He notes the various symptoms of Lassa fever and comments that the 'elucidation of a number of clinical problems in LF (Lassa Fever) requires more information on how strain differences affect the pattern of illness'.

### 296 Anemia of pregnancy in Liberia, West Africa: a therapeutic trial.

Robert Thaddeus Jackson. PhD thesis, Cornell University, Ithaca, New York, 1981. 230p.

Seeks to ascertain the prevalence and causes of nutritional anaemias of pregnancy in Liberia by analysing the results of a trial in which women were given a nutritional supplement during the final stages of pregnancy. The contribution to anaemia of parasitic infection and haemoglobinopathies was also investigated. The conclusion was that iron deficiency was the most important cause of this illness for the sample of 621 women studied. Even after therapy, forty-five per cent of the women studied showed haemoglobin levels below the World Health Organization standard (11.0 g/100 ml).

297 **Improving vaccination completion rates in Liberia: evaluating an intervention trial.**

Rose Jallah-Macauley, Deborah E. Bender. *International Quarterly of Community Health*, vol. 11, no. 4 (1990/91), p. 333-54.

This article evaluates a community-based trial which was designed to extend the Ministry of Health's vaccination programme. The trial involved the use of local chiefs and traditional midwives to increase the size of the vaccination teams.

298 **The distribution of the sickle cell gene in Liberia.**

Frank B. Livingstone. *American Journal of Human Genetics*, vol. 10 (1958), p. 33-41.

The data which forms the basis for this study on the distribution of the sickle cell trait in Liberia was collected largely from workers and their families at the Firestone Plantations Company in Harbel, Liberia, between September 1955 and August 1956. Most of the investigation was carried out at the Liberian Institute of Tropical Medicine which is adjacent to the Firestone plantations. The data suggests 'a northwest southeast decline in the frequency of the sickle cell trait. In the extreme northwest on the Sierra Leone border there is twenty per cent of the sickle cell trait, and the frequency decreases gradually to about twelve per cent in central Liberia' (p. 40).

299 **Cancer occurrence in developing countries.**

Edited by D. M. Parkin in association with A. Arslan, A. Bieber, O. Bouvy, C. S. Muir, R. Owor and S. Whelan. Lyons, France: World Health Organization International Agency for Research on Cancer, 1986. 339. (Scientific Publication no. 75).

This volume brings together in a standard format, data from the publications of seventy-three registries in forty-six countries. Each registry includes information on the cancer patterns in a certain locality, a prerequisite to understanding its importance as a public health problem worldwide. The Liberian section is by A. O. Sobo and is entitled 'Liberia Cancer Registry, 1976-1980' (p. 55-58): tables twenty-seven and twenty-eight show the distribution of cases by age and sex. The Cancer Registry was founded in 1973 in association with the JFK Medical Center in Monrovia. A fuller description of the Registry and results from its first five years of operation has also been published, *see* A. O. Sobo (1982) 'Cancer in Liberia: a review of cases registered from the Liberia Cancer Registry 1973-1977'. *Cancer*, no. 49.

300 **A clinical and laboratory study of leprosy in Liberia.**

Hildrus A. Poindexter. *International Journal of Leprosy*, vol. 19, no. 4 (Oct.-Dec. 1951), p. 395-411.

Although there were four principal leprosy colonies in Liberia when the research for this study was carried out, the author drew most of his observations from one, the Ganta leprosy village. The article represents a detailed clinical and laboratory investigation in 1947 of 269 resident patients with follow-up observations undertaken later. The findings concerning 230 of these are given in the report. The author was director of the United States Public Health Mission in Liberia at the time of publication.

301 **Psychosis in association with possession by genii in Liberia.**
Ronald M. Wintrob. *Psychopathologie Africaine* (Dakar, Senegal)
vol. 2, no. 2 (1966) p. 249-58.
This is a study in transcultural psychiatry which centres on the similarities and points of difference in belief systems in Senegal and Liberia as specifically illustrated by case studies from Monrovia. The author finds striking similarities between a case of mental illness affecting a Senegalese marabout (Islamic religious mystic) which he describes, and certain indigenous Liberian ethnic groups.

302 **Mammy water: folk beliefs and psychotic elaborations in Liberia.**
Ronald M. Wintrob. *Canadian Journal of Psychiatry*, vol. 15 (1970),
p. 143-57.
This article is a product of the author's clinical experience gained during two years as the only psychiatrist at the only modern mental institution in Liberia, the Catherine Mills Rehabilitation Center. Wintrob considers folk beliefs and presents clinical material relating to possession by a spirit called 'mammy water'. Beliefs in 'mammy water' are represented as widespread in Liberia, affecting both indigenous and settler Liberians. The data on which the study is based came from a sampling of both 'normal' subjects and selected patients at the rehabilitation centre in Monrovia.

# Housing

303 **Squatter settlement in Liberia: toward the integration of housing and population policies.**
Linda Lacey. *African Urban Quarterly* (Nairobi), vol. 3, no. 34
(Nov. 1988), p. 219-230.
The article explores the relationship between population growth in Africa and the growth of squatter settlements in the Liberian capital of Monrovia.

304 **Low-income settlements in Monrovia, Liberia.**
Linda Lacey, Stephen Emmanuel Owusu. In: *Spontaneous shelter: international perspectives and prospects.* Edited by Carl V. Patton.
Philadelphia: Temple University Press, 1988. p. 214-34.
Focuses on the problem of housing in urban Liberia. Other African cities have faced similar difficulties which have resulted from rapid industrialization and population growth accompanied by a stagnant economy and a shortage of building materials. The authors examine the evolution and growth of communities in Monrovia pointing out how residents have coped with the problem of shelter, and highlighting the government's role in housing the urban poor. Alternative strategies for addressing the problem are also presented.

305 **Republic of Liberia, shelter sector analysis.**
Washington, DC: United States Agency for International Development,
Office of Housing, 1977. 93p.

After summarizing this USAID-funded report and its recommendations, and supplying
background information on Liberia, the study discusses: 'The role of government in
housing'; 'The housing need'; 'The supply of housing'; 'Housing finance and
development institutions'; and 'Economic outlook and investment capacity'.

# Women

306 **Liberian women: their role in food production and their educational
and legal status.**
Jeanette E. Carter, assisted by Joyce Mends-Cole. A Research project
jointly sponsored by the USAID/Liberia and the Liberian Government,
and implemented by the University of Liberia, March 1982. 194p.
bibliog.

Rice, the staple food in Liberia, has traditionally been produced by women living in
rural areas. The majority of Liberian women are employed in this way, and the report
examines this group with the aim of providing those involved in development policy
with information covering 'the role played by women in food production, their access to
formal schooling, and their legal status'. The authors of the report assert that their
objective is to provide information which is intended to assist in the integration of
women in the development process'.

307 **Liberian women and development: identifying structures for survival
and employment.**
Mary Antoinette Brown Sherman. Paper presented at a Conference on
Empowerment, Gender and Social Change in Africa and the African
Diaspora. Cornell University, Ithaca, New York, May 23-June 3, 1992.
30p.

This excellent paper provides 'a brief account of the situation of women in Liberia,
including their contributions to the development of their country and the constraints
within which they live and work' and aspires 'to identify the structures which they
utilize to aid their survival, especially when they and their families are at risk'. The
manner in which the structures may be employed in order to empower women is also
discussed. This study is perhaps the most current account of the position of Liberian
women, and it draws upon the extant literature on the subject. The author is former
President of the University of Liberia.

**'Vai women's roles in music, masking, and ritual performance'.**
*See* item no. 569.

**'Womanhood, work and song among the Kpelle of Liberia'.**
*See* item no. 574.

# Politics and
# Government

308 **'Black imperialism: Americo-Liberian rule over the African peoples
of Liberia'.**
Monday B. Akpan. *Canadian Journal of African Studies*, vol. 7, no. 2
(1973), p. 217-36.
This is a brief, yet interesting analysis of the domination of Liberian social, economic,
and political life by the descendants of immigrants from the United States. The author
likens the political pre-eminence of black settlers from the New World over the
indigenous Africans of the Liberia area to European imperial rule over African peoples.

309 **The Albert Porte papers.**
West Falmouth, Massachusetts: African Imprint Library Services.
1973-74. 10 reels of film.
Albert Porte is a legendary Liberian political commentator and veteran teacher. These
films contain facsimile reproductions of some of his private papers and documents as
well as samples, and in some instances lengthy runs of more than fifty different Liberian
newspapers. This is perhaps the most extensive Liberian collection of its kind. Roll one
consists of manuscripts and personal documents, and rolls two to ten carry the
newspapers. A complete printed table of contents is included. The film is available from
African Imprint Library Service, 410 West Falmouth Highway, West Falmouth,
Massachusetts, 20574.

310 **Nation-building in Liberia: the use of symbols in national
integration.**
J. Bernard Blamo. *Liberian Studies Journal*, vol. 4, no. 1 (1971),
p. 21-30.
Drawing upon presidential addresses and legislative acts, the author analyses the
manipulation of symbols at various stages in the development of the Liberian state. He
demonstrates how the Liberian political vocabulary has been modified over time to
express changing notions of national purpose, from the initial idiom of 'civilization' to
the post-War emphasis on national unification and integration.

### 311 Liberia: the rise and fall of the first Republic.

George E. Saigbe Boley. London: Macmillan, 1983. 225p.

Between 1883 and 1980 the True Whig Party (TWP) enjoyed a virtual political monopoly. Here the author reveals his opposition to the TWP in the closing stages of its rule. In so doing he sets the scene for the major part he was to play in the military régime that followed the 1980 *coup d'état*. The first six chapters represent a selective history of the 'black colonial' state, while chapters seven to nine describe the Tolbert years (1971-80), in which Boley served as Assistant Minister for education. He was dismissed by the tottering Tolbert government from this post and imprisoned on treason charges along with officials from the Peoples' Progressive Party. Boley makes no criticisms of the military régime in which he served as a senior Minister of State. He does, however, express concern about the need both to reconstruct a national system of values and to avoid the political abuse of power. Many would regard these pronouncements as somewhat misplaced given the brutality of the military government in which Boley served and the political conditions which led to the collapse of the Second Republic and the outbreak of Civil war.

### 312 The Liberian republic.

Raymond Leslie Buell. In: *The native problem in Africa*. London: Frank Cass, 1965, vol. 2, p. 704-888.

This was first published in 1928 by the Bureau of International Research of Harvard University and Radcliffe College. Buell attempts to provide a detailed explanation of the Liberian state through an examination of its political institutions. A student of comparative politics, Buell is expansive on the social issues which influence the political process, the potential impact of foreign investment on the country, and relations between the centre and the periphery of power in Liberia in the 1920s.

### 313 Liberia and Sierra Leone: an essay in comparative politics.

Christopher Clapham. Cambridge, England: Cambridge University Press, 1976. 156p.

This work is 'concerned with the relationship in each country between political activities directed towards controlling the coercive and distributive apparatus of the state, and the social economic features of the society on which that is built'. The author compares the two countries during the 1960s and 1970s and his analysis is interesting given the enormous changes which have taken place since then.

### 314 The politics of failure: clientelism, political instability and national integration in Liberia and Sierra Leone.

Christopher Clapham. In: *Private patronage and public power: political clientelism in the modern state*. Edited by Christopher Clapham. New York: St. Martin's Press, 1982, p. 76-92.

Defining clientelism as a 'set of exchanges conducted through the state hierarchy and lubricated by the proceeds of the export economy', Clapham advances the notion that in the absence of a genuine feeling of national identity, or common ideological identity, 'clientelism provides the only means short of brute force for binding together the disparate power centres within the state, and creating at least the appearance of legitimacy and effectiveness'. Undertaking a comparative study of Sierra Leone and Liberia, the author demonstrates that despite variations in the circumstances of the two countries, there are significant factors which are common to both countries; notably in each case the government is viewed as being neither legitimate nor effective. Liberia's decline came about during the administration of President William R. Tolbert, Jr., while Sierra Leone's occurred under Sir Albert Margai.

### 315 Political parties and national integration in tropical Africa.
Edited by James S. Coleman, Carl G. Rosberg, Jr. Berkeley, California: University of California Press, 1970. 730p.

A study in two parts, the second section 'Parties and national integration', contains an article on Liberia written by J. Gus Liebenow under the subtitle of 'transforming historic oligarchies' (p. 448-81). The article stresses that there has been an 'evolution of privilege' amongst settler-Liberians and that this should be tempered by some reform of the system, however guardedly pursued.

### 316 The April fourteenth crisis in Liberia.
S. Henry Cordor. Monrovia: Published by the author, June 18, 1979. 120p. mimeograph. bibliog.

Cordor, a Liberian writer and journalist, presents here his eye-witness account of the events of the civil disturbance in Monrovia on April 14, 1979, and offers a 'candid discussion of the major issues and crises [within] Liberian society with particular reference to the causes and the aftermath of the . . . crisis . . . and plans for national reconstruction'. The contents includes a detailed coverage of the: demonstrations which took place; military and police involvement; destruction and looting; the casualties; the government's reaction to the disturbance; and the aftermath.

### 317 Death of a Liberian regime.
*West Africa* (London), no. 3274 (April 21, 1980), p. 687.

This is an editorial on the overthrow of the Tolbert régime and the assassination of the President. It briefly reviews the conditions and the political developments which immediately preceded the *coup d'état* and condemns the assassination of Tolbert.

### 318 Liberia reconsidered: a review.
D. Elwood Dunn. *Canadian Journal of African Studies*, vol. 21, no. 2 (1987), p. 259-62.

This review article is based on three books: Yekutiel Gershoni's *Black Colonialism* (Westview Press, 1985), Katherine Harris' *African and American Values* (University Press of America, 1985), and Hassan Sisay's *Big Powers and Small Nations* (University Press of America, 1985). All of the books are criticized for failing to come to grips with the imperative of establishing an analytical link between pre-*coup* and post-*coup* Liberia, a connection considered by the reviewer to be vital for gaining an understanding of contemporary Liberian society and politics.

### 319 Liberia: a national polity in transition.
D. Elwood Dunn, S. Byron Tarr. Metuchen. New Jersey: Scarecrow Press, 1988. 259p.

This important monograph on the development of modern Liberia, covers: the country's history; Liberian society; the first Republic; the military interregnum; the Liberian economy; and foreign relations, especially Liberia's role in the creation of the Organization of African Unity. The authors present an integrated national perspective that emphasizes historical continuity. At the heart of this work is the question of whether the *coup* of 1980 accelerated the process of political reform that began in the 1970s, or whether it abruptly aborted that process. The authors conclude that: 'the *coup* and military rule were not a culmination of seething reformation, much less a revolutionary process, but rather a counteraction to the democratic tendencies that the first Republic could not contain'.

320 **West African states: failure and promise: a study in comparative politics.**
Edited by John Dunn.   Cambridge, England: Cambridge University Press, 1978. 259p.

This study examines political developments in Ghana, Côte d'Ivoire (Ivory Coast), Liberia, Nigeria, Senegal and Sierra Leone, seeking to account for the diversity of the dashed hopes of their citizens since independence. Christopher Clapham's chapter on Liberia employs a core/periphery (patron/client) framework of analysis to explain how the Liberian state performed over the twenty year period preceding 1978, and how it would be expected to perform in the years that followed. He concludes that 'whereas failure and promise is the title of this volume, success and danger might be a more appropriate verdict on the recent Liberian experience'.

321 **Behold Uncle Sam's step-child: notes on the fall of Liberia, Africa's oldest republic.**
Bill Frank Enoanyi.   Sacramento, California: SanMar Publications, 1991. 144p.

Presents a severe but long overdue criticism of Liberian society in the wake of the devastating civil war which began in 1989. The author, a veteran Liberian journalist seeks to identify a national cultural trait which undermines the common good, indulges self-serving public officials, and degrades the human person. This collection of thoughtful essays seems to be directed at all those who will be involved in the task of national reconstruction.

322 **Black colonialism, the Americo-Liberian scramble for the hinterland.**
Yekutial Gershoni.   Boulder, Colorado: Westview Press, 1985. 134p.

Although the original authors are not acknowledged, this study reworks a thesis by Monday Akpan, J. Gus Liebenow and others, which maintains that the settler founders of the Liberian state practised black colonialism by subjugating indigenous Liberians. Focusing on the period between 1900 and 1930, Gershoni compares Liberian state expansion into the hinterland with European colonial expansion in other areas of Africa.

323 **Liberia: the road to democracy under the leadership of Samuel K. Doe.**
Edited by Willie A. Givens.   Abbottsbrook, Bourne End, England: Kensal Press, 1986. 480p.

Reproduces with commentary devoid of serious analysis, some of the public statements of the Liberian military leader, Samuel K. Doe between 1980 and 1985. The work has been compiled by a senior official in Doe's government. Commencing with a brief biography of Doe and an editor's introduction, the compilation has thirteen chapters dealing with such general topics as education and agriculture. An epilogue contains the full text of Doe's 1986 inaugural address.

324 **The inaugural address of the Presidents of Liberia: from Joseph Jenkins Roberts to William Richard Tolbert, Jr. 1848 to 1976.**
Edited by Joseph Saye Guannu.   Hicksville, New York: Exposition Press, 1980. 411p.

This valuable compilation contains all the inaugural presidency addresses except those of 1850, 1854, 1888, 1890, 1892 and 1896 which the editor was unable to locate. There is an introduction but unfortunately no index. These speeches are extremely important for what they reveal about the nature and aims of successive governments in Liberia from independence onwards.

325 **An introduction to Liberian government: the first Republic and the People's Redemption Council.**
Joseph Saye Guannu.   Smithtown, New York: Exposition Press, 1982. 110p.

This primer is intended to introduce students in Liberia's high schools to the structure and operation of Liberian governments from the founding of the state to 1982.

326 **Africa: dispatches from a fragile continent.**
Blaine Harden.   New York: W. W. Norton & Company, 1990. 333p.

The author, an American journalist, reports on socio-economic and political life in seven contemporary African countries, Liberia included. He is merciless in attacking 'The good, the bad and the greedy', in his indictment of both the Doe decade in Liberia and of President Samuel K. Doe personally whom he characterizes as blending 'buffoonery and brutality while bankrupting his country and turning his government into an international laughing stock'.

327 **Liberia's fulfillment: achievement of the Republic of Liberia during the administration of President W. V. S. Tubman 1944-1969.**
Compiled by A. Doris Banks Henries.   Monrovia: [n.p.], 1969. 213p.

Published on the occasion of the silver jubilee of the Tubman presidency, this is a collection of self-congratulatory articles by various government departments. The foreword has been written by the compiler, who was director of higher education and textbooks research at the education ministry and spouse of Richard A. Henries, the speaker of the Liberian House of Representatives.

328 **Development of unification in Liberia.**
A. Doris Banks Henries.   Monrovia: Government of Liberia, Department of Education, 1963. 101p.

This work attempts to refute 'assertions and assumptions that the African immigrants and their descendants who left America and returned to establish the Liberian nation have held themselves aloof from the native tribes'. Henries provides a very useful compilation of excerpts on unification from inaugural addresses and other statements by presidents of Liberia from J. J. Roberts in the 1840s to W. V. S. Tubman in the 1960s which she uses to illustrate her claims. The various statements do indeed show a concern by the presidents for the unification of settler and indigenous Liberians, but these concerns are voiced with the explicit assumption that indigenous Liberians will assimilate themselves into settler-Liberian society.

329 **Class, ethnicity and politics in Liberia: a class analysis of power struggles in the Tubman and Tolbert administrations from 1944-1975.**
Stephen S. Hlophe. Washington, DC: University Press of America, 1979. 316p.

Written from a Marxist-perspective, this work sets out to describe the process and dynamics of social change in Liberia. Perhaps the study's major value is its departure (in parts two and three) from the conventional perception of Liberian society: Hlophe introduces into his social analysis a technocratic class of indigenous Liberians. This class emerged, he contends, 'from an association with repatriate Liberians either through the ward system (whereby settler-Liberians informally adopted the children of indigenous Liberians), marriage, office or religious mentors, political patronage or the educational system used by the repatriates as a source of recruitment or token membership in the upper class'. This class of indigenous technocrats in alliance with 'progressive' descendants of settlers was crucial not only in the process that led to the overthrow of the Tolbert régime in 1980, but also to the stiff opposition that developed to the Doe régime and that led to its demise in unparalleled bloodshed in the Civil War of 1989-90.

330 **Ruling families and power struggles in Liberia.**
Stephen S. Hlophe. *Journal of African Studies*, vol. 6, no. 2 (summer, 1979), p. 75-82.

Provides an interesting class analysis of the power struggles which have determined the composition of the Tubman and Tolbert administrations. Hlophe shows how indigenous 'technocratic' Liberians (q.v.) emerged and this is set against the backdrop of divisions among the ruling settler-Liberian families and growing activism among students and workers.

331 **The political and legislative history of Liberia.**
Charles Henry Huberich. New York: Central Book Company, 1947. 2 vols. maps.

Contains a semi-official documentary account of the first Constitution (1847), and the laws and treaties of Liberia from the early colonial settlement in the 1820s to the declaration of a Republic in 1847. The author sketches the activities of the various American societies for the colonization of the free people of colour of the United States and comments on the Constitution, whilst surveying political and social legislation from 1847 to 1944. The volume also contains appendices which reproduce the Laws of the Colony of Liberia, 1820-1839 (certified by the Liberian Secretary of State) and Acts of the Governor of the Council, 1839-1847. Other appendices contain various maps and illustrations.

332 **Personal rule in black Africa: prince, autocrat, prophets, tyrants.**
Robert H. Jackson, Carl G. Rosberg. Berkeley, California; Los
Angeles: University of California Press, 1982. 316p.

Compares and contrasts the varying degrees of personal rule which have emerged in
sub-Saharan Africa, and considers 'their capacity to produce political goods, basing a
theory of personal rule on an historical analysis of contemporary African political
systems'. After establishing the meaning of personal rule the study includes chapters on:
'princes and oligarchic rule' (both Presidents William V. S. Tubman and William
R. Tolbert, Jr. are featured here); 'autocrats and lordship'; 'Prophets and leadership'; and
'Tyrants and abusive rule'. There is an appendix of black African countries and rulers
dating from September 1980.

333 **National integration and the Liberian political process, 1943-1985.**
Abraham L. James. PhD thesis, University of Pennsylvania,
Philadelphia, Pennsylvania, 1990. 288p.

Provides a conservative assessment of the causes and consequences of the division
which occurred between indigenous and settler Liberians and focuses on the strategies
employed by the Liberian state to minimize the divisions between these groups.

334 **Liberia: underdevelopment and political rule in a peripheral society.**
Robert Kappel, Werner Korte, R. Friedegund Mescher. Hamburg,
Germany: Institute fur Afrika-Kunde, 1986. 292p.

This volume on Liberian political economy is a sequel of sorts to *Dependence,
underdevelopment and persistent conflict – on the political economy of Liberia*, (Edited
by Eckhard Hinzen and Robert Kappel. Bremen, Germany: Bremen Africa Archives,
vol. 11, 1980. 408p.) and reflects an interdisciplinary approach. Six of the eleven
contributions are in German and five in English. Divided into two sections, part one
covers 'Political development, internal power struggles, and the role of the military', and
part two focuses on 'Structural dependence and underdevelopment'. One contributor
argues for more intensive regional co-operation and a dissociation of the Liberian
political economy from industrial capitalism as essential prerequisites for long-term
development.

335 **Liberia: the inside story.**
Luther Henry Lemley. New York: Exposition Press, 1963. 101p.

Subtitled 'a travel report of an American union man', this study is an account of the five
years which the author spent in Monrovia as the general railway superintendent of the
Liberia Mining Company. The author, whose knowledge of Liberian society was merely
superficial, gives a prejudiced view of the entire social and political system in Liberia.
This is one of many such accounts which have been published over the years.

336 **Liberia: the lid blows off.**
*Africa Confidential*, London, vol. 20, no. 11 (May 23, 1979), p. 2-4.

Describes the Liberian revolt against the Tolbert régime which occurred in April 1979,
and highlights the unreliability of the armed forces. In the light of the April 1980 *coup
d'état* this article provides an accurate analysis of the situation in the country at that
time.

337 **Liberia: the slippery slope.**
*Africa Confidential*, London, vol. 21, no. 8 (April 9, 1980), p. 5-7.
Describes the events which immediately preceded the military coup of April 12 1980 and examines the disturbances of March 1980 and the banning of the People's Progressive Party (PPP). Also included are profiles of the two opposition leaders – the PPP's Gabriel Baccus Matthews, a settler-Liberian, and Dr. Togba Nah Tipoteh (head of MOJA – Movement for Justice in Africa), a Kru-Liberian.

338 **Liberia: Tolbert's strategy.**
*Africa Confidential*, vol. 20, no. 6 (March 14, 1979), p. 4-5.
Suggests that President Tolbert (1971-80) was paving the way for his ultimate withdrawal from politics through his attempt to groom a Liberian of indigenous background to succeed him.

339 **The plot that failed: the story of the attempted assassination of President Tubman.**
Monrovia: Liberian Information Service, 1959. 68p.
Presents the official account of the unsuccessful attempt to assassinate President Tubman on 22 June 1955. At this time Tubman had been in power for twelve years. He was to rule for twenty-seven years altogether.

340 **President William V. S. Tubman on African unity.**
Monrovia, Liberia: Liberian Information Service, [n.d.]. 71p.
Contains extracts from President Tubman's public statements on the issue of African unity. This work was published by the government possibly in the early 1960s.

341 **Liberia, the evolution of privilege.**
J. Gus Liebenow. Ithaca, New York: Cornell University Press, 1968. 224p.
One of the major themes in Liberian historiography since the end of the Second World War has been that of 'black colonialism', introduced by Professor J. Gus Liebenow. In this, his major study, he claims that Liberian society is essentially 'colonial' in character, with the settler-Liberian minority (which comprised around five per cent of the population) as the colonizers and the indigenous majority as the colonized. This social division persisted for more than a century. Liebenow attributes both its continued existence and the evolution of an élite to the political skill of President Tubman (1944-71). The author argues that the 1980 *coup* permitted the eradication of privilege (through the removal of the settler élites). Notwithstanding this, there are many who would question this theory, along with the arguments which Liebenow develops in one of his later books (*Liberia: the quest for democracy* [1987]) (q.v.).

342 **Liberia: the quest for democracy.**
J. Gus Liebenow. Bloomington, Indiana: Indiana University Press, 1987. 336p.
A sequel to his magnum opus, *Liberia: the evolution of privilege* (q.v.), Liebenow's thesis reiterates the theme of his original study (q.v.) – that five per cent of the Liberian population who are 'pure' descendants of black settlers established a colonial relationship with the indigenous population and maintained their position of dominance

in society until it was removed by force in 1980. The April *coup d'état* thus represented a 'dissolution of privilege' and opened up the real prospect of establishing equality, given the democratic political forces that had come to the fore in the 1970s (namely the Movement for Justice in Africa – MOJA, and the Progressive Alliance of Liberia – PAL). Liebenow attributes the failure of these forces to the military assault on democracy and the effective imposition of yet another minority on the Liberian people, this time a Krahn minority (representing five per cent of the population). There are many questions which remain unexplained concerning not only the survival of the old patronage party system, and the continued activities of many individuals and institutions of the pre-*coup* era, but perhaps, most significantly, the fact that the removal of the True Whig Party régimes did not lead to the expected empowerment of the 'pure' indigenous majority.

### 343 Politics in Liberia: the conservative road to development.
Martin Lowenkopf. Stanford, California: Hoover Institution Press, Stanford University, 1976. 237p.
Presents a wide-ranging overview of politics in Liberia during the Tubman era (1944-1971). Although the book lacks a coherent and consistent framework it does attempt to explain the many facets of the nation – the systems and sub-systems of its government and the broad outlines of its political economy.

### 344 The Liberian presidential election of 1955.
Townsend M. Lucas. MA thesis, Howard University, Washington, DC, 1960. 165p.
An interesting eye-witness account by an American author of the controversial 1955 presidential election. In this election former President Edwin Barclay (1930-44) stood against the incumbent president William V. S. Tubman (1944-71). It was Tubman who was victorious.

### 345 The new Liberia: a historical and political survey.
Lawrence A. Marinelli. London: Praeger, 1964. 244p.
The uncritical historical, economic, and political survey was intended to provide the background to the achievements of the administration of the then incumbent President Tubman. An introduction is written by Senegalese President, Leopold Sédar Senghor.

### 346 Which way Africa? Notes on the present neo-colonial situation and possibilities for struggling against it.
Dew Tuan-Wleh Mayson. Syracuse, New York: the Clearinghouse for Liberian Literature (P.O. Box 6084, Syracuse, New York 13210), [n.d.] 26p.
This is largely a collection of public speeches made by the author, an important member of the opposition group, the Movement for Justice in Liberia during the 1970s.

### 347 Liberia: the Americo-Liberian elite.
Ozay Mehmet. In: *Economic planning and social justice in development countries.* New York: St. Martin's Press, 1978. p. 123-40.
The author's premise is that underdevelopment and poverty in Liberia are the result of political, not economic factors. He contends that the settler élites, who monopolized

political power, also monopolized economic power as they sustained a lopsided distribution of wealth from the enclave sector. However, what seems unclear in this chapter is the author's definition of the sociological composition of this 'Americo-Liberian élite'.

### 348 Liberian politics today: some personal observations.
Harry F. Moniba.   Monrovia, Liberia. 1992. 79p.

The author who was vice-president of Liberia from 1986 to the outbreak of the Civil War in 1990, contributes his personal reflections on the possible causes of the civil conflict. Whilst he identifies 'the need for patriotic political leadership that can safely take Liberia into the 21st century', he refrains from making any serious reflections on the nature and character of the pre-1980 governments in Liberia, and, more importantly, on the régime of Samuel Doe.

### 349 Seven years of total involvement and fulfilment.
Monrovia: Ministry of Information, Cultural Affairs, and Tourism
(Produced by IMPADS, London), 1978. 64p.

This review of the achievements of the first seven years of the nine-year presidency of William R. Tolbert, Jr. was prepared by a committee, set up by the President, and composed of nineteen deputy ministers. Chaired by D. Elwood Dunn (Minister of State for Presidential Affairs), who compiled and edited the document, the areas covered include: financial performance; foreign policy; economic co-operation; commercial transactions; industrial advances; progress in transportation; public corporations; pursuits in agriculture; efforts in health and social welfare; human resource development; rural development and urban reconstruction; Ministry of Defense activities; labour, youth and sports; administration of justice; administration of lands and mines; and new horizons in communications and culture.

### 350 The first five years of Dr. Samuel Kanyon Doe: a catalog of achievements.
Monrovia: Ministry of Information, 1985. 76p.

Offers an official account of the administration of President Samuel K. Doe five years before its downfall during the 1990 Civil War. The work includes the following chapters: 'An inevitable and providential change'; 'National life and public policy', 'Today's challenge – the making of the Second Republic', and 'Building for the future – the task ahead'. Appendices provide background information.

### 351 President William V. S. Tubman of Liberia: pace-setter for a democratic and stable government in Africa.
*The New York Times*, Nov. 1966. 32p. illus.

This supplement marks the seventy-first birthday of President Tubman. Tubman's career is highlighted and short statements are presented by the cabinet ministers in charge of the various government departments. Greetings from the leaders of Ethiopia and Ivory Coast are also included.

352    **The Liberian bureaucracy: an analysis and evaluation of the environment, structure and functions.**
    Anthony J. Nimley.    Washington, DC: University Press of America, 1977. 314p.

Accounts for the problems and failures of contemporary bureaucracy in Liberia using both indigenous, or 'ancient', and western models. The author offers suggestions for bureaucratic improvements which include the development of a meritocracy which incorporates the concept of social justice.

353    **Government and politics in Liberia.**
    Anthony J. Nimley.    Nashville, Tennessee: Academic Publishers International, 1991. 2 vols. 3,367p. illus.

This voluminous analytical study seeks to present the experience of government in Liberia in terms of an indigenous African system ('African meritocracy') and a black settler or 'foreign' system ('European Amemocracy'). The author asserts that there was a conspiracy at the core of the 'foreign' system to conceal its true nature in order to repress and control the indigenous people and their system. Nimley states that his aim is to unveil 'in written words for the very first time the real nature of the African Meritocracy and the real nature of the European Amemocracy not only in theory but also in practice encompassing their respective systems of public policies in terms of process and substance, encompassing the institutional and substantive foundations of policies concerning natural and material resources ...' (p. xxxvi). The contents of the study include under chapter one: 'The task environment of the state'; chapter two: 'The African meritocracy, government under unwritten constitution'; chapter three: 'The analysis and evaluation of the African meritocracy'; chapter four: 'The European amemocracy, government under written constitution'; chapter five: 'The analysis and evaluation of the European Amemocracy'; chapter seven: 'The Pahndakorian Gbor: government under the people's Redemption Army'; and chapter eight: 'Government in the future, recommendations for implementation by the people and the government'. Among items in chapter eight is a call for a 'National Convention for the reconstruction of the nation' along the lines of the indigenous norms and institutions. There is an extensive bibliography of fifty-one pages and 402 titles of primary and secondary sources, though Nimley stressed in the introduction to the study his heavy reliance on 'African sources' drawn largely from 'the author's family oral archives ...' An appendix of 104 documents is included. Nimley is a Liberian of Kru ethnicity who in 1994 was a Professor of politics at Fisk University in Nashville, Tennessee, USA.

354    **Contemporary West African states.**
    Edited by Donal B. Cruise O'Brien, John Dunn, Richard Rathbone.
    Cambridge, England: Cambridge University Press, 1989. 227p.

This work is the successor to *West African states, failure and promise* (q.v.) edited by John Dunn. Six of the nine countries surveyed in this volume were also examined in the previous volume (Ivory Coast, Ghana, Liberia, Nigeria, Senegal, and Sierra Leone). This edition also covers Burkina Faso, Cameroon, and Chad. For each country there is an analysis of an important aspect of contemporary politics. For Liberia there is also a consideration of the political trends that have culminated in a 'corrosion of the political order' since 'a reasonbly effective and peaceful system of dependent clientelism has ... been replaced by a much less effective and more violent one.'

355  **American imperialism enslaves Liberia.**
George Padmore.   Moscow: Centrizdat, 1931. 45p.

Padmore, a West Indian-born pan-Africanist, expresses here the African nationalist viewpoint regarding the 1927 Firestone concession agreement and the appended loan of the Finance Corporation of America.

356  **Presidential papers, documents, diary, and record of the activities of the Chief Executive, first year of the administration of President William R. Tolbert, Jr.**
Monrovia: Republic of Liberia, Press Division, The Executive Mansion; Barnham, England: Anchor Press, 1972. 574p.

This useful reference work, complete with illustrations, provides a record of the Tolbert Presidency during the period between 23 July 1971 and 31 July 1972. The book contains a reproduction of the President's diary and summary of events, and includes edited extracts from Tolbert's documents and speeches, as well as a record of his daily activities. Successive publications, from the same publisher, covered: the second and third years of his administration (1 August 1972 to 31 July 1974), published in 1975; the concluding period of the first administration (1 August, 1974 to 31 December, 1975), published in 1976; and the first two years of the second administration (1 January, 1976 to 31 December, 1977). Unfortunately, the period between January 1978 and the *coup*, which occurred in April 1980, when Tolbert was overthrown, are not covered by the series.

357  **Effective immediately, dictatorship in Liberia, 1980-1986: a personal perspective.**
Amos Sawyer.   Bremen, Germany: Liberia Working Group Papers, no. 5, 1987. 41p.

The author, a former political activist who was the chairman of the National Commission which wrote the 1984 Liberian constitution, presents his initial assessment of the régime which seized power in 1980. He asserts that 'the greatest threat posed by the military dictatorship to Liberian society lies in the introduction of the military itself as a factor in Liberian political life in the future' (p. 35). Sawyer indicts the régime on the grounds that there was a discrepancy between what it said and what it did, and that it brutally pursued power and self-aggrandizement. The régime claimed to represent the political agenda of the 'progressive' movements of the 1970s, MOJA and PAL of which he writes: 'neither organization had achieved the requisite state of development. Neither had developed a comprehensive national program, a cadre of trained technicians or informed perspectives on all of the salient national issues' (p. 16). This is why, when integrated into the military government in 1980, they quickly degenerated into what the author describes as 'bounty hunters, fortune seekers and ethnicists'. As later events revealed, plunder and pillage would remain the régime's hallmark until its downfall in the Civil War of 1989-90.

358 **The Putu development association: a missed opportunity.**
Amos Sawyer. In: *Rethinking institutional analysis and development: issues, alternatives, and choices.* Edited by Vincent Ostrom, David Feeny, Hartmut Picht. San Francisco, California: ICS Press for the International Centre for Economic Growth, an affiliate of the Institute for Contemporary Studies, 1988, p. 247-78.

The Susukuu Corporation, 'a nonprofit agency designed to study the problems of urban and rural poverty' in Liberia, was established by the Putu Development Association in the Konoba District of Grand Gedeh County in the 1970s. Sawyer, a prominent member of Susukuu, uses the experience of the association to demonstrate 'how traditional institutions can be deployed to achieve development objectives within a framework of local self-organization'. In addition, he reveals the consequences of such autonomy when established as part of a larger autocratic system.

359 **Proprietary authority and local administration in Liberia.**
Amos Sawyer. In: *The failure of the centralized state: institutions and self-governance in Africa.* Edited by James S. Wunsch, Dele Olowu. Boulder, Colorado: Westview Press, 1990, p. 148-73.

By contrasting the notion of a self-governing constitutional order with the traditional forms of patron-client relationships, Sawyer traces the evolution of proprietary authority in Liberia and shows how a structure of local administration was created as an instrument of control. 'The self-governing potentials of the constituent elements of Liberian society were co-opted, or destroyed, while dependency relationships were encouraged'. A final section demonstrates how these patterns led to 'political and economic stagnation' in the country.

360 **The emergence of autocracy in Liberia: tragedy and challenge.**
Amos Sawyer. San Francisco, California: ICS Press, 1992. 418p.

The author breaks new ground in what is perhaps the first attempt to integrate the various interpretations of the Liberian experience, by seeking to come to grips with the 'constitution of the social order'. He combines micro-Liberia (the large body of ethnohistorical and anthropological studies) with macro-Liberia (the Monrovia-centred analyses) in an effort to account for the process which led to the development of an autocratic presidential system which eventually degenerated into Civil War. Sawyer's prescription for an alternative to autocracy (a mode of governance which he sees as typical of contemporary African states), is to reverse the current state-society relationship in ways that increase 'civic capacity'.

361 **The emancipation of the hinterland.**
Robert A. Smith. Monrovia: Star Magazine and Advertising Services, 1964. 126p.

This account of President Tubman's efforts to bridge the socio-cultural and political divide between settler-Liberians and indigenous-Liberians through a policy of national unification and integration, is told from the perspective of one who sympathized with the Tubman régime. It includes a profile of the President, and ten appendices containing public papers relating to the unification effort. Of related interest is Smith's *Unification reconsidered: a contemporary social and political history of Liberia* (Monrovia: Providence Publications, 1971. 77p).

362 **Justice, justice: a cry of my people.**
Edited by Nya Kwianon Taryor, Sr.   Chicago: Strugglers' Community
Press, 1985. 319p.

Presents a collection of essays and speeches by members of MOJA (Movement for
Justice in Africa), a large-scale political movement critical of the government of
President Tolbert during the 1970s, and still currently active in the political arena. The
articles cover social, political, economic and educational issues and Congressional
documents from the second MOJA Congress in 1980 are also included. Contributors
include H. Boima Fahnbulleh, Jr., Dew Tuan-Wleh Mayson, Amos C. Sawyer, Togba-
Nah Tipoteh, and W. Comnany B. Wesseh as well as the editor, Nya Kwianon Taryor.

363 **Democracy: the call of the Liberian people.**
Togba-Nah Tipoteh.   Sweden: Tofters Tryckeri ab., 1982. 212p.

The politics of confrontation among the 'progressive' movements, i.e., Movement for
Justice in Africa (MOJA) and the Progressive Alliance of Liberia (PAL) within the
context of the ruling True Whig Party (TWP) government of President Tolbert in the
1970s are presented from the perspective of the leader of MOJA and its subsidiary,
the Susukuu Corporation. The author's analysis is at the macro level, however, and he
fails to explain the difficult relationship between the 'progressives' and the military
government prior to the removal of the former from the government in 1980. The book
was produced by Tofters of Sweden for the Susukuu Corporation of Monrovia.

364 **President William V. S. Tubman of Liberia speaks: major addresses,
messages, speeches and statements, 1944-1959.**
Edited by E. Reginald Townsend.   Consolidated Publications, 1959.
301p. (for the Department of Information and Cultural Affairs).

Covers the first fifteen years of Tubman's twenty-seven-year presidency, and portrays a
president who was relatively popular until faced with serious opposition in 1951 (from
D. Twe and the Reformation Party) and in 1955 (from the Independent True Whig Party
and from an alleged assassination attempt). This is nonetheless a very useful resource.

365 **The official papers of William V. S. Tubman, President of the
Republic of Liberia.**
Edited by E. Reginald Townsend, Abeodu Bowen Jones.   London:
Longmans Green, 1968. 687p.

Presents a collection, with annotations of the addresses, messages, speeches and
statements of President Tubman for the period 1960 to 1967. Published for the
government's Department of Information and Cultural Affairs the volume portrays a
Tubman worried about the Liberian 'revolution of rising expectations', and threatening
authoritarian measures.

366 **The love of liberty: the rule of President William V. S. Tubman in
Liberia, 1944-1971.**
Tuan Wreh.   London: C. Hurst & Co., 1976. 138p.

A critical account by an eminent Liberian journalist and Law professor, of the political
career of a dictator who served as president for twenty-seven years. The writer includes
an account of the repression and torture he experienced at the hands of the Tubman
administration because of his controversial writings as a journalist.

# Human Rights

367 **Best friends: violations of human rights in Liberia, America's closest ally in Africa.**
New York: Fund for Free Expression Report, 1986. 54p.

Based on visits to Liberia by the journalist, Michael Massing (who apparently wrote the report), and sponsored by the Fund, this is a dismal account of the atrocities of the régime of President Samuel K. Doe. This report is similar to the Lawyers Committee's *A Promise Betrayed* [q.v.] (1986) although it lacks the graphic quotations from interviews and the detail of the latter. *Best friends* is available from the Fund for Free Expression, 30 West 44th St., New York, NY 10036.

368 **Liberia: human rights violations in Liberia, 1980-1990.**
Edited by Robert Kappel, Werner Korte. Bremen, Germany:
Informationszentrum Afrika, Liberia Working Group, 1990. 308p.

A collection of some 200 documents which surveys over a decade of human rights violations under the Samuel K. Doe administration. It includes news analysis, narrative reports, historical extracts, personal recollections, and appeals from organizations such as Amnesty International. The sources are almost all in English, with a few in German.

369 **Liberia: a promise betrayed – a report on human rights.**
New York: Lawyers' Committee For Human Rights, 1986. 179p.

Apparently acting upon reliable reports of flagrant violations of human rights in Doe's Liberia, the Lawyers Committee sent a fact-finding team to visit the country from March 9 to April 9, 1986. The book is a product of the Committee's findings and subsequent research. Written by consultant journalist, Bill Berkeley, it is a searing account of the rule of a murderous dictator. Undoubtedly these events were the precursors of the civil war, which broke out some four years later. The address of the Lawyers' Committee is: 36 West 44th Street, New York, NY 10036, USA.

370 **Uprooted Liberians: casualties of a brutal war.**
Haram A. Ruiz.   Washington, DC: United States Committee for
Refugees, 1992. 32p.

This is a good summary of the refugee dimension of the Liberian civil war that began in
December 1989 and still remains unresolved in 1994. The war 'has fanned ethnic hatred,
uprooted half the country's population, left tens of thousands dead, injured, or orphaned,
derailed an already ailing economy.' Recommendations for ending the tragedy are
advanced by the author. This publication is available from 1025 Vermont Avenue, NW,
Washington, DC 20005.

# Law and the Legal System

### 371 Constitutions of the countries of the world.

Edited by Albert P. Blaustein, Gisbert H. Flanz. Dobbs Ferry, New York: Oceana Publications, various paginations.

First published in 1971, this series consists of updated texts of constitutions, constitutional chronologies and annotated bibliographies, presented in a loose-leaf format so that each section may be easily updated. Liberia features in the ninth section prepared by Albert P. Blaustein and Michael G. Kitay (p. 1-120). Issued in September 1985, the contents include a constitutional chronology and Decrees (1861-1985) and the 1984 Constitution (Approved Revised Draft Constitution of the Republic of Liberia, and 'Draft Constitution of the Republic of Liberia as published by the National Constitution Commission'). There is also a brief annotated bibliography (p. 173-75).

### 372 Flags of convenience: an international legal study.

Boleslaw A. Boczek. Cambridge, Massachusetts: Harvard University Press, 1962. 323p.

This is the first publication to appear which comprehensively discusses the problems associated with flags of convenience; where a ship owned by one country is registered by another, thus avoiding financial charges and creating commercial and legal advantages. Using the example of Liberia, along with that of Panama and Honduras, the book focuses on the international legal aspects of foreign registration.

### 373 Regulation of insurance in the republic of Liberia: a study and proposed insurance law prepared for the government of Liberia by Checchi and Company, Washington, DC, final report.

Checchi and Company. Washington, DC: Government publication, 1967. 105p.

This study contains legal proposals for regulating the business of insurance in Liberia. It was prepared for the government by Checchi and Company and drafted by Ronald A. Jacks, a member of the District of Columbia Bar. The Liberian insurance law of 1967 seeks to accomplish three objectives, according to the report: to ensure that only responsible insurers will be allowed to do business in Liberia; to guarantee that all insurers and alien carriers in particular, pay their fair share of tax on revenue derived from Liberia; and to promote investment in Liberia. 'This is accomplished by requiring all insurers to retain in Liberia at least 10% of the gross premium income derived from that country' (p. 47-50). The appendix includes the 'Liberian Insurance Law of 1967' and the 'Charter of the Insurance Company of Africa'.

374 **The constitution of the Republic of Liberia and the Declaration of Independence.**
Edited by Alfonso K. Dormu. New York: Exposition Press, 1970. 119p.

Provides an account of the drawing up of the 1847 Constitution and the Declaration of Independence and reproduces in their entirety both documents with explanatory comments. The author, a Liberian lawyer, discusses why the democratic principles embodied in the documents were not realized in practice.

375 **The trial of Henry Fahnbulleh.**
Victor D. DuBois. American Universities Field Staff Reports (AUFS), West Africa Series, Vol. 11, nos. 3-7, Parts I-IV, 1968 (various pagination).

In early 1968 the Vai-Liberian Ambassador to East Africa, Henry Boima Fahnbulleh Sr., was arrested, tried and convicted for treason. To many foreign observers and Liberians alike, it was the Liberian régime itself which was effectively seen to be on trial for the injustices it had shown to its indigenous majority and for the alienation of Liberian youth. DuBois, an American political scientist witnessed the trial and he presents his observations in five parts: Background of the trial; The case for the prosecution; The defense's rebuttal; The closing of the trial; The trial in retrospect.

376 **Reports and opinions of the Attorney-General of the Republic of Liberia, December 15, 1922 – July 31, 1930.**
Louis A. Grimes. Ithaca, New York: Cornell University Press, 1969. 2nd ed. 423p.

First published by the author in the 1930s, this is a collection of the judicial opinions and decisions of one of Liberia's foremost jurists, Louis Arthur Grimes, who was Attorney General (1922-30) and later Chief Justice of Liberia (1934-48). The book underscores the successful efforts of Grimes to ensure the impartial administration of justice to all, including indigenous Liberians. It also demonstrated his position as a focal point for the judicial resolution of public issues. See also *Opinions of the Attorney-General of the Republic of Liberia, September 10, 1964 – August 13, 1968* (q.v.).

377 **Ethiopia and Liberia vs. South Africa: the South West Africa case.**
Ernest A. Gross, D. P. de Villiers, Ambassador Endalkachew Makennen, Richard A. Falk. Los Angeles: African Studies Centre, University of California, 1968. 41p. (Occasional Paper, no. 5).

With a preface by Paul O. Proehl, this is an interesting collection of articles written by those close to the confrontation which occurred in the 1960s between Ethiopia and Liberia, on the one hand, and South Africa, on the other, and which was placed before The International Court of Justice. Ethiopia and Liberia instituted contentious proceedings against South Africa regarding 'the continued existence of the mandate for South West Africa and for the duties and performance of the Union as mandatory thereunder'. The proceedings lasted nearly six years before the court finally ruled that the applicants had no *locus standi*, whereupon the case was dismissed. Ernest Gross, the American international lawyer hired by Liberia analyses the 1966 decision in 'The South West Africa cases: an essay on judicial outlook'. The South African government's lawyer, de Villiers, urges great caution relative to the international community's acceptance of 'dynamic law-creating processes' in 'The South West Africa case: the case for rectification'. Ethiopia's United Nations Ambassador E. Makennen calls the 1966 decision a 'technical ruling which amounted to nothing more than a decision not to decide'; and Professor Falk of Princeton University argues in 'The South West Africa case: the limits of adjudication' that the applicants had placed their charge against South Africa in 'a setting appropriate for judicial settlement'.

## 378 The Cassell case: contempt in Liberia.
Geneva: International Commission of Jurists (ICJ), 1961. 19p.

Liberia's former Attorney General, C. Abayomi Cassell (1944-57), was disbarred in 1961 by the Supreme Court on grounds of 'gross constructive contempt' because of critical remarks he made in January 1961 at the African Conference on the Rule of Law which was held in Lagos, Nigeria. This is a brief ICJ study of the law of contempt of court in relation to the Cassell case. The inquiry concludes that Cassell 'did not exceed the limits of reasonable criticism' (p. 19).

## 379 Courts and trial in the republic of Liberia (as related to law enforcement and the treatment of criminals).
E. Sumo Jones. New York: Carlton Press, 1979. 71p.

In its examination of the administration of justice in Liberia, this study covers the institution and trial of criminal suits in the lower courts. It also describes, and attempts to evaluate, Liberia's court system, the methods of trial and the treatment of criminals. Jones is a former Liberian commissioner of immigration and naturalization as well as being a former senator of Lofa County.

## 380 What future for flags of convenience?
Roy Laishley. *Africa Business* (March 1980), p. 13-14.

This is a brief report on a United Nations Conference on Trade and Development (UNCTAD) which proposed a phasing out of flags of convenience, namely the arrangement involving the ownership of a vessel in one country with registration in another to assure commercial and legal advantages. Claiming that the arrangement brings little benefit to developing countries, UNCTAD wanted the programme ended by 1991. The proposition was stoutly challenged by Liberia which called a rival conference in Monrovia to challenge the UNCTAD initiative (see p. 14-15 of *Africa Business*, March 1980).

## 381 The Liberian labour law and labour policies: an explanation of rights of employers and workers.
Victoria Flamma-Sherman Lang. Monrovia: Published by the author, 1985. 2nd ed. 185p.

The author, a former official of the Liberian government's Ministry of Labour, presents here a useful manual on Liberian labour law and practices. The contents include:

'Scope of the labour practices law'; 'The labour practices law and labour policies'; 'Procedure governing the settlement of labour disputes'; and 'International labour standards applicable in Liberia'. There is also an appendix which includes details about regulations, conventions and decrees on labour matters. The author indicates that copies of the study can be purchased through her law firm at the Liberia Finance & Trust Corporation Building, Broad Street, Monrovia, Liberia.

382 **First steps: rebuilding the justice system in Liberia.**
New York: Lawyers Committee for Human Rights/Africa, A report, 1992. 39p.

Reviews 'the justice system in Liberia, including the roles of the Ministry of Justice, the Courts, the legal profession and the Police, as well as the administration of the prisons'. Since the team which researched and wrote the report was unable to meet the representatives of the National Patriotic Front of Liberia (NPFL), or visit the sizeable territory under its control, attention is focused on the efforts of the Interim Government of National Unity (IGNU), based in Monrovia, 'to develop institutions which guarantee official accountability and to encourage the growth of an independent non-governmental community' (p. 3).

383 **Cases and materials on Liberia's interstate succession and wills.**
Johnnie N. Lewis. Published by the author, 1978. 2 vols.

Largely intended to introduce students to the law dealing with the transfer of property by interstate succession and/or will, the first volume contains the first four chapters and the second volume contains the last two chapters, and appendices. The author is a prominent lawyer and law professor at the University of Liberia.

384 **Liberian code of laws of 1956.**
Edited by the Liberian Codification Project under the direction of Milton R. Konwitz. Ithaca, New York: Cornell University Press, 1957. 3 vols.

This work is the product of a project commissioned in 1952 by the Liberian government to make arrangements for the systematic codification, compilation and publication of the laws of Liberia. The project was undertaken by the School of Law of Cornell University and subsequently by a codification division of Liberia's Department of Justice before being adopted by the Legislature on March 22, 1956. A fourth volume containing a complete index was later published; as well as a fifth volume of statutes enacted by the Legislature between 1957 and 1958.

385 **Liberian code of laws revised.**
Edited by the Liberian Codification Project under the direction of Milton R. Konwitz. Ithaca, New York. Cornell University Press, 1973-1979. 6 vols.

These six volumes incorporating thirty-nine titles were published under the authority of the Liberian Legislature and the President; they supercede the old Code of 1956. Attorney General Clarence L. Simpson, Jr. wrote in the preface to the first revised volume in 1973 that the new Code represented 'a complete revision of the existing statutory law of Liberia formulated with a view to its culture and traditions, its growing economy, and its place in the modern world'. The subjects covered are: constitution; civil procedure law; criminal law; agriculture law; aliens and nationality law; associates law; banking law; commercial and bankruptcy law; descendants estate law; domestic relations law; education law; election law; executive law; foreign relations law; general business law; general construction law; insurance law; labour law; legislative law; local government law; maritime law; national defense law; national social security and welfare law; natural resources law; patent, copyright, and tradesmark law; patriotic and cultural observances law; penal law; postal service law; private wrongs law; property law; public authorities law; public contracts law; public employment law; public health law; public lands law; public safety law; revenue and finance law; transportation and communications law; vehicle and traffic law; and zoning law.

386  **Liberian law reports.**
Edited by the Liberian Codification Project under the direction of Milton R. Konwitz. Ithaca, New York: Cornell University Press, 1961-1978. 27 vols.

These volumes contain the published decisions of the Liberian Supreme Court from 1961 to 1978. Circuit court decisions are available in mimeographed form in the libraries of the Supreme Court and the University of Liberia, respectively. The earlier volumes are reprints, with the more contemporary being compilations of a Codification Project which the Liberian government contracted to Cornell University under the direction of Law Professor, Milton R. Konwitz. Volume one, for example, was compiled and annotated by associate justice, James J. Dossen, and published in 1908 by The Boston Book Company. Volume twenty-seven and the bulk of the other volumes were compiled by the Codification Project. All of the Reports feature a Table of Cases Reported, and a subject-index.

387  **Understanding the Liberian Constitution.**
Compiled by Harry T. F. Nayou, Isaac M. Randolph.  Monrovia: National Advance Press, [n.d.]. 69p.

Contains the basic text of the Constitution of the Republic of Liberia as approved on July 20, 1984 and enforced from January 1986. The compilers indicate that their aim in undertaking the compilation was to instruct Liberians about their constitutional rights and obligations. Besides the forty-six page constitutional text, the twenty-three preceding pages include a preface, introduction, questions on each of the constitutional chapters, and an index of the text.

388  **Constitutions of nations.**
Compiled by Amos J. Peaslee. (*Africa*, vol. 1, revised 4th edition by Dorothy Peaslee Xydis and Martinus Nijhoff). The Hague, The Netherlands, 1974. 1141p. bibliog.

Contains entries for forty-three African countries. The basic information for the volume is supplied by each Foreign Ministry. The Liberia section (p. 415-28) includes a summary highlighting its international status, form of national government and the rights of the people. There is a full text of the Constitution of 1847 as amended to May 1955.

389  **Opinions of the Attorney-General of the Republic of Liberia, September 10, 1964-August 13, 1968.**
James A. A. Pierre.  Ithaca, New York: Cornell University Press, 1969. 208p.

The author was the Attorney-General during this period (1967-71). Most of the opinions contained in this work relate to economic issues and problems associated with foreign concessions in Liberia. On the whole the opinions do not portray a jurist respectful of the separation of powers. Pierre was also Chief Justice of Liberia, 1971-80.

390 **Liberia under military rule – decrees of the People's Redemption Council and Interim National Assembly governments: 1980-1986.**
Edited by James Teah Tarpeh. Monrovia: Liberian Educational & Professional Services, 1986. 320p.

This is a generally useful compendium of the decrees of the military government of Samuel K. Doe. Of the eighty-nine decrees promulgated by the military council five (numbers eight, twenty-four, twenty-six, forty and forty-five) could not be located and are therefore not included in this compilation. All twenty-five edicts of the Interim National Assembly government, also headed by Doe, are included along with appendices containing other useful information on military rule.

391 **Pluralism, constitutionalism, and law in Africa: a Liberian view.**
Winston B. Tubman. In: *Democracy and pluralism in Africa.* Edited by Dov. Ronen. Boulder, Colorado: Lynne Rienner Publishers, 1986, p. 109-17.

A good article on Liberia's painful experience in attempting to establish a constitutional pluralistic democracy and the rule of law. Presented in two parts, the first part reviews pre-1980 Liberia and seems to extol the 'chieftaincy presidency' (p. 111) of President W. V. S. Tubman (1944-71). Part two analyses Liberia's difficult quest for a new order in the aftermath of the 1980 *coup*, pointing out that for Liberia, as for all of Africa, three vital concerns must be dealt with if constitutional pluralistic democracy is to have a future – the role of the military establishment; the role of the educational establishment in the political arena; and 'how to minimize corruption and ensure a more equitable distribution of the national wealth'. Tubman, a former Liberian justice minister, is a relative of former President Tubman.

392 **The legal system of the republic of Liberia.**
Jan Werner. In: *Africa (vol. 6, Modern Legal Systems Cyclopedia).* Edited by Kenneth Robert Redden. Buffalo, New York: William S. Hein, Law Publisher, 1990 (6.290.3-6.290.43).

Liberia appears in part one (6.290.3-6.290.43) chapter 8A of this useful analytical survey of countries and organizations. The author covers: the form of government; legal education; admission to, and organization of, the Bar; the judicial system; sources of Liberian law; the ship registry corporate law; and taxes. A good, partially annotated, bibliography and nine pages of notes are also included together with an introduction.

393 **Trial by ordeal in Liberia.**
Tuan Wreh. *Liberian Law Journal,* vol. 6, no. 1 (1975), p. 1-10.

This brief article by a noted Liberian jurist examines the attempts to establish the judicial and statutory regulation of trial by ordeal, a trial method traditionally employed by some indigenous Liberian peoples to adjudicate civil and criminal matters. Wreh suggests that the system be discontinued through government prohibition, and the education of its advocates in 'the benefits of modern legal procedure'.

394 **Statutes and cases on Liberian maritime law.**
Tuan Wreh. Monrovia, Liberia: Wreh News Agency, 1975. 150p.

The author, a distinguished Professor in the University of Liberia Law school, writes that 'the need to publish this book arose from the fact that Liberian maritime statutes are scattered in various titles of the Liberian Code of Laws, in legislative enactments and in the National Port Authority regulations ...' (Preface). The contents include: general policy (chapter 1); documentation and identification of vessels (chapter 2); preferred ship mortgages and maritime liens on Liberian vessels (chapter 3); carriage of goods by sea (chapter 4); limitation of shipowners' liability (chapter 5); radio (chapter 6); rules of navigation (chapter 7); wrecks and salvage (chapter 8); merchant seamen (chapter 9); penal law (Crimes affecting foreign relations) (chapter 10); admirality jurisdiction (chapter 11); violation of revenue laws (chapter 12); and smuggling (chapter 13).

### 395 Statutes, cases and materials on aliens, immigration and naturalization law of Liberia.

Tuan Wreh.    Monrovia, Liberia: Wreh News Agency, 1976. 224p.

During the early 1970s the author was Liberia's Commissioner of Immigration and Naturalization. At that time he perceived that there was a need for a compendium which presented Liberia's laws concerning aliens, immigration and naturalization. This work was the result. The compilation (accompanied by commentaries, summaries and textual explanations) includes the new Aliens and Nationality Law followed by pertinent citations of statutory laws aliens should know. Landmark judicial cases dealing with the rights and liabilities of aliens in Liberia as decided by the Supreme Court then follow. The contents include: aliens and nationality law; general business law; labor law; foreign relations law; property law; public land law; revenue and finance law; public health and safety law; natural resource law; penal law; and civil procedure law.

### 396 Evidence law of Liberia: statutes, cases and materials.

Tuan Wreh.    Monrovia, Liberia: Wreh News Agency, 1979. 2 vols.

This two-volume study of the evidence law of Liberia 'is designed not only to give easy access to all the statutory evidence law of Liberia, as well as the applicable common law and the relevant constitutional provisions, pertinent rules and principles of law, but to ... provide ... background and analysis, plus appropriate reporting of Liberian Supreme Count cases' (p. iii). It is written in the style of a textbook and was apparently meant for use by students at the Louis Arthur Grimes School of Law at the University of Liberia where the late author was a professor.

### 397 Liberia.

Gerald H. Zarr.    In: *African Penal Systems.*    Edited by A. Milner. New York: F. A. Praeger, 1969, p. 193-212.

This study pays particular attention to criminal law, the objectives of the penal system, the prison system, alternative methods of dealing with offenders, young offenders, and capital and corporal punishment in Liberia.

# Foreign Relations

### 398 Liberia: America's African friend.

R. Earle Anderson. Chapel Hill, North Carolina: University of North Carolina Press, 1952. 305p.

This book, written in a rather paternalistic tone, is based largely on interviews with three Liberian presidents (C. D. B. King, Edwin Barclay, and W. V. S. Tubman), an American medical missionary, and a number of American officials and businessmen. Anderson presents an episodic account of early post-Second World War Liberia that highlights both the Liberia-American connections, and the dichotomous culture of the hinterland and coastal dwellers. Liberia stands out as America's friend in Africa in a world caught up in the Cold War.

### 399 Liberia in world politics.

Nnamdi Azikiwe. Westport, Connecticut: Negro Universities Press, 1970. 406p.

Originally published in 1943 by A. H. Stockwell, in London, Azikiwe (then a lecturer at Lincoln University), and later the first president of Nigeria, sets out the rationale for Liberia's foreign relations as 'an inevitable obeisance to the dictates of colonial imperialism'. This study provides a comprehensive survey of Liberia's foreign relations which includes a sympathetic rendering of the charges made between 1929 and 1930 by the League of Nations that the Liberian government was involved in the practice of forced labour. Whilst admitting the need for political and social reform in Liberia, 'Zik' felt it was necessary to emphasize pan-Africanist values which the lone African republic should assert as 'the fount of black hegemony.'

### 400 The foreign policy of the United States in Liberia.

Raymond W. Bixler. New York. Pageant Press, 1957. 143p.

Details the ways in which American diplomacy contributed to the creation, and maintainance, of the Liberian state in the nineteenth and early twentieth centuries. Bixler describes how the Liberian state developed under the 'fostering guardianship of the United States' and shows how, as a consequence, it was protected both from European

Imperialism and British financial control. Other topics covered include: the early years of American involvement in Liberia; the First and Second World Wars; the world rubber crisis; and the Great Depression.

401 **American foreign relations since 1700.**
Edited by Richard D. Burns. Santa Barbara, California: ABC-CLIO, 1983. 1,311p.

In this voluminous but useful reference work, only chapters eighteen and thirty-seven have direct relevance for Liberia. Chapter eighteen, 'United States and sub-Saharan Africa to 1939' (p. 511-19) covers: American merchants and commerce; the slave trade; 'from colonization society to pan-Africanism'; the American Colonization Society 1816-1965; Back-to-Africa movements from the 1880s until 1929; and US-Liberian relations. In chapter thirty-seven 'The United States and sub-Saharan Africa' (p. 1,093-105), sub-sections examine: black Americans and pan-Africanism; US Africa policies; the Roosevelt-Truman years, 1941-1952; the Eisenhower-Kennedy-Johnson years, 1953-1968; the Nixon-Ford years, 1969-1976; the Carter years, 1977-1980; and the sub-Saharan countries (grouped mainly by region). This publication in association with the Society for Historians of American Foreign Relations has extensive author and subject indexes, twelve maps and other useful features.

402 **Clash of titans: Africa and United States foreign policy, 1783-1974.**
Edward W. Chester. Maryknoll, New York: Orbis Books, 1974. 316p.

The major emphasis of this volume concerns the years between the American Revolution and the Second World War. In this comprehensive survey economic, religious, and cultural relations are considered as well as political affairs. An important conclusion of the study is that American policy was a mix of humanitarian and economic interests tempered by 'a number of colorful but essentially inconsequential episodes'.

403 **Dynamics of the African, Afro-American connection: from dependency to self-reliance.**
Edited by Adelaide M. Cromwell. Washington, DC: Howard University Press, 1987. 161p.

The proceedings of a conference held in Monrovia in 1983 of scholars and policymakers from five West African states and their *African-American* counterparts are included in this volume. Fifteen papers and responses are concerned with addressing the conference's objective of furthering collaborative research and dialogue between continental and diaspora Africans. Topics covered include: 'Key issues and changing dynamics of the African/Afro-American connection . . .'; 'Personal networks and institutional linkages in the global system'; 'The world economy and African/Afro-American connection'; 'How long Africa's dependency? Strategy for economic development and self-reliance'; and 'Teaching and research resources on Afro-Americans in Africa'.

404 **The foreign policy of Liberia during the Tubman era, 1944-1971.**
D. Elwood Dunn. London: Hutchinson Benham, 1979. 255p. bibliog.

A pioneer study of Liberia's foreign relations during the twenty-seven-year rule of William V. S. Tubman, in which the author posits two attitudes which guided policy throughout this period: namely, a policy affinity with the Western world on the issues of war and peace; and a stance of anti-colonialism. Special attention is paid to the position adopted by the Liberian government on six issues placed before the United Nations General Assembly. These issues were: Apartheid in South Africa; the representation of China in the United Nations; the Congo Crisis of 1960-61; the disposal of the former Italian colonies; the question of Algeria; and the question of South West Africa. The volume includes a foreword by Rocheforte L. Weeks, a former minister for foreign affairs (1972-73).

405 **The 1975 Vorster visit to Liberia: implications for free Africa's relations with Pretoria.**
D. Elwood Dunn. *Liberian Studies Journal*, vol. 10, no. 1 (1982-83), p. 37-54.

Following a controversial visit to Liberia by the South African pro-apartheid Prime Minister, John Vorster, in February 1975, there emerged a wave of resentment against the Liberian régime of President William R. Tolbert, Jr. One African newspaper printed the headlines 'Liberia receives Africa's Enemy Number One'! This article reviews the background of Vorster's 'secret' visit to Liberia, examines the substance of the discussions which took place, and describes both domestic and foreign reaction to the visit and the diplomatic responses of the Organization of African Unity. The author, who was as surprised by the visit as others, was an assistant minister in the Liberian Foreign Ministry at the time and used state papers to help write this article.

406 **The diplomacy of prejudice: Liberia in international politics, 1945-1970.**
H. Boima Fahnbulleh, Jr. New York: Vantage Press, 1985. 234p.

Written by a former Liberian foreign minister, this work offers a new perspective on Liberian foreign relations presented in the form of an interesting reworking of the theme of 'black colonialism' in Liberian historiography. He analyses the 'effect of prejudice as a governing force, not only in the founding of a state, but in the subsequent functioning of one congenitally influenced by prejudice.' Fahnbulleh argues that the unequal treatment of Liberians by their Western colonial neighbours has as its analogy the unequal treatment of indigenous Liberians by their settler overlords and suggests that foreign relations in Liberia under President W. V. S. Tubman were simply a projection of this prejudice.

407 **'Non-benign neglect': the United States and black Africa in the twentieth century.**
E. Gerald, K. Haines, J. Samuel Walker. In: *American foreign relations: a historiographical review.* Edited by Thomas J. Noer. Westport, Connecticut: Greenwood Press, 1981, p. 271-92.

A non-controversial review of the literature concerning US relations with sub-Saharan Africa. This area is 'usually dismissed by diplomatic historians with a few words about the founding of Liberia and the mandate system after the Second World War. They occasionally rediscover Africa in the 1960s to mention America's role in the Congo crisis and to illustrate the problems of US adjustment to Third World independence' (p. 271-72). Works cited on Liberia specifically are Earle Anderson's *Liberia: America's Friend* (Chapel Hill, North Carolina: University of North Carolina Press, 1952) and Raymond W. Bixler, *The Foreign Policy of the United States and Liberia* (New York: Pageant Press, 1957).

408   **Liberian diplomacy in Africa: a study of inter-African relations.**
Joseph E. Holloway.   Washington, DC: University Press of America,
1981. 230p.

Reviews the background to the unequal and discriminatory domestic relations which
exist within Liberia and considers how these have affected foreign relations. In addition,
Holloway suggests that the guiding principles behind Liberia's domestic policy
decisively shaped the course of its continental relations as institutionalized in the
Organization of African Unity (OAU). The latter suggestion attributes more influence to
Liberia than her size and resources would warrant, while at the same time omitting many
other factors that explain the nature of the OAU such as the considerable Western
influence on a large number of African countries, and the conservative instincts of a
majority of the African leaders.

409   **Liberia: a report on the relations between the United States and
Liberia.**
Robert L. Keiser.   Washington, DC: US Government Printing Office,
1928. 371p. (US Department of State. Second series B, no. 1. Liberia).

This work documents American-Liberian relations, from the founding of modern Liberia
to 1926. Drawing heavily from primary sources, Keiser divides his study into five
sections: the background to Liberian history; financial and economic history before
1923; the Firestone agreements; the ensuing concessions; and finally US interests in
Liberia after 1923. He covers in detail the transactions involving the Firestone Rubber
Company and the governments of Liberia and the US which led in 1926 to an agreement
between Harvey Firestone and the Liberian government. By this agreement the Liberian
government agreed both to lease a million acres of land to Firestone to develop his
rubber plantation and to take out a loan of $5 million through the Firestone-created
Finance Corporation of America.

410   **Dependency and the foreign policy of a small power: the Liberian
case.**
George Klay Kieh, Jr.   Lewiston, New York: Edwin Mellen Press,
1992. 224p.

Most Third World states are economically dependent on other nations and this
dependency has a profound impact on the formulation of foreign policy by developing
nations. Using the indices of foreign aid, trade and investment, Kieh applies his theory
to Liberia through its relationship with four capitalist (USA, France, Britain and West
Germany) and four socialist states (USSR, China, Romania and East Germany).

411   **Vorster's gamble for Africa: how the search for peace failed.**
Colin Legum.   New York: Africana Publishing Company, 1976. 127p.

Presents an account of the attempt by the pro-apartheid régime in South Africa to end its
isolation on the African continent by engaging in secret personal diplomacy. Among
South African Prime Minister John Vorster's several secret visits to African capitals was
one to Monrovia in February 1975 to confer with President William R. Tolbert, Jr.
Tolbert was severely criticized at home and abroad for what was considered an ill-
advised action.

412 **Ministers to Liberia and their diplomacy.**
James A. Padgett. *Journal of Negro History*, vol. 22, no.1 (1937), p. 50-92.

This essay includes a considerable amount of biographical material on American diplomats accredited to Liberia between 1863 and 1931. The author concludes: 'Perhaps in no small country, especially in an out of the way backward country, has the ministerial and consular work been carried on in a more satisfactory manner than in this little Republic'.

413 **Liberia's place in Africa's sun.**
Hilton Alonzo Phillips. New York: Hobson Book Press, 1946. 156p.

A most sympathetic presentation of Liberia, Africa's lone republic, in the immediate aftermath of the Second World War. The author portrays a long-despised Liberia on the verge of becoming a strategic asset to the Western World. Topics covered include: background information; the dawning of Nationalism; the strategic importance of Liberia; and Liberia's struggle for independence.

414 **Transnational non governmental organizations: a new direction for United States Policy.**
Pearl T. Robinson. *Issue, Journal of Opinion*, vol. 18, no. 1 (1989), p. 41-50.

The article represents fresh thinking about the provision of new resources to assist international development. It advocates a shift of focus from state-centred development to 'strategies for strengthening transnational relations'. This is an important development for Liberia which will need to engage in major reconstruction after the Civil War in a new post-Cold War era. Robinson observes that African NGOs seem to have made remarkable progress, in spite of considerable official reluctance, in exploring co-operative activities which among several benefits, have contributed to grassroots economic development and democratic renewal.

415 **Big powers and small nations: a case study of United States-Liberian relations.**
Hassan B. Sisay. Lanham, Maryland: University Press of America, 1985. 202p.

Describes US-Liberian relations between 1923 and 1947. The work is based on extensive use of primary source materials, especially US government documents and presidential papers. The book lacks a clear thesis or hypothesis, although the author has attempted to categorize the relationship in four phases: phase one – 1820-1862 (from the origins of Liberia to US official recognition.); phase two – 1862-1929 (characterized by more active US involvement in Liberian affairs); phase three – 1929-1933 (marked by the entry of the Firestone Rubber Company into Liberian affairs and accelerated American involvement); phase four – 1933-1980 (when Franklin D. Roosevelt's 'New Deal' apparently translated into improved relations with Liberia), the Cold War also took place during this era, at a time when Liberia was an ally of the West.

416 **African Americans and US policy toward Africa, 1850-1924: in defense of black nationality.**
Elliot P. Skinner. Washington, DC: Howard University Press, 1992. 555p.

The prime purpose of the book is 'to disprove the charge that, unlike many other ethnic groups in the United States that attempt to influence American policy to help their embattled homelands, African Americans have done little or nothing to aid the continent of their ancestors' (p. ix). The author describes 'activities largely unknown to contemporaries and to later generations' which demonstrate how African-Americans employed 'their limited political power and their considerable symbolic means to influence United States foreign policy toward Africa' (p. 516).

417 **Black scandal: America and the Liberian labor crisis, 1929-1936.**
Ibrahim K. Sundiata. Philadelphia: Institute for the Study of Human Issues, 1980. 230p.

*Black scandal*, which is written by an African-American historian, is 'a history of political evolution in Africa, of morality on the world stage, of imperialism and policy-making in the United States, and of the struggle by American blacks to come to terms with both their own society and the continent of their origin'. The author analyses the crisis that faced Liberia in the early 1930s, stemming from the charges of domestic slavery and forced labour levelled at the Liberian government by the United States, Great Britain and the League of Nations. This controversy threatened the sovereignty of what was the only black republic in Africa at this time. Accordingly, the situation aroused the concern of African-Americans and pan-Africanists. Of related interest is *Forced labour and migration: patterns of movement within Africa* (Edited by Abebe Zegeye and Shubi Ishemo. London: Hans Zell, 1989. 405p.).

418 **Africa and unity: the evolution of pan-Africanism.**
Vincent Bakpetu Thompson. London: Longman, 1971. 412p.

Chapters seven to ten of this historical study deal with the role played by Liberia in the pan-African movement's attempt to create unity throughout the continent. The author describes the movement from its early years until the advent of independence in many African nations and the subsequent efforts to unite both individual countries and the continent as a whole.

419 **United States Commission to Liberia.**
Washington, DC: Government of the United States, 61st Congress, 2nd Session, 1910. 37p.

Following the Deficiency Act of March 4, 1909, a commission visited Liberia with the aim of investigating the interests of the US and its citizens within the country. Recommendations were made by the commission with regard to increased aid and it was suggested that the US should enable Liberia to refund outstanding debts by assuming, as a guarantee for the payments of obligations under such an arrangement, the control and collection of Liberian customs dues.

# The Economy, Economic Development and Finance

### 420 The Mano River Union: a study of sub-regional strategy for economic cooperation and development in West Africa.
Mohammed Allieu Abdullah.    PhD thesis, University of Maryland, 1984. 257p.

Examines and attempts to evaluate the Mano River Union, a customs union which was established in 1973 by Liberia and Sierra Leone, with Guinea becoming a member in 1980. The author's conclusions are largely theoretical and over-optimistic and gloss over the many real problems faced by the member states because of the economic crises and political conditions of the time. However, the author describes the idea as an 'unqualified success in the establishment of a complete customs union and its education and institutional components'.

### 421 The evolution of the Monrovia strategy and the Lagos Plan of Action: a regional approach to economic decolonization.
Adebayo Adedeji.    United Nations Economic Commission for Africa, 1983. 25p.

In this revised text of a lecture delivered under the auspices of the Nigerian Institute of Social and Economic Research, Distinguished Lecture Series (University of Ibadan, March, 1983), the Executive Secretary of the Economic Commission for Africa reviews the many African strategies and plans for addressing the development of the continent. It is emphasized that the 1979 Monrovia strategy and the 1980 Lagos Plan were the most comprehensive collective African statement of plans designed to achieve the objectives of self-reliance and self-sustainment. The occasion of the lecture was the Silver Jubilee of the ECA (1958-1983).

422 **Readings and documents of ECOWAS: selected papers and discussions from the 1976 Economic Community of West African States Conference.**
Edited by A. B. Akinyemi, S. B. Falegan, I. A. Aluko. Lagos: Nigerian Institute of International Affairs with Macmillan Nigeria, 1984. 779p. bibliog.

Thirty writers contribute to this full discussion of the Economic Community of West African States (ECOWAS). Topics covered include: the basic concept of ECOWAS; economic issues and industrial development; customs and trade; agricultural and natural resources; transport; labour migration; and basic socio-political problems. The full text and related protocols of the treaty of ECOWAS are also included (p. 669-766).

423 **The size distribution of income in Liberia.**
E. K. Akpa. *Review of Income and Wealth*, no. 4 (Dec. 1981), p. 387-400.

The article finds that 'income inequality in the Liberian economy is high, it follows economic-sectoral lines'. Akpa argues that the greatest wealth lies with those who own the greatest money-making industries leaving others, such as rural workers, worse off. As a result one county (Montserrado) is set apart from all the others as the industrial as well as political seat of the country. An update of this survey would produce radically different results.

424 **The development of Liberia.**
Louis P. Beleky. *The Journal of Modern African Studies*, vol. 2, no. 1 (1973), p. 43-60.

Assesses Liberia's expansion during the 1950s and early 1960s, especially its impressive growth rates. Though primarily quantatitive in nature, the author contends that qualitative change through gradual and subtle modernization was an integral component of the development which took place. This, Beleky asserts, is borne out by increased *per capita* income and improvements in national health care, education, wages, and energy consumption. He maintains that such changes are part of a reciprocal relationship between development and growth and that the continued encouragement of foreign investment in the export sector should therefore remain the thrust of Liberia's economic policy.

425 **Development problems in Putu Chiefdom (Liberia).**
Nii K. Bentsi-Enchill. *West Africa*, no. 3266 (25 Feb. 1980), p. 344-46. (Liberia notebook).

This short commentary includes a review of the Susukuu Corporation-aided development project, organized by the Putu Development Corporation (PUDECO), in Putu Chiefdom, and assesses the Liberian government's reaction to it. The project was apparently a community effort at economic self-help but was perceived by the government as being politically motivated by Susukuu to expose a lack of government help in rural development.

### 426 Accelerated development in sub-Saharan Africa: an agenda for action.

Elliot Berg, K. Y. Amoako, Rolf Gusten, Jacob Meerman, Gene Tidrick. Washington, DC: World Bank, 1981. 198p. map. bibliog.

This report by the World Bank African Strategy Review Group, headed by Berg, 'highlights the severity and complexity of the problems facing many of the countries of Sub-Saharan Africa in their efforts to raise the living standards of their people' (foreword, p.v.). Requoting the goals of the Lagos Plan of Action, the report stresses that scarce resources must be used more efficiently and that African governments should rely more on the private sector. The volume consists of the following nine chapters: 'Introduction'; 'Basic constraints'; 'External factors'; 'Policy and administrative framework'; 'Policies and priorities in agriculture'; 'Human resources'; 'Other productive sectors'; 'Longer-term issues'; and 'External assistance in the 1980s'. In the statistical annex (p. 134-98) forty-three tables present a wealth of data on each of the thirty-nine countries covered in the report, including Liberia.

### 427 The impact of external domination on the Liberian Mano economy: an analysis of Weber's hypothesis of rationalism.

David G. Blanchard. PhD thesis, Indiana University, Bloomington, Indiana, 1973. 299p. (UMI order no. 73-22-988).

Employs Max Weber's hypothesis of economic rationalism to explain how the Mano-Liberians changed their 'household economy' to a wage-labour economic order operating under national, political, and bureaucratic domination. The author contends that the Mano benefitted through a marked rise in their living standards over and above the traditional ideal.

### 428 Multinational corporations and culture in Liberia.

T. H. Bonaparte. *Journal of Economics and Sociology*, vol. 38, no. 3 (1979), p. 237-51.

The principal argument of this article is that the number of multinational corporations in a developing country has little to do with the degree of corruption of local culture that takes place. Instead, it is the policy decisions of the governments of developing countries that determine whether or not multinationals have a positive or negative impact. Based on research in Liberia among foreign industrial managers, African supervisors, and Liberian workers, the author contends that, in spite of Liberia's 'Open Door' policy towards foreign investment, very little damage has been done to Liberian culture, due to the enclave character of the multinationals, and a *laissez-faire* government policy *vis-à-vis* the foreign corporations.

### 429 Rural resources and Liberian economic development.

Patrick D. Bropleh. PhD thesis, Duke University, Durham, North Carolina, 1974. 203p.

Set against the background of Liberia's dual and enclave economy which is characterized by monetary and traditional sectors, the study investigates the agricultural, forestry, and iron ore industries in order to estimate their contributions to employment, income, and output, as well as to assess their potential for expansion. In order to generate economic growth in the traditional or rural sector, the author presents a descriptive model which involves a rural-urban commercial mechanism and secondary industries in the enclaves, as well as a co-ordinated development programme for agriculture and forestry.

### 430 The economic history of Liberia.

George W. Brown. Washington, DC: Associated Publications, 1941. 366p.

Although now somewhat dated, this comprehensive review analyses the Liberian economy up until 1940. It covers both traditional and modern aspects and presents the background to the immediate post-War developments; heightened foreign influence in the private and public sectors and an apparent marginalization of the 'parallel' or indigenous economy. Towards the end of the work Brown concludes that the Liberian economy at that time was clearly the product of three systems: 'the self-sufficient economy of the African, the parasitic capitalism of the ruling class of Liberia; and the financial exploitation of the American and European industrialist' (p. 231).

### 431 The Mano River Union: an experiment in economic integration.

Augustus F. Caine. *Liberian Studies Journal*, vol. 13, no. 1 (1988), p. 6-41.

Assesses the Mano River Union of 1973 (see also item no. 420). Caine, a Liberian anthropologist, concludes that the hoped-for sectoral co-operation and integration of the economies of the member countries was not realized in 1980 due to their deteriorating economic circumstances. This deterioration prevented member states from keeping up-to-date with their contributions to the Union budget. The problem was compounded by the reduced level of assistance from foreign donors.

### 432 The limits to structural change: a comparative study of foreign direct investment in Liberia and Ghana, 1950-1970.

Jerker Carlsson. Uppsala, Sweden: Scandinavian Institute of African Studies (in co-operation with the Department of Economic History, University of Gothenburg), 1981. 299p.

Carlsson concludes that during this period foreign investment had little impact in terms of promoting structural change in these two economies. This was because of the nature of the foreign investment and the financial interests of the dominant social groups who wished to preserve the existing economic order.

### 433 Granges and the undermining of Liberia: a critique of a joint venture agreement.

Jerker Carlsson. *Review of African Political Economy*, vol. 23, no. 1 (1982), p. 72-84.

In this case study of a joint venture between a transnational corporation, Granges of Sweden, and the Liberian government the author sets out to demystify the intricate corporate structural arrangement. The Liberian government contended that, contrary to the fifty-fifty partnership arrangement set out in the legal codes, Liberia in actuality received only twenty per cent of the profits while yielding full operational control to Granges.

434 **Growth without development: an economic survey of Liberia.**
Robert W. Clower, George Dalton, Mitchell Harowitz and A. A. Walters
(with the assistance of Robert P. Armstrong, Johnetta Cole, Robert Cole
and George Lamson). Evanston, Illinois: Northwestern University
Press, 1966. 385p.

This economic survey of Liberia by a team of scholars from Northwestern University
was undertaken at the behest of the Liberian government and the United States Agency
for International Development. The objective was to offer a structural analysis and
policy recommendations to further Liberian development. One of the report's basic
conclusions is that Liberia has the domestic resources to develop, but will not do so
because of a stifling socio-political structure that keeps power and resources 'among a
small group of families of settler descent' to the evident detriment of the indigenous
majority of the population. It is asserted that although there had been some growth in the
economy, there had been hardly any development because there had been so few
beneficiaries of that growth.

435 **West German transnationals in tropical Africa: the case of Liberia
and the Bong Mining Company.**
William D. Coale, Jr. Munich: Institut für Wirtschaftsforschung/
Weltform Verlag, 1978. 240p. bibliog.

Examines the issue of the control of transnational corporations by host countries with
specific reference to Liberia and the Bong Mining Company, a German iron ore mining
enterprise situated in Bong County, Liberia.

436 **The Liberian elite as a barrier to economic development.**
Robert Eugene Cole. PhD thesis, Northwestern University, Evanston,
Illinois, 1967. 336p. (UMI Order no. 68-3167).

Positing a single explanation for the behaviour of the Liberian economy, and suggesting
that, despite 'large financial resources', economic development eluded Liberia, Cole
hypothesizes that a settler aristocracy ('the Liberian élite') had impeded development.
This élite is assumed to have espoused the following values: that only the welfare of the
élite should count; that economic inequality should be encouraged; and that the *status
quo* with regard to economic, social, and political institutions should be preserved. As a
result it has used its political domination to monopolize economic resources and render
national economic development impossible.

437 **Peasants and rural development in Liberia.**
Stephen K. Commins. In: *Africa's crisis: the roots of famine.* Edited
by Stephen K. Commins, Michael F. Lofchie, Rhys Payne. Boulder,
Colorado: Lynne Rienner Publishers, 1986, p. 133-52.

Examines various rural development projects and discusses how they reflect the interest
of both the state and international bodies. Particular mention is made of the Bong
County Agricultural Development Project and the Lofa County Agricultural Development Project, which were established by the Liberian government, the US agency for
International Development and the World Bank. The author notes that even though
changes were made in the scope and management of the projects there still remained a
divergence between the aims of the development group and the peasantry. He also
stresses the need for the sponsors of the projects to involve the local inhabitants much

more and to gain their cooperation. Indeed a more sensitive approach to the background and culture of each ethnic group was required. This work was one of a number of studies which called for a grassroots influence on national policy.

### 438  Essays on the economic anthropology of Liberia and Sierra Leone.

Edited by Vernon R. Dorjahn, Barry L. Isaac. Philadelphia: Institute for Liberian Studies, 1979. 283p.

Contains twelve essays on the economics of the 'countryside' based on field research undertaken by each of the authors nearly all of whom are anthropologists. The introductory and concluding essays are theoretical, whilst the remaining essays are a series of micro-level economic analyses. Among the titles in the latter category are: 'Economic activities in the Liberia area: the pre-European period to 1900' (S. E. Holsoe); 'Land, labour, and capital in Loma agriculture' (G. E. Currens); and 'The economics of Mende upland rice farming' (A. O. Njoku).

### 439  Country Report: Ghana, Sierra Leone, Liberia.

London: Economist Intelligence Unit, 1986. quarterly. (Reports nos. 1, 2 and 4).

Presents an overview of important political and economic events and provides information on energy, agriculture and industry, foreign trade and investments as well as statistical appendices. The reports also include quarterly indicators of economic activities in Ghana, Sierra Leone and Liberia. Additionally, an invaluable *Country Profile* is published, also by the EIU. At the time of publication the most recent issue (1986-87) covers Sierra Leone and Liberia jointly, and contains political backgrounds, a survey of every economic sector, and a profile of regional organizations of which Liberia is a member, as well as a brief bibliograpy (p. 45). The EIU's address is: 40 Duke Street, London WIA SDG, England.

### 440  From growth to development: planning in Liberia.

Richard Melvin Fulton. *African Urban Studies*, vol. 13 (1982), p. 55-74.

Outlines the emergence of development planning in Liberia during the Tolbert presidency (1971-80), details the planning structure and discusses the constraints under which development planning was implemented.

### 441  Export commodities and economic development: the Liberian rubber industry.

Animesh Ghoshal. PhD thesis, University of Michigan, Ann Arbor, Michigan, 1974. 205p. (UMI Order no. 74-25, 208).

This microeconomic analysis of the role of the rubber industry in the economic development of Liberia, pays particular attention to the Liberian-owned sector (as opposed to the foreign concessions).

### 442  The Liberian internal market system.

Winston Penn Handwerker. PhD thesis, University of Oregon, Eugene, Oregon, 1971. 423p.

Seeks to determine how the elements of the Liberian market system have been drawn together. The author analyses historical changes in the spatial and temporal integration of producers, consumers and intermediaries prior to 1970. The principal topics include market places, market sellers and the flow of foodstuffs from producers to urban consumers.

443  **Area development in Liberia: toward integration and participation.**
John W. Harbeson, Annette L. Binnendijk, Svend E. Holsoe, Robert W. Roundy.   Washington, DC: United States Agency for International Development (AID), 1984. 59p. appendices. (Project Impact Evaluation Report, no. 53).

'AID, the World Bank, and the Government of Liberia collaborated in setting up two large-scale, multisectoral agricultural development projects in Liberia. The Lofa County project began in 1976 and the Bong project in 1978. Using semi-autonomous Project Management Units (PMU), the two projects were designed to improve incomes, productivity, and standards of living for poor, rural Liberians who have been essentially spectators in any development which the country had previously achieved. This report assesses the impact of these projects on the lives of the intended beneficiaries'. (p. 1).

444  **Modeling the macroeconomy/energy economy relationship in developing countries: the case of Liberia.**
Lawrence J. Hill.   *The Journal of Developing Areas* (Macomb, Illinois), vol. 22, no. 1 (Oct. 1987), p. 71-84.

Discusses the construction of a model which was employed to simulate energy demand by sector and fuel type in Liberia. The period covered is 1982 to the year 2000.

445  **Dependence, underdevelopment and persistent conflict – on the political economy of Liberia.**
Edited by Eckhard Hinzen, Robert Kappel.   Bremen, Germany: Obersee Museum, 1980. 408p. (Bremen Africa Archives, series F, vol. 11).

The old indigene/settler dichotomy provides the framework for this compilation which is presented in a Marxist perspective. The authors seek 'to contribute to a critical discourse which identifies socio-economic contradictions and conflict in their long-term historical context'. The work is divided into three parts, with contributions from European and African scholars, as well as leading Liberian political figures in the 'progressive' movements of the 1970s. Part one portrays Liberia as a black colonial state; part two underscores the role of foreign capital in fostering dependency and therefore underdevelopment; while part three contains statements by Liberian politicians about their efforts to effect radical change. These Liberian politicians include Gabriel Bacchus Matthews of the Progressive Alliance of Liberia (PAL), H. Boima Fahnbulleh, Togba-Nah Tipoteh and Dew Tuan-Wleh Mayson of the Movement for Justice in Africa (MOJA).

446  **An economic history of West Africa.**
A[nthony] G. Hopkins.   New York: Columbia University, 1973. 337p. 17 maps. bibliog. (Columbia Economic History of the Modern World Series).

A comprehensive account of the region with an interdisciplinary perspective which seeks 'to direct attention away from the adventures and triumphs of great leaders, past and present, and towards the activities of the overwhelming majority of Africans' (p. 296). Hopkins describes traditional domestic economies and their involvement in external and colonial trade up until 1960, with particular reference to the study's central theme which deals with 'the interaction of the various internal and external factors which have determined the structure and performance of the market economy' (p. 293).

447 **Liberia: recent economic developments and medium-term prospects.**
Washington, DC: International Bank for Reconstruction and Development (World Bank), Dec. 1982. 112p. (World Bank Report, no. 4178-LBR).

This report by the World Bank assesses the state of the Liberian economy in the aftermath of the *coup d'état* of April 1980. The investigators found a military government willing to take the necessary austerity measures to alleviate the economic crisis which it inherited. Attention is paid to: the implementation of a programme of graduated reductions in public sector salaries; the need for improvement in tax administration; the strengthening of development administration; the enforcement of concession agreements; and the expansion of forestry, rubber, and upland rice production. Although the point is conceded that future development of the country was dependant in large measure on the world market prices for Liberia's principal commodities, the military government is given credit for its initial internal management efforts.

448 **Toward a political economy of Liberia.**
Khafre Kadallah. *Review of African Political Economy*, vol. 12 (1978), p. 105-13.

Writing from a Marxist perspective, the author traces the historical development of the economy from the establishment of Liberia as a colony in 1822 to its emergence as a 'neo-colony' in the twentieth century. The emphasis is on the post-Second World War period when, it is argued, a true class system emerged.

449 **Transformation of Liberian peasantry under peripheral capitalism.**
I. Sorie Kondowa Kajue. PhD thesis, University of Manchester, Manchester, England, 1987. 304p. (UMI order no. BRD-83928).

Explores the impact of capitalism on the peasant economy and society of Lofa county, Liberia. The broader context of the study is that of the development of colonial capitalism in developing countries, using the Mende social organization to demonstrate the economic impact of capitalism.

450 **The investment climate in three West African countries: Liberia, the Ivory Coast and Ghana.**
Erasmus H. Kloman. PhD thesis, University of Pennsylvania, Philadelphia, Pennsylvania, 1962. 448p. (Order no. 62-4316).

Presents a comparative appraisal of the domestic attitude to foreign private capital investment in three west African countries, Liberia, the Côte d'Ivoire (Ivory Coast) and Ghana during the 1950s.

451 **The Open Door policy of Liberia: an economic history of modern Liberia.**
Fred van der Kraaij. Bremen, Germany: Ubersee-Museum Bremen. 1983. 2 vols. (Series F. Bremen Africa Archives 17/1, XXI and 17/2, IV).

The first volume constitutes the main body of work, while the second volume contains endnotes, annexes, a bibliography, and an index, etc. The work is an overall study of a country moving from a subsistance to a market economy. The author's main aim seems to be to show how capitalist corporations, which had been invited into an 'open economy', removed all the constraints which were holding back the export sector and therefore created in Liberia a dependency on foreign investments and export-oriented production. The book details the arrival of Firestone, LAMCO (Liberian-Swedish-American-Mining Company), the Bong Mining Company, and the logging companies, among others and shows how each contributed to the 'economics of dependency'. Moreover, it is asserted that the assumed motive for the government's Open Door policy was to ensure that a ruling élite, responsible for selling Liberia to the multinationals, would remain in power. This work essentially supports the thesis of Clower, Dalton (et al.) in *Growth Without Development* (q.v.) which discusses the principle of dubious growth without development in Liberia. Proposals are made for reversing this trend of economic dependency.

452 **Liberia economic survey.**
*African Development* (London), July 1976, p. 719-46.

The contents of this interesting survey include: 'Liberia's resilient economy'; 'Iron ore mining – waiting for the new projects'; 'Liberia's first five-year plan'; 'Hopeful prospects in rubber'; 'National bank and the currency chestnut'; 'Diamond mining/insurance industry', all by A. Rake; 'Transport problems' by Warkeh T-Toe; 'Steady growth of co-operatives' by R. Goodridge; and 'Labour and employment' by J. Makobi.

453 **Foreign investment and development in Liberia.**
Russell U. McLaughlin. New York: Praeger Publishers, 1966. 217p.

Surveys the Liberian economy of the 1960s and emphasizes the controlling role of foreign investment in the private sector, and foreign, particularly American, aid in the public sector.

454 **Administrative machinery for development planning in Liberia.**
Ozay Mehmet. *Journal of Modern African Studies*, vol. 13, no. 3 (1975), p. 510-18.

Citing statistics that attest to Liberia's striking economic performance in the 1950s and early 1960s, the author asserts that local management and institutions played only a marginal role in development. Although the profit motive and Tubman's Open Door tax concession policy provided the initial stimulus for investment, it was the engine of foreign capital and management that propelled the growth of an enclave economic sector upon which the national economy rested. To reverse this trend of 'growth without development', fundamental administrative reorganization through the government's ministry of planning and economic affairs was required. The author explains that reorganization along these lines must also be linked to political reforms and he focuses in particular on the patronage political system which had stifled development.

455  **Lagos Plan of Action for the economic development of Africa, 1980-2000.**
Organization of African Unity.   Geneva: International Institute for Labour Studies, 1981. 132p.

Presents a strategy for development adopted by the Heads of State and Government of the OAU summit meeting at Lagos, 28-29 April 1980, which stressed co-operative, internal and inter-African approaches to development, considering 'sectoral integration at the continental level, and particularly in the fields of agriculture, food transport and communication, industry, and energy' (p. 128). For a good sequel, see the workshop proceedings edited by David Fashole Luke and Timothy M. Shaw, entitled *Continental crisis: the Lagos Plan of Action and Africa's future* (Lanham, Maryland: New York: University Press of America, and Dalhousie University Centre for African Studies, 1984. 231p).

456  **Gender and population in the adjustment of African economies: planning for change.**
Ingrid Palmer.   *Women, Work and Development*, Series no. 19, 1991, 187p.

Maintains that gender issues should be taken systematically into account when planning structural economic change, because, without a gender perspective in development and population policy analyses, resource misallocation will persist and possibly impair the chances of achieving sustainable growth in Africa.

457  **Political economy as adapted to the republic of Liberia.**
James Spriggs Payne.   Monrovia: G. Killian, Printer – *Liberia Herald* office, 1860. 186p.

This is a 'prize essay' written by Liberia's fourth president, The Rev. James S. Payne (1868-70), with an introduction by Liberia's second president, Stephen Allen Benson (1856-64). Contents include: the claim of political economy upon the nation; the circumstances influencing the creation of capital; the circumstances influencing the creation of capital, continued; the creation of capital; obstacles to the creation of capital; the effect of encouragement upon production; and essential accompaniments of production.

458  **The economies of West Africa.**
Douglas Rimmer.   New York: St. Martin's, 1984. 308p. map. bibliog.

In this examination of the economies of the sixteen sovereign states of ECOWAS (Economic Community of West African States) the author dwells on the period from 1960 to the early 1980s as he examines economic structures, population and the labour force, external trade, policy instruments, and development policies. Rimmer is Director of the Centre of West African Studies, University of Birmingham, Birmingham, England.

### 459 The Mano River Union.

Peter Robson. *Journal of Modern African Studies*, vol. 20 (Dec. 1982), p. 613-23.

Examines the structure, progress, and potential of the Mano River Union, which was inaugurated in October 1973 by Liberia and Sierra Leone. Guinea became a member of this customs union in 1980.

### 460 The tax system of Liberia: report of the tax mission.

Carl S. Shoup, assisted by Douglas Dosser, Rudolph G. Penner, William S. Vickerey. New York: Columbia University Press, 1970. 189p.

This is a report produced by a group of American tax experts commissioned by the government of Liberia to conduct a comprehensive examination of the national tax system with a view to recommending measures for improvement. A number of recommendations were advanced, all of them designed to: ensure that Liberia's tax revenue would rise more rapidly as its national income increased; eliminate some of the tax burden on low-income families; and facilitate national economic development.

### 461 The Liberia-Lamco Joint Venture partnership: the future of less developed country and multinational corporation collaboration as a national strategy for host country development.

James Teah Tarpeh. PhD thesis, University of Pittsburgh, Pittsburgh, Pennsylvania, 1978. 662p.

The primary purpose of this study is to explore the economic and social effects of the Lamco Joint Venture Company (LJVC) and Lamco on Liberia's development potential. Among the findings of the study were that LJVC made useful contributions to the economic and sociocultural development of Liberia – namely, improving employment opportunities and social amenities such as schools and hospitals in the enclave communities of the LJVC, etc.

### 462 Public economic development policy and practice in contemporary Liberia.

Togba Nah Tipoteh. *Journal of African Studies*, vol. 1, no. 2 (1974), p. 158-74.

The author, a professor of economics and a leading critic of the Tolbert administration of the 1970s, asserts that although the government's stated policy was to promote economic self-reliance, the very opposite occurred and Liberia experienced 'under-development'. This was due to the country's Western institutional biases and its free enterprise economy which fostered dependency on foreign capital.

### 463 Liberia: need to improve accountability and control of US assistance.

Gaithsburg, Maryland: United States General Accounting Office. Report to the Honorable Edward M. Kennedy, US Senate, 1987. 43p.

This report was produced as the result of an investigation into US economic, food and security assistance programmes to Liberia since 1980 in an attempt to determine whether or not controls over US funding are adequate. It shows that, between 1980 and 1986, Liberia received almost US$434 million in aid. The report concluded that 'control' problems did exist. The Liberian government had failed to comply with 'established assistance agreements' and in some cases funds had been misappropriated.

### 464 Untying technical assistance: a Liberian illustration.
*International Development Review, Focus Technical Cooperation*
(Washington, DC), no. 1 (1975), p. 19-23.

An analysis of foreign assistance programmes in Liberia accompanied by illustrated data. The article concludes that providing technical assistance on an unconditional basis would be a considerable improvement over the conditional aid arrangement then in existence. Suggestions are advanced as to how to bring about the desired change.

### 465 Decentralization and culture: the case of Monrovia, Liberia.
Herbert Werlin. *Public Administration and Development*, vol. 10 (1990), p. 251-61.

'The World Bank's urban development project in Monrovia, Liberia, attempted to pay for services and infrastructure provided [for] under this project. Because of cultural barriers and a blueprint approach, the project resulted in charity rather than institutional reform. However, effective approaches and procedures require more attention to the underlying causes of existing problems. In as much as politics, even more than culture, affects decentralization, the World Bank needs to be more open with its borrowers about political requirements' (author's summary, p. 251).

# Commerce, Industry and Trade

### 466 Liberia's rubber outgrowers: an economic appraisal.
Christopher M. Brown.    PhD thesis, Fletcher School of Law and Diplomacy, Tufts University, Medford, Massachusetts, 1989. 279p. (UMI order no. DA8919377).

In 1988, Liberia was the largest rubber-producing country in Africa, and the fourth largest rubber exporter in the world. Against this background, this study assesses the profitability and the international comparative advantage position of outgrowers to determine the extent to which private rubber farming might continue as a source of employment and exports for Liberia. It finds that outgrowers farming may continue to be profitable for the farmers and the economy providing: aging tree stocks are replanted; there is a closer alignment between farmers' financial incentives and the government's economic benefit; and the government supports the privatization of some 6,000 acres of prime plantations seized in 1980 from officials of the deposed Tolbert régime and other presumed 'élites'.

### 467 Realizing the development opportunity created by an iron ore mining concession in Liberia: the Yekepa model.
George P. Butler.    Monrovia: Sebanoh Print Press, 1978. 109p.

Prepared under the auspices of the Partnership for Productivity Foundation in Liberia, this article attempts to establish a model to limit the exploitive impact of concessionaires dealing with depletable resources. This is achieved by obliging the concessionaires to implement development opportunities for the local communities and their residents.

### 468 Liberia: open door to travel and investment.
Monrovia: Department of Information and Cultural Affairs, 1967. 95p.

This compilation of basic information on the country was intended at this time both to promote and to provide information on travel and investment in Liberia.

### 469  Iron ore in the Liberian economy.

William Amara Freeman. *The Liberian Economic and Management Review*, vol. 2, no. 2 (1973), p. 59-71.

Presents a summary of the growth of the iron ore industry in Liberia and assesses its impact on the economy in terms of government revenue, infrastructure development, technical training, and foreign exchange earnings.

### 470  'Entrepreneurship in Liberia'.

Winston Penn Handwerker. *Liberian Studies Journal*, vol 5, no. 2 (1972), p. 113-47.

Emphasizes the importance of small-scale businesses and the part that they play in the community especially in providing a service which cannot be obtained elsewhere. Through profit redistribution amongst the family, it is more than just the entrepreneur who profits. Handwerker comments on what he sees as 'the largest concentrated pool of talent and energy in Liberia'.

### 471  History of mining in Liberia.

A. E. Nyema Jones. *The Liberian Historical Review*, vol. 5 (1969), p. 53-59.

The author, a pioneer Liberian geologist, presents in this brief article a historical survey of mining activities in Liberia. Following a cursory commentary on indigenous Liberia's 'mining methods', Jones surveys the mining industry in Liberia beginning with exploratory efforts in the 1930s through to: the establishment of the Liberia Mining Company in 1946; the Liberian-American-Swedish Mining Company (LAMCO) in 1953; the German-Liberian Mining Company (DELIMCO or Bong Mines) in the 1950s; and the National Iron Ore Company in the 1960s. A brief history of the government's Bureau of Natural Resources and Surveys is also included.

### 472  The Firestone story: a history of the Firestone tire and rubber company.

Alfred Lief. New York: McGraw-Hill, 1951. 437p.

Based on an impressive list of company sources, documents on Liberia, biographies, US government sources, and documents connected with litigations, this study highlights various periods in Firestone's history starting with the foundation of the Firestone Tire and Rubber Company in Akron, Ohio, on 3rd August 1900. The work also chronicles the commencement of the company's activities in Liberia in 1924 and the fiftieth anniversary celebrations. Several of the book's chapters deal with Liberia in detail, particularly chapter eleven 'Liberia and Restriction', and chapter twenty-one 'Liberia and the offensive'.

### 473  The evolution of energy planning in Liberia.

Miedi-Himie Neufville, William F. Barron, Patricia Koshel. *Energy System and Policy*, vol. 10, no. 2 (1987), p. 149-66.

Suggests how the institutional machinery used in energy planning in Liberia could be improved. Although the authors advise against adhering rigidly to any one 'model' of planning, given the unique context of Liberia's policy formulation they suggest that 'Liberia's experience offers useful lessons for other countries and donor institutions'.

474 **The ports of Liberia: economic significance and development problems.**
W. Schulze. In: *Seaports and development in Tropical Africa.* Edited by B. S. Hoyle, D. Hilling. New York: Praeger, 1970, p. 75-101.

Discusses the geographical and technical characteristics of the Liberian ports of Monrovia, Buchanan, Greenville, Harper and Robertsport, as well as problems associated with development.

475 **The Lebanese in Liberia: a study of their influence upon the agricultural marketing process.**
William Richard Stanley. *Abstracts, Annals of the Association of American Geography,* (New York State University, Cortland) vol. 59, no. 1 (1969), p. 203. map.

In spite of their importance in the economy, this minority group of residents in Liberia has received very little scholarly attention. Arriving in Liberia toward the end of the nineteenth century, Lebanese have operated as traders, large-scale wholesale entrepreneurs, and agricultural marketeers. They have played a part in rubber, iron ore and lumber enterprises as they established themselves in various parts of the country. Stanley also comments: 'the distribution and density of Lebanese stores in Liberia not only indicate a close relationship to the road pattern, but also to those areas of relatively high agricultural development'.

476 **Transport expansion in Liberia.**
William Richard Stanley. *Geographical Review,* vol. 60, no. 4 (1970), p. 529-47.

Surveys the events which stimulated the development of transport in Liberia. Covering trade contacts between Liberia and Europeans from the fifteenth through to the nineteenth century, Stanley points out how these contacts led to the emergence of small ports along the coast, only a few of which – Monrovia, Buchanan, Greenville and Harper – survived into the twentieth century. These entry ports and the economic activity they engendered encouraged road construction. The stationing of US troops in Liberia during World War II, and the discovery of iron ore deposits in commercially exploitable quantities at several locations in the interior of Liberia encouraged the development of the transport system. Both events necessitated the expansion of the port facilities in Monrovia, construction of a port at Buchanan, and the development of road and rail links to the interior. The unevenness in the development of transport is stressed.

477 **Rural transport development in Liberia.**
W. R. Stanley. *Rural Africana,* vol. 15 (1971), p. 89-96.

Outlines the history of road construction in rural Liberia. Road-building began in 1906 with the development of the nation's first rubber plantation at Mount Barclay, but transport facilities seriously lagged behind developments in neighbouring countries until the 1960s largely because of the absence of an overall cohesive policy. Even then it took many years of divergent philosophies, priorities, and methods advocated by the Liberian government and donor agencies before a shared realization developed that no real development in the agricultural and other sectors could be achieved without a concerted effort in rural road construction.

478 **Changing export patterns of Liberia's seaports.**
William Richard Stanley.   In: *Seaport systems and spatial change:
technology, industry, and development strategies.*   Edited by B. S. Hoyle,
D. Hilling.   New York: John Wiley, 1984, p. 435-59.

Building upon the work of the late Professor Willie O. Schulze of Giessen, Germany,
(q.v.) this chapter attempts to document the connection between the development of
Liberia's ports and economic growth and social development.

479 **Africa and the sea.**
Edited by Jeffry C. Stone.   Proceedings of a colloquium at Aberdeen
University, United Kingdom, March, 1984. 412 columns. (Aberdeen
University African Studies Group).

This colloquium opens with an introductory overview regarding the role of the sea in
African history and economic development in the continent. Of particular relevance to
Liberia are papers on the Kru Coast Revolt by Jo Ann Sullivan, fisheries in Sierra Leone
by M. K. Hendrix, and other contributions on continent-wide issues such as fisheries, the
law of the sea, and international maritime transport.

480 **The Firestone operation in Liberia.**
Wayne C. Taylor.   Washington, DC: National Planning Association,
1956. 115p. illus.

This is the fifth in a series of case studies by the National Planning Association on US
business performance abroad. The study considers what was one of the first American
experiments involving investment and large-scale plantation operations in tropical
Africa. Taylor devotes the first third of the book to a survey of Liberian geography,
history, economics, society and politics. The steps leading to the Firestone concession of
1926 are then related from the perspective of the American investors. The final section
of the book evaluates Firestone's impact on the country and the implications for the
company and for the future of Liberia. The book's publication coincided with the
thirtieth anniversary of Firestone's commercial endeavours in Liberia.

481 **Marketing in Liberia.**
John Crown.   Washington, DC: US Department of Commerce,
International Trade Administration, 1982. 22p. (International Marketing
Information Series, Overseas Business Report, OBR 82-12).

Provides basic information (which was valid at the time) on distribution and sales
facilities, trade regulations, commercial practices, marketing aids, taxation, government
procurement, investment, industrial property protection, business organization, employment as well as more general notes for business travellers to Liberia.

# Agriculture and Forestry

482 **Rice production and marketing in Liberia.**
C. Roy Adair, Herschel B. Ellis, Fred T. Cooke, Jr., Armin Grunewald.
Washington, DC: USAID, Survey Report, United States Department of
Agriculture co-operating with the Agency for International Development.
March 16-April 24, 1968. 51p.
Liberia was reported to be self-sufficient in rice production in 1945 but after 1948 there
was a gradual but steady increase in the amount of rice imported. To address this
growing deficit, the Liberian government, with the assistance of the American
government, undertook a study of rice marketing and production. The US Department of
Agriculture conducted the study on behalf of USAID and this report is the result of that
study. It attributes the rice deficit primarily to the movement of farm workers from rural
areas to the capital city and into industry and recommends policies that 'will provide
incentives to farmers to increase their rice production', and 'develop and extend to
farmers new technologies for growing rice' (p. 2).

483 **Liberian agricultural programmes: the theory and practice of
marketing and food distribution systems.**
Austin Kwaku Amegashie. PhD thesis, University of Florida,
Gainesville, Florida, 1978. 186p.
Focuses on the key topics of food, markets and marketing, production factors, and socio-
economic considerations. Against the background of the world's food production
problems, Liberia's food supplies are reviewed in the light of its increasing population.
One important conclusion of this thesis is that national agricultural programmes must be
integrated into other major development programmes.

484  **Stand and Problematik der Agrarforderungsinstitutionen in Liberia.**
(Institutional aspects of agricultural development in Liberia.)
E. Baum.  *Tropenlandwirt*, no. 78 (1977), p. 47-61.

Asserts that the institutional infrastructure for agricultural development in Liberia is inadequately financed, staffed, and organized. Accordingly, agricultural reform measures designed to increase food supply cannot have a meaningful impact. This study describes agricultural training and research particularly at the Agricultural Extension Training Centre, the Booker Washington Institute, the University of Liberia's College of Agriculture and Forestry, and the government's Agricultural Research Station. It is highly critical of the government's agricultural policies during the 1970s.

485  **Social institutional profile: management practices and prospects, a study of the Liberian agricultural sector.**
Jeanette Carter, Martin Ford, Winston Penn Handwerker, Svend Holsoe (et al.).  Binghamton, New York: Institute for Development Anthropology, 1984. 155p.

This is an important collaborative study involving American and Liberian academics. The work focuses on public administration in the country and the consequences of Liberia's patron-client structure. Consideration is also given to the prospects for change in the agricultural sector and notes are provided on land tenure, small commercial farmers, the extension service of the ministry of agriculture in Bong County, a Bong County Agriculture Development Project and a private agriculture concession institution in Liberia.

486  **Small farmers' response to economic incentives: a case study of small farmers in Liberia.**
Florence Alletta Chenoweth.  PhD thesis, University of Wisconsin, Madison, Wisconsin, 1986. 445p.

Presents the results of a research programme carried out between 1970 and 1980 which investigated the activities and requirements of small-scale subsistence farmers, upon whom the country is dependent for its agricultural production. It found that national polices were not directed toward the needs of these farmers. Rather than creating a food-pricing policy that took its cue from these food producers, the policies of the government favoured urban consumers instead. The author, who was Minister of Agriculture during the late 1970s concludes: 'a reorientation of this policy is seen as the most important step that the government of Liberia can take to raise agricultural productivity and attain a more equitable distribution of the fruits of development'.

487  **The evergreen forests of Liberia.**
George Proctor Cooper, Samuel J. Record.  New Haven, Connecticut: Yale University Press, 1931. 167p.

During the late 1920s areas of Liberia's timberland were cleared to meet the requirements of the Firestone Plantations Company in Harbel. This study was the product of a financial offer to the Yale University School of Forestry by Harvey S. Firestone and was originally suggested by Rudolph Block, an ardent collector of rare and unusual woods. Some 500 specimens were obtained, representing 300 species (eighteen of which were new discoveries), 222 genera, and 68 families of woods. Six types of terrain were identified: coastal mangrove swamps; tropical evergreen forests; fringing forests; deciduous forests; parkland forests; and savannah grassland.

### 488 Agricultural land development in Liberia.

Robert L. Curry. *Journal of International Law and Economics*, vol. 6, no. 1 (1971), p. 125-37.

This article criticizes agricultural land development in Liberia, the primary objective of which has been to maximize rubber exports from large concessions. The author's chief argument is that in the context of price decline for crude rubber in the 1964-68 period, Liberia can ill-afford increased acreage devoted to that crop. It is, however, asserted that if rubber is to remain a primary commodity, public policy should provide greater assistance to independent farmers who collectively own more land than the concessions, but lack the capital to develop it. Alternatively, it is argued the government should seek to transform small-scale farming into a surplus-producing commercial sector.

### 489 Farming systems research in three counties in Liberia: a reconnaissance survey in Grand Gedeh, Nimba, and Bong Counties.

Timothy R. Frankenberger. Farming System Support Project.

Gainesville, Florida: University of Florida, April 1985. 178p.

This multidisciplinary study focuses on nineteen villages in three Liberian interior counties during 1984. The survey of farming systems shows that within the study area there were differences in rice planting methods, the degree of crop diversity, and the length of fallow. Also revealed was the significance of tree cropping and intercropping as regards rice and cassava production.

### 490 Liberia: ministry of planning and economic affairs: 1971 census of agriculture summary report for Liberia (preliminary).

Monrovia. Government of Liberia, 1973. 70p.

Presents a general summary of the agricultural characteristics of the major administrative divisions of Liberia. This publication has become widely recognized as the first complete census of Liberian agriculture.

### 491 Forest resources of Liberia.

Karl R. Mayer. Washington, DC: United States Department of Agriculture (Office of Foreign Agricultural Relations) and United States Department of State (Technical Cooperation Administration). US Government Printing Office, Washington, DC, October 1951. 69p.

This United States government-funded survey of Liberia's forest resources aimed 'to determine the approximate area, volume, composition, quality, distribution, and operability of Liberian forests'; and 'to recommend a program for the protection, development, and rational utilization of the forest resources' (p. 3). Appendixes include a field identification of Liberian tree species; an alphabetical list of tree species identified; and a tree and timber guide.

492 **Producing rice in Liberia: the farmer's case.**
Monrovia: Ministry of Agriculture, 1979. 7p.

This pamphlet was released by the government in response to the initial controversy surrounding the Ministry of Agriculture's annual report of 1978, which recommended an increase in the price of rice in order to stimulate domestic production. The publication's purpose was to contain further public protest by explaining the plight of the farmer, 'the orphan of agriculture in Liberia' (p. 4). It failed in its objective and indeed the proposed increase in the price of rice, Liberia's staple food, remained a major issue and one of the factors that led to the collapse of the government of Liberia in April 1980.

493 **Rice in West Africa: policy and economics.**
Edited by Scott R. Pearson, J. Dirok Stryker, Charles Humphreys.
Stanford, California: Stanford University Press, 1981. 482p.

Examines rice production, consumption and trade in five west African countries: the Ivory Coast; Liberia; Sierra Leone; Senegal; and Mali. It includes a mix of 'country-by-country' and comparative analysis. Chapters three and four, by Eric A. Monke cover Liberia, tracing the evolution of rice production policy, pointing out that it was only with the slow-down in income from the mining and rubber sectors of the economy toward the end of the 1960s that the government began turning its attention toward agriculture, although this change in emphasis produced few important results during the 1970s. Among his recommendations is increased government promotion of more efficient rice production technologies.

494 **Reconnaissance soil survey of Liberia.**
William E. Reed. Washington, DC: United States Department of Agriculture, Office of Foreign Agricultural Assistance, and United States Department of State, Technical Cooperation Administration, June 1951. 107p. (Agriculture Information Bulletin, no. 66).

This is a scientific inventory of Liberian soil, which classifies, maps and explores the factors that determine soil use. Topics covered include: general physiography and geology; classification of soils; agriculture and soil management; and policies for future land use. The study divides Liberian crops into three groups on the basis of their adaptability to climate and soil.

495 **The proposed Sarpo national park in Liberia: a field survey of prospects and problems.**
Phillip T. Robinson. In: *National Geographic Society research reports: on research and exploration projects supported by the National Geographic Society, for which an initial grant or continuing support was provided in the years 1980-1983*, vol. 21. Compiled and edited by Winfield Swanson. Washington, DC: National Geographic Society, p. 425-35.

The proposed Sarpo National Forest is a 419-square mile location in Sinoe County considered 'of sufficient size, biologic diversity, low non-renewable natural resource potential, and zero population density available for national park development. Moreover, a high percentage of its land area is unmodified primary forest containing significant populations and diversity of wildlife characteristic of the Liberian forest biome' (p. 425). Based on field work carried out between the 6th of January and the 6th of April 1982, recommendations were advanced through the Division of Wildlife and National Parks within the Liberian Forestry Development Authority to the Liberian government that the Sarpo Forest be made a National Park.

496  **A history of agriculture in Liberia, 1822-1970: transference of American values.**
Santosh C. Saha.  Lewiston, New York: Edwin Mellen Press, 1990. 128p.

Presents a brief but interesting outline of the history of the Liberian state with particular emphasis on the development of agriculture. Focusing on the nineteenth century, Saha attempts to dispute a thesis advanced by some historians that agricultural activities were sublimated by the settler ruling class because of a bias toward trade. Unfortunately, the study pays little attention to the more modern period.

497  **Local participation and institution building: the case of the Lofa county agricultural development project in Liberia.**
Dominic Nmah Tarpeh.  DPA thesis, State University of New York at Albany, Albany, New York, 1984, 542p. (Order no. DA8414325).

The stated purpose of this study was to examine the extent of local participation, especially by farmers, in decision-making associated with the project. A further aim was to discover to what degree local wherewithal was developed in order to sustain the project. The results were that the original blueprint of the project hindered effective local involvement in decision-making. The agricultural inputs and services provided through the project did reach the targeted small farmers but there was a preoccupation with the desire to protect the large capital investment and show quick visible results. Indeed this overriding aim overshadowed the need to develop local capabilities to sustain the project.

498  **Liberia: agricultural sector review.**
World Bank.  Washington, DC: World Bank Report, no. 4200-LBR, April 20 1984. 4 vols. 479p.

This World Bank report is one of the most comprehensive reviews of Liberian agriculture ever published. It provides general background information, details the major constraints facing production on a crop-by-crop basis, outlines the framework of agricultural institutions, critically assesses past development objectives, and advances alternative strategies. 'Food security', a policy of crop diversification is recommended in preference to rice self-sufficiency, which was at this time a government objective which had met with failure. Volume I is the 'main report' and consists of 74 pages. Volume II has two 'supporting papers' respectively entitled 'Food economy' (1-92p.) and 'Forestry sub-sector' (93-132p.) Volume III, 'Supporting papers', is broken down into 'Treecrops production' (1-137p.) and 'Treecrops processing and marketing' (138-166p.). The final volume's 'Supporting papers' cover such topics as 'Institutional framework' (1-74p.) and 'Problems and possibilities of privatization of marketing and import supply' (75-107p.).

# Employment and Labour

499 **Employment and multinational enterprises in export processing zones: the cases of Liberia and Ghana.**
George Botchie. Monrovia: University of Liberia. Published by the International Labour Office (ILO) Geneva, Switzerland, 1984, 74p. (Working Paper, no. 30).

This is one in a series of working papers prepared for an ILO study on multinationals in Export Processing Zones (EPZs). Botchie seeks 'to evaluate the direct and indirect employment effects of direct MNE (Multinational Enterprise) investment in EPZs in the two west African countries, Liberia and Ghana' (p. 1). He concluded that experience of the EPZ in Ghana in the context of the multinationals promoting employment has been positive, while for Liberia it has been negative. With high expectations, Liberia had invested US $15 million to equip the zone yet only one multinational enterprise had invested and this had resulted in the direct employment of only fifty workers.

500 **Schooling, work experience and earnings: a study of determinants of earnings in a Third World Corporate Setting.**
Roland Durberg. Stockholm, Sweden: Institute of International Education, 1982. 165p.

With special reference to the activities of the Liberian-Swedish-American Mining Company in Liberia the aim of this study is 'to investigate determinants of earnings ..., to estimate the relative importance of these determinants, [and] to compare the determinants between different sectors'. Among the conclusions of the study is the evidence that there is a threshold effect of education, with very little payoff to basic education. Instead, 'work experience and specific on-the-job training is a much more powerful predictor of earnings than formal education' (Abstract).

501 **Collective bargaining and security of employment in Africa: English-speaking countries: proceedings of, & documents submitted to, a symposium (Victoria Falls, Zimbabwe, 4-8 May 1987).**
Washington, DC: International Labour Office, 1988. 259p.

This is a report of the proceedings of a regional symposium on the promotion of collective bargaining and the protection of security of employment in English-speaking African countries. It is available from ILO, 1828 L. Street, NW, Washington, DC 20036.

502 **Multinationals and employment in a West African sub-region: Liberia and Sierra Leone.**
Olukunle Iyanda. Geneva: International Labour Office, 1984. 49p.
(Working Paper, no. 29).

This ILO study, conducted by a Nigerian professor at the University of Lagos, focuses on the employment generated by multinational enterprises in Liberia and Sierra Leone and makes the following conclusions: that foreign direct investment is unevenly distributed in favour of more advanced countries; that multinationals do not constitute the major source of employment; that multinationals are concentrated in the primary sector of mining (including agriculture for Liberia); and that in both countries multinationals 'operate largely as foreign enclaves, with little or no traditional linkages or integration with the local economy' (p. 33).

503 **Civil Service Development Project, Government of Liberia final report: a cooperative effort between Civil Service Agency of the Republic of Liberia and California State Personnel Board.**
Available from Library of Congress, Washington, DC, 1979. 47p.

In September 1974 the California State Personnel Board entered into a contract with the United States Agency for International Development (USAID) to provide technical assistance and training to the Civil Service Agency of Liberia. As an integral part of the contract, this final report was to be prepared at the conclusion of the contract summarizing the results and the co-operative effort made to create an effective government personnel management system. The report covers activities which occurred during the contract period from September 1974 to February 1979.

504 **Labour in Liberia.**
Dew Tuan-Wleh Mayson, Amos C. Sawyer. *Review of African Political Economy*, vol. 14 (1979), p. 3-15.

Traces the development of peripheral capitalism in Liberia. The authors emphasize: the totally dependent nature of the country's export economy which is dominated by multinational corporations; the deteriorating economic position of the workers and peasants; and the growing power of the ruling class. The growth of the working class and its increasing militancy since 1961, the legislative response to this in the form of anti-strike legislation and the consequent worsening of workers' conditions and standards of living is also discussed. Mayson, now a wealthy Liberian businessman living in Paris, was a militant politician in Liberia during the 1970s. Sawyer, President of the interim government of Liberia in Monrovia (1990-94) was a close associate of Mayson.

505 **Civil service pay in Africa.**
Derek Robinson. Washington, DC: International Labour Office, 1990.
220p.

This book, which is based on evidence gathered from a sample of civil servants, provides data on wage levels and hierarchies, job classification, recruitment, promotion and fringe benefits.

506 **Labour in Liberia.**
United States Department of Labour. Washington, DC: Foreign Labor Information, Bureau of Labor Statistics, May 1960. 22p.

This government compilation examines the conditions experienced by workers in Liberia during the 1950s. Topics covered include: wages and conditions of work; labour–management relations; and labour legislation. The primary source of information for this study is cited as being an unpublished US Foreign Service report dated 6 January 1959.

507 **Foreign labor trends: Liberia.**
United States Department of Labour. Washington, DC: Bureau of International Labour Affairs, 1987. 9p. (FLT 87-44).

Prepared by the US Embassy in Monrovia, this annual survey of labour trends includes key labour indicators, as well as updates on the political economy, employment, education and training, labour unions, and recent labour activities. Most of the information is drawn from Liberian government sources. Of related interest are the issues from 1988-89 (FLT 89-40); 1989 (FLT 90-48); and 1987-88 (FLT 89-11).

508 **Cases, statutes, and materials on Liberian labor law.**
Tuan Wreh. Monrovia: Wreh News Agency, 1977. 281p.

This is a compilation of cases, statutes and other materials dealing with 'the evolution of labor problems and labor policies within the Republic of Liberia since the 1850s and up to the 1970s and the Liberian government's umpire role in regulating and adjudicating labor-management frictions, practices and grievances' (p. v). The contents include: The history of industrial relations (chapter 1); Illegal dismissals (chapter 2); Workmen's compensation (chapter 3); The rise of the labor unions (chapter 4); Recrudescence of strikes (chapter 5); and Government employees (chapter 6). Seven appendices cover such items as 'An Act creating the Civil Service Agency', and 'Ministry of Labor, regulations on collective bargaining and representation election'.

**The economies of West Africa.**
*See* item no. 458.

# Education

509 **The trustees of donation for education in Liberia: a story of philanthropic endeavor, 1850-1923.**
Gardner Weld Allen. Boston, Massachusetts: Thomas Todd Co., 1923. 132p.

This is perhaps the first account of the history of Liberia College, now the University of Liberia. It was written at the instance of the Trustees of Donation for Education in Liberia, the American philanthropic organization that founded the educational institution in Liberia. Upon the initiative of the Massachusetts State Colonization Society and the endorsement of the American Colonization Society, a board of the Trustees of Donation was formed and locally chartered. These developments were then conveyed to the Liberian national leadership whose president, Joseph Jenkins Roberts, expressed in a reply his delight 'at the prospect of having permanently established in Liberia the means of education – a Collegiate Education'. Eventually an Act of the Legislature was passed and approved (24 December 1851) establishing Liberia College and incorporating a Board of Trustees with the necessary powers. Roberts became the College's first president in 1856, but the institution was not formally opened until 2 February 1863.

510 **Vocational guidance for Liberian schools.**
Bertha Baker Azango. London: Macmillan, 1966. 176p.

This booklet is one of the few publications about vocational counselling and it provides information for Liberian students especially at the secondary education level. Issues highlighted include the background knowledge and qualifications required for various types of vocational training at this time (1966).

511 **Educational laws of the Republic of Liberia.**
Bertha Baker Azango. Monrovia: Ministry of Education, 1968. 173p.

Contains a random compilation of laws, or legislative enactments, relating to education. Some of these laws deal with educational administration such as the creation of the Ministry of Education, teacher education, and other areas of educational activities in Liberia.

512 **The present socio-economic situation in Liberia and its implications for the educational system.**
Bertha Baker Azango. *Liberian Research Journal*, vol. 6, no. 3 (1971), p. 1-34.

This important study relates socio-economic problems to the educational development of Liberia. The article considers such subjects as national integration, illiteracy, population growth, rural and industrial development, agriculture and mining, in the context of the critical needs of education in Liberia.

513 **Education and national development in Liberia, 1800-1900.**
Mary Antoinette Hope Grimes Brown. PhD dissertation, Cornell University, Ithaca, New York, 1967. 240p.

This major work is one of the few comprehensive studies on 19th-century Liberian education. It addresses the issues of traditional and western education and explores the need to create a synthesis of the two systems. The thesis contains a lengthy bibliography on education in Liberia.

514 **A consolidated school system for Monrovia, Liberia: report of a survey for the International Cooperation Administration.**
Leo F. Cain, John C. Connelly, Arch D. Lang, Robert R. Smith. San Francisco, California: San Francisco State College, 1961. 67p.

In 1961 a four-man team of educators from San Francisco State College was commissioned, through an agreement between the governments of Liberia and the United States, to determine the feasibility of consolidating Monrovia's scattered school districts at both the elementary and secondary levels into a single system. The report is based on information provided by the government of Liberia, and information gained by the American personnel in Liberia during their time in Monrovia and elsewhere in Liberia. Specific recommendations were advanced to create the consolidated school system and the subsequent implementation of the recommendations led to the creation of the Monrovia Consolidated School System (MCSS).

515 **Rural education and research in Liberia: an evaluation.**
Augustus F. Caine. *Rural Africana*, vol. 15 (1971), p. 37-50.

The author, a Liberian minister of education (1965-70) contends that rural education in Liberia can only be understood against the historic settler/indigene or urban/rural divide of the country. Though an independent country since 1847, the first government attempt to initiate rural education was the creation, in 1929, of the vocational training institute, the Booker Washington Institute (BWI). No other major measure was taken before the advent of the Tubman presidency (1944-71). Though the author cites some of the improvements in rural education during the Tubman years, it must be pointed out that they were accompanied by problems, among them a poor teacher/pupil ratio, poorly-prepared teachers, and greater access to resources on part of urban schools compared with their rural counterparts. Some of these difficulties contributed to a rural-urban exodus. The author asserts that if these problems are to be overcome there must be a comprehensive government policy for rural transformation and an integrated rural development programme.

516 **The cultural context of learning and thinking: an exploration in experimental anthropology.**
    Michael Cole (et al.) in association with Thomas Ciborowski (et al.).
    New York: Basic Books, 1971. 304p.

Based on an interdisciplinary effort that drew on psychology, anthropology, education and linguistics, the authors sought to understand the difficulties experienced by Kpelle-Liberians in learning Western mathematics. It is unclear what they achieved except for the assertion that the effort was experimental and consequently 'at the cutting edge of anthropological work'.

517 **Arts and crafts education for Liberian schools.**
    Cecily Delafield.   PhD thesis, Columbia University, New York. 1967.
    267p. (UMI order no. 58-2417).

The author identifies the requirements of arts and crafts education, the difficulties involved in teaching this subject in Liberian schools at this time (ca. 1967) and makes a number of recommendations.

518 **The new mathematics and an old culture: a study of learning among the Kpelle of Liberia.**
    John Gay, Michael Cole.   New York: Holt, Rinehart & Winston, 1967.
    100p.

Mathematics instructor, Gay, and psychologist, Cole, collaborated to study the cultural factors influencing learning among Kpelle-Liberians. Examining a culture undergoing rapid change in the 1960s due to various forms of Western influences, the authors discovered that the classrooms were forums for severe cultural disorientation. Remedies are suggested.

519 **Civics for Liberian schools.**
    A. Doris Banks Henries.   New York: Collier-Macmillan International,
    1966. 121p.

Considers how Liberian schoolchildren are taught about the concept of Liberian nationhood, the operation of the government, the responsibilities of the citizen, the place of Liberia in the community of nations, and the functions of the Liberian government. The perspective is largely limited to the experience of Liberians of settler background.

520 **Education and politics in Liberia and the United States: a socioeconomic comparison of colony and colonizer.**
    Stephen S. Hlophe, Randle W. Nelson.   *UMOJA: A Scholarly Journal of Black Studies*, vol. 1, (spring 1977), p. 51-71.

The authors present the findings of this case study comparing the interrelationships between the growth of higher education and the development of government policies in both countries between the 1940s and 1960s. Hlophe and Nelson assert that in the United States and Liberia there was an attempt by the socio-economic élite 'to maintain their dominant position within the prevailing socio-economic system'.

521 **A short history of Liberia college and the university of Liberia.**
Advertus A. Hoff. Monrovia: Consolidated Publications, 1962.
128p.

A short historical study of Liberia College (established 1862) and the University of
Liberia (created in 1951) from their early days until 1960. The book lists the
accomplishments of the country's oldest institution of higher education, the problems it
has faced and its role in the growth of the Liberian nation. Hoff served as President of
the University of Liberia in the early 1970s.

522 **The psychology of literacy.**
Sylvia Scribner, Michael Cole. Cambridge, Massachusetts: Harvard
University Press, 1981. 335p. bibliog.

This is a study of the Vai people of Liberia and their script which was carried out
between 1973 and 1978. The authors evolved from their 'early gropings for a functional
approach to the psychology of literacy' to 'a theoretical framework' which they 'hope
will contribute to a deeper understanding of the way in which different kinds of socially
organized practices help shape human thought' (p. ix). Included in the appendices is a
brief history of the Vai script.

523 **Education in Liberia.**
Mary Antoinette Brown Sherman. In: *Education in Africa: a
comparative survey.* Edited by A. Babs Fafunwa, J. U. Aisiku.
London: George Allen & Unwin, 1982, p. 162-87.

Surveys the history of modern education in Liberia highlighting its problems and
prospects. It is written by one of Liberia's foremost contemporary educators who was
also the first female president of the University of Liberia.

524 **The University in Modern Africa: toward the twenty-first century.**
Mary Antoinette Brown Sherman. *Journal of Higher Education,*
vol. 61, no. 4 (July–Aug. 1990), p. 363-85.

A former president of the University of Liberia, the author draws from her experience of
higher education in Liberia in her background sketch of higher educational development
on the continent. She then focuses on the problems facing the university in
contemporary Africa, 'principal among them [being] the inability as yet to integrate the
university into the life of the continent'. Her stated purpose is to establish why this is the
case and to explore ways of bringing about the desired integration of the traditional
African environment and the modern Western sector.

525 **The politics of miseducation in Liberia: the Booker Washington
Institute of Liberia, 1929-1984.**
Donald Spivak. Lexington, Kentucky: University of Kentucky Press,
1986. 177p.

Using the Booker Washington Institute (BWI) of Liberia as a case study, the book's
hypothesis is that vocational education, used in the United States to breed an economic
and politically submissive black population, was extended to Africa by Americans and
Europeans with the same intention. In the Liberian case, according to the author, black
settlers (pejoratively now called Americo-Liberians) encouraged the establishment of the
BWI in Liberia as a means of maintaining their 'hegemony' over the indigenous

population. The underlying theme of settler supremacy in Liberia and the author's own heavy reliance on conditioned American sources have been considered the norm in Liberian scholarship. However, this approach is increasingly coming under scrutiny by revisionists scholars and fresh insights are being provided by other scholars, some of whom are themselves Liberians. This development might be considered the 'Liberian phase' of the reappraisal of the history of Africa and of black America.

526 **Education and other determinants of income among heads of households in rural Liberia.**
Henrique F. Tokpa.   PhD thesis, Florida State University, Tallahassee, Florida 1988. 125p. (UMI order no. DA8822474).
Explores the effects of education and other variables on the earnings of individuals in rural Liberia, and recommends reforms to further education as a means of promoting material development in rural Liberia. The author is Vice-President of Cuttington University College.

527 **Education as related to civic progress: valedictory address on graduation at Liberia College.**
William R. Tolbert, Jr.   Monrovia: Printing Division, Ministry of Information, Cultural Affairs and Tourism, 1974. 22p.
This pamphlet contains President Tolbert's valedictory address of April 1934 at Liberia College. The work includes a foreword by Henry B. Cole, a government journalist.

# Literature

**528 An obituary for Hawa Barchu.**
C. William Allen. Monrovia: Central Printing, 1983. 100p.
This novel seeks to address the identity problem that is often experienced by the urban dwellers of Liberia who are rooted in an ethnic culture but have a Western cultural orientation. The main character, Hawa, represents the generation of young Liberians who grew up in the city and are thus largely alienated by the rapidly changing settler-Liberian dominated social order of the capital. Allen imagines, through the feelings of a woman, acute cultural alienation which leads to depression and eventually to murder.

**529 The African interior mission.**
C. William Allen. Stone Mountain, Georgia: Strugglers' Community Press, 1992. 195p.
This is a contemporary novel that dramatizes 'significant events in the lives of typical secondary school students in Liberia'. Portraying genuine friendship that transcends the indigene/settler social cleavage, the book explores some of the complexities of Liberian society, including the themes of rural *versus* urban values, and the impact of Christian missionaries on the Liberian educational system.

**530 After long silence and other Liberian stories.**
Robert H. Brown. New York: Vantage, 1979. 105p.
A collection of six short stories including some which have been published in an assortment of periodicals and anthologies.

**531 A guide to the study of Liberian literature.**
Similih M. Cordor (formerly S. Henry Cordor). Monrovia: Liberian Literary & Educational Publications, 1971. 82p.
Presents a compilation of important information concerning the study of Liberian literature, including bibliographical data on major sources and biographical information about Liberian writers.

532 **Towards the study of Liberian literature.**
Edited by Similih M. Cordor (formerly S. Henry Cordor). Monrovia:
Liberian Literature Studies Programme, 1972. 230p.
This is an anthology of critical essays on the study of Liberian literature; its contributors
include A. Doris Banks Henries, Bai T. Moore, Kona Khasu, John Payne Mitchell, and
J. Bolton Williams. The essays consider poetry, fiction writing, regional literature
(literary works from the counties of Liberia), drama, and the historical study of Liberian
literature.

533 **New voices from West Africa: an anthology of Liberian stories.**
Similih M. Cordor (formerly S. Henry Cordor). Monrovia: Books for
Africa Press, 1980. 77p.
A collection of short fictional works by nine contemporary Liberian writers including
Bai T. Moore, Wilton G. S. Sankawulo, Robert Brown, and Elizabeth Mitchell. This is
one of the earliest anthologies of Liberian modern fiction.

534 **Folk tales of Liberia.**
J. Luke Creel. Minneapolis, Minnesota: T. S. Dennison, 1960. 144p.
This collection of folktales includes some traditional stories. It was prepared in
collaboration with Dr. Bai Gai Kiahon, a Vai Liberian. The sixteen stories are
introduced by Oscar S. Norman, who, at the time of publication, was a member of the
government's Bureau of Folkways (folklore).

535 **Liberia's contribution to world literature.**
Roland T. Dempster. Monrovia, 1940. (unpublished manuscript).
This work has been highly praised both by Liberians and foreigners. It was reviewed by
Henry B. Cole, and was mentioned in *Time* magazine (May 14, 1942) at the time when
Dempster received a degree of Master of Literature *Summa Cum Laude* from Liberia
College. The manuscript has been mentioned in several other papers and books but it
seems never to have been published and unfortunately manuscript copies are very
difficult to locate. Dempster was a professor of World Literature and of Latin at the
University of Liberia as well as being a literary critic, a poet, a journalist, and a Liberian
legislator.

536 **The mystic reformation of Gondolia.**
Roland T. Dempster. London: Dragon Press, 1953. 71p.
This is a satirical treatise on moral philosophy with implications for the whole of
Liberian society. It contains a detailed listing of Dempster's literary works and a lengthy
biographical sketch.

537 **A song out of midnight.**
Roland T. Dempster. London: Dragon Press, 1960. 42p.
Presents a small collection of Dempster's poems.

538 **Folk-tales and proverbs of Liberia.**
Peter G. Dorliae. New York: Carlton Press, 1965. 65p.
A collection of folktales and proverbs of northeastern Liberia, largely associated with the Mano (Maah) and Gio (Dan) ethnic groups.

539 **The leopard's claw.**
George Washington Ellis. New York: International Authors Association, 1917. 172p.
This novel, written by a former black American diplomat who was accredited to Liberia, is an adventure story which attempts to provide an insight into those African cultural and social institutions which centre around the mysterious power and significance of the leopard's claw.

540 **More Liberian tales.**
Edwin O. K. Freeman. London: Sheldon Press, 1941. 69p.
A collection of Liberian folktales.

541 **Poems of Liberia 1836-1961.**
A. Doris Banks Henries. London: Macmillan, 1963. 114p.
A collection of poems by an array of Liberian poets including Hilary Teage, Daniel B. Warner, Edwin J. Barclay, H. Carey Thomas, Roland T. Dempster, and Bai T. Moore. The poems are arranged in chronological order. This collection is one of the few anthologies of poems written by Liberians.

542 **Liberian folklore.**
A. Doris Banks Henries. London: Macmillan, 1966. 152p.
An anthology of 99 folktales and 119 proverbs stemming from a variety of Liberian ethnic groups.

543 **Liberian writing as seen by her own writers.**
A. Doris Banks Henries, Bai T. Moore, S. Jangaba M. Johnson (et al.).
Tübingen, West Germany: Horst Erdman Verlag, 1970. 238p.
Presents a collection of the writings by the authors themselves as well as by a few German writers. This volume is described as 'the first comprehensive anthology presenting an almost complete survey of Liberian literature, past and present'. It incorporates Henries's *Survey of Liberian literature* which contains brief historical comments on both traditional and contemporary Liberian writing. Also included are poems and extracts from writings by E. W. Blyden, Nettie Sie Brownell, Hilary Teage and others. The two pieces by Moore which are included are his short fictional work, *Murder in the Cassava Patch*, and a long article on Liberian traditional songs, while Johnson's biographical sketch of a Liberian warrior, Sao Boso, is also reproduced. The German authors include Jahneinz Jahn, Werner Junge (a missionary doctor), and Eugen P. Plotzki (an industrialist). All the German pieces are extracts and are mostly reminiscences.

# Literature

544 **Jabo proverbs from Liberia.**
George Herzog.   London: Oxford University Press, 1936. 272p.
These are Kru proverbs written in collaboration with Charles G. Blooah, a Liberian. The book, which also attempts to provide an interpretation of the proverbs, is a good source of traditional literature. The author was for many years an anthropologist at Indiana University whilst Blooah was educated in America and served as an adviser and interpreter for several other anthropologists.

545 **Liberian poets and their poems.**
Reginald I. Hodge.   Monrovia: University of Liberia, 1957. 78p.
An anthology of poems which includes short biographical sketches of some of the poets, and introductory comments on Liberian poetry.

546 **Poems from black Africa: Ethiopia, South Rhodesia, Sierra Leone, Madagascar, Ivory Coast, Nigeria, Kenya, Gabon, Nyasaland, Mozambique, South Africa, Congo, Ghana, Liberia.**
Langston Hughes.   Bloomington, Indiana: Indiana University Press, 1963. 158p. illus. (UNESCO Collection of Contemporary Works).
An anthology of poems by Africans, which includes the work of two Liberian poets, Roland T. Dempster and Edwin Barclay. Also included in the collection is one Liberian proverb from the Kru ethnic group.

547 **Love in Ebony.**
Varfelli Karlee (*pseudonym* for Charles Edward Cooper, a Liberian diplomat).   London: John Murray, 1932. 136p.
This novel, which is one of the earliest full-length fictional works to be written by a Liberian, is based on Liberian indigenous romantic and social interactions. Topics featured in the novel include Poro rites, sorcery, Islam in Liberia, and some aspects of missionary Christianity.

548 **The emergence of drama in the African cultural reconstruction.**
Kona Khasu.   *Liberian Studies Journal*, vol. 1, no. 1 (Dec. 1967), p. 34-36.
An interesting article on drama in West Africa that also touches on similar activities in other regions of the continent. The final section, 'Theatre in Liberia', provides a brief review of drama in Liberia. Reference is made to plays by Lester R. Parker, Edith Bright and the University of Liberia Players, a dramatic group at the University of Liberia principally composed of students.

549 **Ebony dust.**
Bai T. Moore.   Monrovia: Ducor Publishing House, 1976. 11p.
This collection of Liberian poems is presented in three sections which include the 'African scene', and 'American scene' and the 'Various scenes'. Each part illustrates the background which inspired the collection. The third section addresses the author's vision of the world and man, and life and death.

### 550 The money doubler.

Bai T. Moore. Lagos: Unicom Books, 1976. 105p.

A novella on aspects of Liberian life, especially in urban Monrovia.

### 551 Murder in the cassava patch.

Bai T. Moore. Monrovia: Ducor Publishing House, 1976. 64p.

First published in 1968 by N. V. D. Bosch (Holland), this novel presents essentially a love-story gone wrong. 'It tells a story about the humiliations, the frustrations and abysmal despair, the amorous and often crucial relationship between a young man and his unrequited love for a beautiful and faithful young lady, and the blood-curdling act of murder'. The book's central theme 'is the evocation of one's past, the bitterness it awakens in the individual and the painful realization that one cannot repudiate that past'.

### 552 Legends of Liberia: a collection of folktales told by the people of Liberia and written down by Peter Pinney.

Compiled by Peter Pinney. Monrovia: Society of Liberian Authors, 1973. 2nd ed. 299p.

The author, a New Zealander, first visited Liberia in the 1950s, at which time he undertook the collection and compilation of folktales and legends emanating from the country's various ethnic groups. He acknowledges the sponsorship of the work by the government of Liberia and the editorial assistance of Oscar Norman and Varney Jakema Fahnbulleh of the Bureau of Folkways. This edition was mimeographed in 1972 by the Society of Liberian Authors as part of its International Book Year activities. Its contents discuss such topics as the origins of African People and of the Liberian tribes. The tales themselves are arranged by ethnic groups (Bandi, Gola, Kissi, etc.) and most are identified by their author.

### 553 Marriage of wisdom and other tales from Liberia.

Wilton G. S. Sankawulo. London: Heinemann, 1974. 80p.

A collection of Liberian folktales. The title of the book is also the title of one of the important folktales included in the volume.

### 554 The rain and the night.

Wilton G. S. Sankawulo. London: Macmillan Education, 1979. 172p.

This novel depicts aspects of traditional Liberian society focusing on the Kpelle ethnic group. Sankawulo attempts to show the essence of tradition and mores and their place in the leadership of the key character, Kortuma.

### 555 Why nobody knows when he will die and other tales from Liberia.

Wilton G. S. Sankawulo. London: Macmillan Education, 1979, (reprinted 1982). 80p.

This collection of folktales has been rewritten by the author in modern essay style. There are ten stories in the anthology and the most important ones reflect the traditional culture of the Kpelle people.

556 **Myths and legends of Liberia.**
Wilton Sankawulo. Monrovia: self-published, 1982. 211p.
This compilation of Liberian tales was largely written by the author. Without clearly indicating the sources, he acknowledges the following which form part of the collection – from Moses Pelima: 'Never trust a woman'; 'The girl who must marry a wise man'; 'Hatred and jealousy'; 'Never fool a child'; and 'Marle'; from Weinpie Wongbe: 'Lies save'. Sankawulo also includes some tales which were from a collection made by Peter Pinney: 'The origin of the Wubomai'; 'The story of two brothers'; 'Jungle rivals'; 'An egg for a kingdom'; and 'How a wise man reformed a village'.

557 **The role of the state in the development of literature: The Liberian government and creative fiction.**
John Victor Singler. *Research in African Literature*, vol. 11, no. 4 (winter 1980), p. 511-28.
An important study of Liberian fiction writing which analyses the development of novels and short stories. Writers discussed in this article include Bai T. Moore, Robert H. Brown, Similih M. Cordor (formerly S. Henry Cordor), Wilton Sankawulo, Charles E. Cooper and Roland T. Dempster.

558 **The anthology of Liberian literature.**
Monrovia: Society of Liberian Authors, 1974. 161p.
A collection of short stories, poems, plays, and essays by Liberian writers, including Bai T. Moore, H. Carey Thomas, Wilton G. S. Sankawulo, A. Doris Banks Henries, Joseph Gbadyu, Fatima Massaquoi-Fahnbulleh, and Alice Perry Johnson. The foreword is by Jackson F. Doe, Liberian Minister of Education.

559 **Echoes of the valley, being odes and other poems.**
H. Carey Thomas, Bai T. Moore, Roland T. Dempster. Robertsport, Liberia: Douglas Muir Press, 1947. 48p.
This collection of poems by three prominent Liberian authors contains an interesting introduction by Edwin Barclay. The volume was published in 1947 to commemorate the Liberian centennial.

560 **Libretto for the Republic of Liberia.**
Melvin B. Tolson. London: Collier-Macmillan, 1970. 80p.
Contains poems written in celebration of Liberia's centenary in 1947 by Tolson, a distinguished black American poet. Allen Tate, the writer of the preface observes: 'In the end I found that I was reading *Libretto* . . . not because the poem has a Negro subject but because it is about the world of all men. And this subject is not merely asserted; it is embodied in a rich and complex language, and realized in terms of poetic imagination' (p. 12). Tolson was Professor of Creative Literature at Langston University up until his death in 1966.

561 **Africa in modern literature, a survey of contemporary writings in English.**
Martin Tucker. New York: Frederick Unger, 1967. 316p.
This is a good critical survey of modern African literature. It refers to Liberian literature by non-Liberian nationals and highlights the work of Esther Warner.

562 **The voice of my silence.**
J. Warkreh T-Toe. Monrovia: Liberian Literary & Educational Publications, 1980. 49p.

Brings together short stories and poems by a young Liberian writer, poet, and journalist which deal with traditional African life, modern Liberian issues, and the writer's personal reflections on many aspects of his own experiences.

563 **Guanya Pau: a story of an African princess.**
Joseph J. Walters. Cleveland, Ohio: Lauer & Mattil, 1891. 146p.

The central message of this story, according to the author, concerns the plight of women in Liberia. 'The truth is, men are ever exercising their prerogatives to the letter, and we accept it without a question: but as soon as we assert ours, they brand us with transcending our sphere. So long has woman been deceived that her condition seems to be organic. I may not even now secceed; but . . . the day will come, the day will come' (p. 123-24). Sounding the unusual feminist note for a late nineteenth century Christian missionary-educated Liberian, Walters continues: 'In short, our women must be educated. The infamous system of betrothing girls when three and four years old must be obliterated. Polygamy must be wiped out of the land. There are women in that country (Liberia) who would be as pure and good, who would make as blessed wives and noble mothers, as those of any land were is not for the . . . pandemonium in which they are incarcerated' (p. 6-7).

# Culture and The Arts

564 **The artist archetype in Gola culture.**
Warren L. d'Azevedo.   Newark, Delaware: Liberian Studies
Association, University of Delaware, 1975. 80p.

A leading American scholar specializing in the interpretation of Gola culture attempts to explain the role of the artist in Gola society, drawing some parallels with Western society. An earlier version of the work was produced by the Desert Research Institute, University of Nevada, preprint no. 14, 1966 and 1970.

565 **Cultural policy in Liberia.**
Kenneth Y. Best.   Paris: UNESCO Press, 1974. 59p.

In this UNESCO-sponsored study designed to show the process of planning and implementing cultural policies in member states, Best analyses Liberia's experience in coming to grips with its cultural diversity. He also considers the challenges and opportunities that await a fuller national appreciation of this diversity and how it might be harnessed to promote development.

566 **Africa's contemporary art and artists: a review of creative activities in painting, sculpture, ceramics, and crafts of more than 300 artists working in the modern industrialized society of some of the countries of sub-saharan Africa.**
Evelyn S. Brown.   New York: Harmon Foundation, 1966. 135p.

The aim of this publication is to provide an opportunity for the 'more than 300 artists' from sub-Saharan Africa to tell their own stories and relate their own aspirations. Accordingly, for each country represented there is a general country overview followed by the artists' biographical information. Among the Liberian artists featured are Joseph W. Bailey, Sr., John Barbor Bulu, Lawrence Mawolo Cassell, Peter Gondro Dorliae, Salia Duckley, R. Vahnjah Richards, Ahmadu V. Sirleaf and John Nemle Thompson.

567 **The arts of the Dan in West Africa.**
Eberhard Fischer, Hans Himmelheber, translated from the German by
Anne Buddle, edited by Susan Curtis. Zürich: Museum Rietberg
Zürich, 1984. 192p. illus. bibliog.

This is the English version of *'Die Kunst der Dan'* (1976). The original work was
written in collaboration with George Wowoa W. Tahmen, Tiemoko Gba, Isabelle
Wettstein, and Brigitte Kauf. The study primarily depicts the art of the Dan, though the
art of the artistically-related We, Mano, Kono, Kpelle, and Tura are also highlighted.
Chapters include: 'Habitat and community of the Dan'; 'Cosmology'; 'Masquerades of
the Dan'; 'Other artifacts made of wood'; and 'Artistic tradition among the Dan'. A
bibliography completes the study.

568 **A short history of African art.**
Werner Gillon with a preface by Roy Sieber. Harmondsworth,
England: Penguin Books, 1986. 405p. illus. maps. bibliog.

Essentially a reference work, this volume provides coverage in a broad sweep of some
30,000 years of African art. It is illustrated with over 250 photographs and fourteen
detailed maps and includes an extensive bibliography and an index. The volume
highlights the visual arts of Africa: sculpture, painting and architecture; textiles, pottery
and other household objects; and jewellery, ceremonial and religious dress and body art.
Specific references to Liberia are found in 'The art of the Sherbro, Bulom and Kissi'
(p. 113-20).

569 **Vai women's roles in music, masking, and ritual performance.**
Lester P. Monts. In: *African musicology – current trends*, vol. 1.
Edited by Jacqueline Cogdell Djedje, Wilham G. Carter. Los Angeles:
African Studies Center and African Arts Magazine, University of
California, Los Angeles; Los Angeles: Crossroads Press/African Studies
Association. 1989. p. 219-35.

Provides important insights into Vai culture and the changing role of women therein.
Monts detects three major developments which have influenced the role played by
female musicians over the years: the advent of Islam; the decline of the men's secret
society known as *Beli*; and the mass rural-urban migration of the Vai after 1930.
Amongst his conclusions is the observation that the 'processes of musical adaptation
reflect other adaptive strategies in the wider realm of society' (p. 233).

570 **Liberian culture at a glance: a review of the culture and customs of
the different ethnic groups in the republic of Liberia.**
Bai T. Moore. Monrovia: Ministry of Information, Cultural Affairs &
Tourism, 1979. 48p.

This is a good presentation of the basics of contemporary Liberian culture. At the outset
there is an overview of the efforts taken over the years to bring to light, and preserve,
the country's cultural heritage. Brief statements, accompanied by illustrations, follow on
stone carvings, wood sculptures, handicrafts, the performing arts, secular dancing,
masked dancing, ritualistic dancing, cow feasts, traditional and popular songs,
indigenous music, theatre and performing arts groups, and the role of private
organizations in promoting Liberian culture. Though sources are cited within the text,

there is no bibliography. The author was an Assistant Minister for Culture at the Ministry of Information.

571  **Folklore, music and communications.**
Edited by Joseph O. Okpaku.  In: *New African literature and the arts*, vol. 3.  New York: Published by T. Y. Crowell in association with the Third Press, 1973, p. 363-94.

The contents of this work include 'The collection, notation and arrangement of Liberian folk songs' by Agnes Nebo von Ballmoos, and 'Liberia's contribution to the science of communication' by Bai T. Moore. Of related interest is Agnes Nebo von Ballmoos, 'Liberian music' in the *Liberian Research Association Journal*, vol. 3 (1970), p. 30-39.

572  **When the devil dances.**
Harrison Owen.  Los Angeles: Mara Books, 1970. 78p. illus.

This pictorial work depicts elements of the social life and customs of Liberia.

573  **Spirit of Africa: traditional art from the Nokes collection.**
Edited by James R. Ramsey, Maude S. Wahlman.  Memphis, Tennessee: Murdock Printing Co., 1982. 68p. map. bibliog. (Memphis State University Gallery).

This catalogue illustrates work from the Nokes collection, which was assembled by Neil Nokes (whilst he was Defense and Naval Attache at the United States Embassy in Monrovia) and his wife Phillis. On permanent loan since 1974 to the Art Department of Memphis State University, Tennessee, the collection contains over 100 works from Liberia and other African countries. The text states that catalogue entries follow a route from western Sudan, across to the Ivory Coast and Nigeria, and finally to Zaïre, in Central Africa and comments that 'within this sequence, more attention is devoted to the Mende, Dan, Wee, since the art of Liberia forms the heart of the Nokes Collection' (p. 8).

574  **Womanhood, work and song among the Kpelle of Liberia.**
Cynthia E. Schmidt.  In: *African musicology – current trends*, vol. 1. Edited by Jacqueline Cogdell Djedje, Wilham G. Carter.  Los Angeles: African Studies Center and African Arts Magazine, University of California; Los Angeles: Crossroads Press/African Studies Association. 1989, p. 237-63.

Asserting that 'among the Kpelle of Liberia, the lines drawn between gender roles are as deeply incised in music as they are in labour, marriage patterns and social institutions' (p. 237), the author describes and explains the roles of Kpelle women in musical events involving associations such as rural work co-operatives and the *Sande* secret society.

575 **Patchwork gowns, a state regalia in Western Liberia.**
William C. Siegmann. In: *Man does not go naked: Textilien und Hanwerk aus Afrikanischen und anderen Landern.* Edited by Beate Engelbrecht and Bernhard Fardi. Basel: Ethnologischen Seminar der Universität und Museum für Volkerkinde, in Kommission bei Wepf, 1989, p. 107-116. illus. bibliog.

Examines ten examples of gowns tailored from red and black cloth squares interspersed with squares of leopard and antelope skin. Four of the gowns are currently in museum collections, one in a private collection and five are known only from early twentieth-century field photographs. They show certain conceptual similarities with Mande hunters' gowns and like them, they frequently incorporate talismans of animal horns and the feet of birds of prey. The striking visual display presented by such gowns was appropriate to their use as part of the regalia of state for war chiefs who were the principal secular political leaders in a relatively small but multi-ethnic area of western Liberia during the late nineteenth and the early twentieth centuries (taken from the original abstract).

576 **To dance the spirit: masks of Liberia.**
Edited by Christopher B. Steiner, Jane I. Guyer. Cambridge, Massachusetts: Peabody Museum, Harvard University, 1986. 45p.

This illustrated catalogue to an exhibition held at Harvard University contains an interpretative commentary by a dozen scholars explaining the meaning and context of the masks which were displayed.

577 **Dried millet breaking: time, words, and song in the Woi epic of the Kpelle.**
Ruth M. Stone. Bloomington, Indiana: Indiana University Press, 1988. 150p.

This study examines the exploits of Woi, a mythical culture hero in the epic traditions of Kpelle-Liberians. In her discussion of this tradition, Stone considers basic issues in ethnomusicology, analyses the epic as a performance event, and discusses the connections between music and other artistic traditions.

578 **Traditional hairstyles in Liberia.**
George W. W. Tahmen. Self-published in Liberia, 1980. 14p. (A copy is held at the National Museum of African Art, Smithsonian Institution Libraries, Washington, DC 20560, USA).

'Hairstyling among Liberian women has social implications apart from beautification. All women keep their hair well groomed, and the social activity of plaiting is itself a sort of informal ritual. By contrast, mourning women intentionally neglect this aspect of grooming as a visible sign of bereavement' [see item no. 653, p. 172]. The author classifies traditional hairstyling techniques in Liberia into country plait, corn row and wrapping. He briefly describes each, providing their 'tribal names', and indicating the traditional cosmetics and ornaments employed. Extolling traditional hairstyling as the only body art that has survived the westernizing trend in Liberia, he is critical of the contemporary use of wigs and the Afro hair cut. See also *African art: a bibliographic guide*, compiled by Janet Stanley. New York, London: Africana, 1985. 55p, Smithsonian Institution Libraries Research Guide, no. 4.

# Cuisine

579 **Cooking Kwi style in Liberia.**
Kathleen Addison d'Azevedo. Pittsburgh, Pennsylvania: The author for the U.S. Peace Corps project to Liberia 1962. 34p.

This is a very interesting compilation of Liberian recipes and cooking hints. Though the author, the spouse of the noted American Liberianist, Warren d'Azevedo, entitles her work 'Kwi-style cooking', presumably meaning cooking in Westernized Liberia, the work does, in fact, include a great deal of 'country chop', or indigenous, cooking. Moreover, the distinction between the two is not always clear. For example there is no difference between 'Kwi' and 'country chop' palm butter or cassava leaf. Included in the select list of references is a related work by Eugenia Simpson-Cooper entitled *Chop and Chatter*, ELWA Radio Village, Monrovia, Liberia, 1947.

580 **Liberian cooking with Tete Alma.**
Alma K. Harris (with the assistance of Varnie N'Jolah Karmo). Lower Buchanan, Liberia: N'Jolah Publishing, 1974. 33p.

According to the author, the idea for this compilation developed from her six-year-long involvement with teaching expatriate employees of LAMCO/Buchanan how to prepare Liberian food. The work includes various recipes for both food and drink, along with an index of ingredients.

581 **African recipes: Liberian cook book.**
Selena Horace Hoffman. Petersburg, Virginia: Ebonics Publishers International, 1989. 65p.

Compiled by a Liberian, this recipe book provides tips on how to achieve authentic Liberian cooking. The volume's geographical and historical material is now very dated. Notwithstanding this, the work provides interesting recipes for main courses and deserts and a glossary of cooking terms unique to Liberia is provided on p. 56-58.

582 **Kitchen talk: a collection of Liberian and international recipes.**
Hawa Knuckles. Brooklyn, New York: Atlas Communications
Services, 1991. 42p.
This cookbook brings together some 130 recipes accompanied by clear instructions.
Among the recipes are those for preparing rice bread, guava jelly, bread fruit stew,
deepa, cassava cake, gaygba, coconut candy, Kpolon, cassava custard, ginger beer,
pepper soup, pawpaw jam, jollof rice, pawpaw pie, fried pepper sauce, golden plum jam,
banana bread, pumpkin stew, tugborgee, okra palavar sauce, pineapple beer, etc. Copies
can be obtained from the following address: ATCOM, P.O. Box 488, Brooklyn, NY
11230.

583 **1979 Liberian cooking ideas and international thoughts dedicated to
'the international year of the child'.**
Corina Van Ee, Eva George, Matilda G. Dunn, Victoria Tolbert, Gladys
Richardson. Monrovia: Annual Calendar Tea Committee. 1979. 37p.
First produced in 1977, this book contains many recipes for a variety of different dishes.
The Annual Calendar Tea Committee comprised a few prominent Liberian women under
the patronage of the First Lady of Liberia, Victoria A. Tolbert.

584 **A West African cook book: an introduction to good food from
Ghana, Liberia, Nigeria and Sierra Leone, with recipes collected and
adapted by Ellen Gibson Wilson.**
Ellen Gibson Wilson. New York: M. Evans, distributed by
J. B. Lippincott, Philadelphia, 1971. 267p. bibliog.
Contains a compendium of West African recipes, some indicating their country of
origin. Regional culinary characteristics are discussed, such as the use of pepper, and
general West African cooking methods and ways of eating are also described. The
recipes themselves are grouped under headings such as 'Classic main dishes', 'Starters';
and 'Small Chop'.

# Libraries, Museums and Archives

585　**African publications on microfilm – Liberia.**
West Falmouth, Massachusetts: African Imprint Library Services (P.O. Box 350, W. Falmouth, Massachusetts 02574, USA).

This very varied collection on Liberia includes: writings of S. Jangaba M. Johnson (former district commissioner of five Liberian counties, and research officer with the Bureau of Folkways – one reel); works by Wilton Sankawulo (two novels and a collection of Kpelle tales – one reel), papers of Chief Justice Louis Arthur Grimes (1883-1948 – six reels); publications in the Loma language – three reels; publications of the Society of Liberian Authors – one reel; writings of A. Doris Banks Henries (former director of higher education and textbook research at the Ministry of Education – one reel); writings and papers of Fatima Massaquoi Fahnbulleh (founder and Director of the University of Liberia's Institute of African Studies – one reel); the Albert Porte Papers – ten reels; issues of *The Liberian Age*, 1973-1977 and the *Liberian Star*, 1973-1976 (complete runs containing all issues published); documents and newspapers from the collection of C. Abayomi Cassell (former Attorney General, 1944-1957 – ten reels); budgets of the government of Liberia (1974-1978 – four reels); and decisions of the Supreme Court of Liberia, 1861-1898 – one reel.

586　**The library and archives of the Church Historical Society.**
V. Nelle Bellamy. *Historical Magazine of the Protestant Church*, vol. 39, no. 1 (March 1970), p. 91-95.

The author, archivist of the historical society of the American Church until 1992, describes the Society's holdings on Liberia and Haiti. Particular reference is made to the papers of the Domestic and Foreign Missionary Society for the period 1822-1939: 'These records consist mainly of correspondence sent by missionaries in Liberia to the Domestic and Foreign Missionary Society of the Episcopal Church and of related material pertaining to the affairs to this church in Liberia' (p. 92). Files on Liberia have subsequently been opened up to the year 1952. The Haiti papers cover the period 1855-1939 and are found on p. 94-95 of the article.

156

587  **Directory of archives and manuscript repositories in the United States.**
National Historical Publications and Records Commission.  Phoenix, New York: ORYX Press, 1988. 853p.
Each entry provides the name and address of the institution along with a brief description of the scope and contents of its archives. The directory, which contains many references to Liberian material, is arranged alphabetically by state and then by city.

588  **A guide to manuscripts and documents in the British Isles relating to Africa.**
Edited by J. D. Pearson, compiled by Noel Matthews, M. Doreen.
London: Oxford University Press, 1971. 321p.
Covering Africa South of the Sahara, this guide (prepared under the auspices of the London School of Oriental and African Studies) includes both official and unofficial papers which cover a wide variety of subjects. The volume also includes a list of manuscript repositories arranged by county and city. Material on Liberia can be found on pp. 36-38, 49 (Church Missionary Society and Liberia); 91, 108-110, 131, 140, 150, 166, 205, 119 (anthropology); 194 (missionaries), and 248.

589  **A catalogue of the African collection in the Moorland Foundation, Howard University Library.**
Edited by Dorothy B. Porter.  Washington, DC: Howard University Press, 1958. 398p.
This compilation of some 4,865 book entries is an extremely useful reference work, especially for Liberia. Its contents cover Africa generally, followed by regional listings, periodicals, and newspapers. In the 'Western Africa' (p. 196-210) section there are numerous references to the American origins of the Liberian state, and to the nineteenth and early twentieth centuries. Periodicals are listed alphabetically by title, and newspapers by geographical areas. Papers such as *Liberia Herald*, *The Liberian Age*, and *Africa's Luminary* are included.

590  **Guide to Federal archives relating to Africa.**
Compiled by Aloha Smith.  Los Angeles: Crossroads Press, 1977. 556p.
The aim of this guide is 'to make available the vast quantity of Africa-related material housed in the National Archives in Washington, DC'. Arranged according to the United States Government's functional departments and agencies, the compilation features 'country numbers used in Department of State decimal classification scheme for African nations'. There are also indexes of subjects, places, personal names, ships, ethnic groups, etc.

# Media and Periodicals

**591  Africa Report.**

New York: African-American Institute, 1956- . bimonthly.

*Africa Report*, 'America's leading magazine on Africa', continues the publication *Africa Special Report: Bulletin of the Institute of African-American Relations* which began publication on 5 July 1956. Each issue features articles on current issues, an 'update' section highlighting events in several countries, as well as important interviews with leading African personalities. The editorial address is Africa Report, 833 United Nations Plaza, New York, NY 10017.

**592  Liberia: 125 years of independence.**

London: *African Development*, July 1972, p. 5-42.

The contents of this promotional presentation include: 'How Liberia kept its independence', 'Tolbert brushes the cobwebs away', and 'Grappling with the debt problem', all by Alan Rake; 'Rice may be key to updating agriculture' by Alistair Hill; 'Good prospects for the Palm Oil industry' by Douglas Feninmore; 'Foreign operations threaten fisheries' by Harry Jaquar; 'Economic map-companies in the news – how Liberia rules the waves' by Rufus Darpoh; 'Liberia's many-faceted trade in diamonds' and 'Mining: from basis for an expanding economy' by Bobby Naidoo; 'The search for oil continues' and 'Rubber is the main money crop' by Douglas Greves; and 'Monrovia's Freeport: most efficient in West Africa' by J. Powell.

**593  The African Repository.**

Washington, DC: American Colonization Society, 1825-92. quarterly.

This publication was the organ of the American Society for the Colonization of the Free People of Colour of North America and was re-named *Liberia* after 1892. *The African Repository* and *Liberia* constitute a quarterly chronicle of events in, and connected with, Liberia extending over a period of more than eighty years.

594 **African newspapers in selected American libraries.**
Compiled by Rozanne M. Barry. Washington, DC: 1965. third edition.
135p.
Pages 36-39 of this work contain information on Liberian newspapers.

595 **The press of Africa: persecution and perseverance.**
Frank Barton. London: Macmillan, 1979. 304p.
Provides a dated but useful background description of 'what has happened and what is happening to the press in Africa'. Of particular interest for students of Liberia are chapter two; 'West Africa: a black press for black men' (p. 13-30); and chapter eleven; 'Unconquered Africa (Liberia: Tammany Hall in the tropics)' (p. 250-56). Of related interest is Rosalynde Ainslie's *The Press in Africa: Communications Past and Present* (New York: Walker & Co., 1967. 264p) which features Liberia on pages 21-22; 26, 71-72 and 236.

596 **National development in Liberia and the role of the broadcast media, 1950-1980: a descriptive study.**
Jerome Z. Boikai. PhD dissertation, Wayne State University, Michigan, 1983. 251p.
A descriptive study of radio and television broadcasting in Liberia between 1950 and 1980 which emphasizes the functions of radio and television operations in nation-building. It covers such subjects as the role of the media in promoting unity and national integration, and in advancing cultural and educational programmes. Technical, man-power, and socio-political problems associated with radio and television in Liberia are also discussed.

597 **The press in Liberia.**
Henry B. Cole. *Liberian Studies Journal*, vol. 4, no. 2 (1971-72), p. 147-55.
This is basically a historical description of some of the principal Liberian newspapers in the nineteenth and twentieth centuries.

598 **Liberian Diaspora.**
Columbia, Maryland: Diligent Associates, 1990- . monthly.
A Liberian magazine that seeks to address issues of concern both to Liberians at home and those forced into exile as a result of the civil war of 1989-90. *Liberian Diaspora* first appeared in Freetown, Sierra Leone, in July 1990 but the publication has been based in the United States since early 1991. The magazine's editor and publisher is Reginald B. Goodridge, and the contact address is P.O. Box 7124, Silver Spring, Maryland 20907, USA. Of related interest is the *West African Journal*, a monthly published by Maulay Entertainment Communications of California, which focuses on events in Sierra Leone and Liberia since the onset of civil war in the latter country. Publication began in 1991, under the Managing Editor, Joe S. Kappia. The journal's contact address is P.O. Box 110311, Campbell, California 95011-0311, USA.

599 **The press on Liberia.**
John H. Hanson. MA thesis, Syracuse University, Syracuse, New York. 1972. 115p.

This historical study of print journalism in Liberia, details such issues as the development of the press, economic and technical problems of the press, freedom of the press, and government ownership of newspapers.

600 **The Liberian Professional Exchange.**
Monrovia: INMARCO, 1984- . irregular.

This Liberian magazine for 'thinking people' was established on the initiative of its editor, D. Evelyn S. White-Kandakai, former professor of education at Cuttington University College. Its stated purpose is to cater for the needs of professionals in 'research and evaluation, training and education, development and auxiliary areas'. The editorial address is INMARCO, P.O. Box 1143, Monrovia, Liberia.

601 **The role of research in developing communication at the Liberian rural communications network.**
D. Evelyn S. Kandakai. *African Media Review* (Nairobi, Kenya), vol. 3, no. 1 (1988), p. 64-82.

Consistent with the emphasis of the government of Liberia on rural development in the 1970s, a rural communications network was envisaged. Implemented in the 1980s, the Liberian Rural Communications Network (LRCN) sought to achieve the following: to promote the increased use of government services particularly by people in rural areas; to foster increased communications between government agencies at local, regional and national levels; to promote the participation and involvement of rural people in self-help activities and national development; to educate rural people in development-oriented areas such as health, agriculture and literacy; and to serve as a medium of exchange of information and experience among rural people. Kandaki explores the place of research in developing communications, especially with regard to the LRCN.

602 **The press in Africa.**
Edited by Helen Kitchen. Washington, DC: Ruth Sloan Associates, 1956. 96p.

This brief study on journalism in Africa includes a short chapter on Liberian journalistic writing and activities. Also included are comments on press censorship, development programmes and their relationship to Liberian journalism.

603 **Liberia-Forum.**
Bremen, Germany: Liberia Working Group, 1981-90. biannual.

*Liberia-Forum* is a publication of the Liberia Working Group, a German-based association of scholars which aims to cover 'the economic, political, social, cultural, and anthropological aspects of Liberian society'. Most of its articles are in English, though some have appeared in German and French. Its Editors are Robert Kappel and Werner Korte, and the contact address for Liberia-Forum is: Liberia Working Group/Liberia-Forum, c/o W. Korte, Grubenbacherstr. 40, D-6315, Mücke, Germany.